MINING *for* MEANING

A Guide to the Unseen for 'N' and 'O' Level Students

Suzanne Choo | Robert Yeo

Editor
Peter Ellison

LEARNERS PUBLISHING

a division of
SCHOLASTIC

© 2007 Learners Publishing Pte Ltd
Learners Publishing Pte Ltd is a division of Scholastic Inc.

First published 2007 by **Learners Publishing Pte Ltd**
81 Ubi Avenue 4, #02-28 UB.One, Singapore 408830

Reprinted 2008 (twice), 2009, 2010, 2011, 2012

Email: learnpub@learners.com.sg
Visit our website: http://www.learners.com.sg

ISBN 978 981 4151 11 5

Printed by B & Jo Enterprise Pte Ltd, Singapore

Contents

Preface

Mining for meaning refers to the reader, whether a student or teacher, in the process of approaching a text for the first time. The text could be a poem or a prose extract or an entire novel. The reader is like a miner digging for a precious metal.

To effect the process, the miner has to be prepared with the proper tools, be trained to dig in the right places, to dig carefully, to dig deep—and in the end to find, as a reward for hard work, the precious ore ... Unravelling the meaning of an "unseen" text is like striking gold. Hence, the title of this book.

But that is not all. After discovering the raw metal, the miner has to extract it, refine it, sell it: this refers to the further process of the reader going beyond locating the meaning of the text to appreciate its efficacy and share its qualities with others (like answering a question appropriately or writing a good essay); in other words, evaluate the writer's use of language, the various devices for achieving intended effects, and the intrinsic value of the text or its message. This is what reading or engaging with literature is truly about.

Every chapter in this book contains the following features, each represented by its particular iconic symbol:

Trigger activity
Introduces the content of the chapter, and is aimed at rousing interest in students and relating Literature to real life, the visual arts and popular culture.

Definition
Gives the definition of a literary term in a clear, succinct manner.

Purpose
Offers a rationale on why writers employ specific devices.

Method
Provides a structured, practical method which students can use to analyse a text.

Group work
Involves various activities such as cooperative learning, debate and research, which teachers can conduct in the classroom.

Point to note
Summarizes the main point(s) to remember in the chapter.

Links to real-world issues
Encourages students to discuss moral or ethical values and issues related to National Education (NE).

Exercise
Affords students practical activities where theories and a range of skills may be applied.

As it will become apparent when the student uses this book, its aim is to provide a structured—step-by-step—approach to handling unseen poems and prose passages. To continue with the image of mining, the objective of this book is to make available appropriate implements, that is, specific skills, to deal with the Unseen for GCE 'N' and 'O' levels.

We, the present authors, and on behalf of the our publisher, would like to thank the following officers from the English Unit, Curriculum Planning & Development Division, for their advice and input:

Ms Fiona Tan
Ms Meenakshi Palaniappan
Ms Janet Liew

Suzanne Choo
Robert Yeo

Acknowledgements

Poems: "In a station of the metro" by Ezra Pound, from *Personae*, copyright © 1926 by Ezra Pound. Reprinted by permission of New Directions Publishing Corp; "The Road Not Taken" from *The Poetry of Robert Frost*, edited by Edward Connery Lathem. Copyright 1969 by Henry Holt and Company. Reprinted by permission of Henry Holt and Company, LLC; "The Secret Sits" from *The Poetry of Robert Frost*, edited by Edward Connery Lathem. Copyright 1969 by Henry Holt and Company. Copyright 1942 by Robert Frost, copyright 1970 by Lesley Frost Ballantine. Reprinted by permission of Henry Holt and Company, LLC; "The beginning of eternity" from *The Guess Book*, published c. 1820; "We are little airy creatures" by Jonathan Swift; a poetic riddle from *The New Exeter Book of Riddles* by K. Crossley-Holland, published by Enitharmon Press, 2000; two poetic riddles from *The Tolkien Trail* by J.R.R. Tolkien. Reprinted by permission of HarperCollins Publishers Ltd, © J.R.R. Tolkien, 1937; "Tropics" by Muhammad Haji Salleh, published by Heinemann Educational Books (Asia) Ltd; "Remembering Grandma" from *An Acre of Day's Glass: Collected Poems* by Wong Phui Nam, 2006. Reproduced with the kind permission of Wong Phui Nam; "Barbara Allen's Cruelty" by Thomas Percy; "Driving to Town Late to Mail a Letter" by Robert Bly from *Silence in the Snowy Fields*, © by Robert Bly and reprinted by permission of Wesleyan University Press; "mirror, mirror" by Chung Yee Chong from *Five Takes*. With the permission of the National University of Singapore Society; "When you are old" by W.B. Yeats, from *The Rose*, 1893. Reprinted by permission of A P Watt Ltd on behalf of Michael B. Yeats; "old house at ang siang hill" and "letter from a youth to his prospective employer" from *The Space of City Trees* by Arthur Yap, published by Skoob Books Ltd, 2000; "The Death of the Ball Turret Gunner" from *Selected Poems* by Randall Jarrell, published by McClelland & Stewart Ltd, 1964; "Those Winter Sundays", copyright © 1966 by Robert Hayden, from *Collected Poems of Robert Hayden*, edited by Frederick Glaysher. Used by permission of Liveright Publishing Corporation; "The First Day" by Christina Rossetti and "Juliet" by Hilaire Belloc from *Great Love Poems*, edited by Shane Weller, published by Dover Publications, 1992; "in Just-" is reprinted from *Complete Poems 1904–1962* by E.E. Cummings, edited by George J. Firmage, by permission of W.W. Norton & Company. Copyright © 1991 by the Trustees for the E.E. Cummings Trust and George James Firmage; "Singapore River" from *The Brink of an Amen* by Lee Tzu Pheng. Published by Times Editions, an imprint of Marshall Cavendish International (Asia) Pte Ltd. Email: te@sg.marshallcavendish.com, Website: www.marshallcavendish.com/genref; "A Poison Tree" by William Blake, from *Songs of Innocence and Experience,* published in 1794; "Marina Bay" by Robert Yeo; "Child on Top of a Greenhouse" from *Roethke: Collected Poems* by Theodore Roethke, copyright 1946 by Editorial Publications, Inc; "An Irish Airman Foresees His Death" by W.B. Yeats, from *The Wild Swans at Coole*, 1917. Reprinted by permission of A P Watt Ltd on behalf of Michael B. Yeats; "A Brief History of China" from *Peninsular: Archipelagos and Other Islands* by Daren V.L. Shiau,

of C. Day Lewis. Reprinted by permission of The Random House Group Ltd; "Women without Men" by Leong Liew Geok; "The Man in the Bowler Hat" from *The Collected Poems of A.S.J. Tessimond*, translated by Jacques Prévert and edited by Hubert Nicholson, published by Whiteknights Press, 1985; "To My Landlord" from *Nearing a Horizon* by Ee Tiang Hong, published by UniPress and The Centre for the Arts, NUS, Singapore, in 1994; "Dulce et Decorum Est" by Wilfred Owen, from *Wilfred Owen: Poems,* with an Introduction by Siegfried Sassoon, published by Chatto and Windus, 1920; "Boys in Jungle Green" from *Leaving Home, Mother: Selected Poems* by Robert Yeo, published by Angsana Books, an imprint of Flame of the Forest Publishing, 1999; "Do not go gentle into that good night" by Dylan Thomas, from *The Poems of Dylan Thomas*, published by J.M. Dent; "Night Shift" by Yeow Kai Chai, published by Landmark Books; "Digging" from *Death of a Naturalist* by Seamus Heaney, published by Faber and Faber, 1990; "AIDS Diary" from *A History of Amnesia* by Alfian Bin Sa'at, published by Ethos Books, an imprint of Pagesetters Services Pte Ltd, copyright © Alfian Bin Sa'at, 2001; "Mushrooms" from *Selected Poems* by Sylvia Plath, published by Faber and Faber; "Quieter than snow" from *Walking on Air* by Berlie Doherty, published by HarperCollins Publishers, 1993; "Hide and Seek" by Vernon Scannell. Reproduced with the kind permission of Vernon Scannell; "My Grandmother" from *Collected Poems* by Elizabeth Jennings, published by Carcanet, 1987; "First Day at School" from *In the Glassroom* by Roger McGough (Copyright © Roger McGough 1976) is reproduced by permission of PFD (www.pfd.co.uk) on behalf of Roger McGough; "War Photographer" from *Standing Female Nude* by Carol Ann Duffy, published by Anvil Press Poetry, 1985; "The Jaguar" from *The Hawk in the Rain* by Ted Hughes, published by Faber and Faber, originally published in 1957; "The Astigmatic" by Philip Hobsbaum; "My Box" from *Letting in the Rumour* by Gillian Clarke, published by Carcanet Press, 1989; "The Choosing" from *Dreaming Frankenstein & Collected Poems 1967–1984* by Liz Lochhead, published by Polygon Books, 1984.

Prose extracts: "The Wind and the Sun" from *Aesop's Fables*, edited by Jack Zipes, copyright © 1992 by Jack Zipes. Used by permission of Dutton Signet, a division of Penguin Group (USA) Inc; "The Story of a Mother" by Hans Christian Andersen from *The Complete Fairy Tales and Stories,* translated by Erik Haugaard, published by Random House, Inc; "Gimpel the Fool" by Isaac Bashevis Singer, translated by Saul Bellow, copyright 1953, 1954, renewed © 1981, 1982 by Viking Penguin Inc., from *A Treasury of Yiddish Stories*, edited by Irving Howe & Eliezer Greenberg. Used by permission of Viking Penguin, a division of Penguin Group (USA) Inc. "The Temple Bells" by Goh Poh Seng and "The Glittering Game" by Lee Kok Liang from *Twenty-Two Malaysian Stories*, first published by Heinemann Educational Books (Asia) Ltd, 1968; *Emma* by Jane Austen, first published by John Murray, 1815; *Wuthering Heights* by Emily Bronte, first published in 1847; "What you asked" by Nalla Tan and "The English Language Teacher's Secret" by Catherine Lim from *in Blue Silk Girdle: Stories from Malaysia and Singapore*, published by Universiti Putra Malaysia Press, 1998; *Memoirs of a Geisha* by Arthur Golden, published by Chatto & Windus. Reprinted by permission of The Random House Group Ltd; *The Grass Is Singing,* copyright © 1950 Doris Lessing, and *Through the Tunnel*, © 1990 Doris Lessing. Reprinted by kind permission of Jonathan Clowes Ltd, London, on behalf of Doris Lessing; "Patriotism" by Yukio Mishima, translated by Geoffrey W. Sargent, from *Death in Midsummer*, copyright © 1966 by New Directions Publishing Corp. Reprinted by permission of New Directions Publishing

Faber and Faber, 1989; "The Scholarship" from *Malaysian Short Stories* by Stella Kon, published by Heinemann Educational Books (Asia) Ltd, 1981; *The Hound of the Baskervilles* by Sir Arthur Conan Doyle, first published in 1902, reprinted by courtesy of the Estate of Dame Jean Conan Doyle; Selection, pages 19-21 from "The Man Who Lived Underground" from *Eight Men* by Richard Wright. Copyright 1944 by L. B. Fischer Publishing Corp.; copyright © 1961 by Richard Wright. Reprinted by permission of HarperCollins Publishers; *Interview with the Vampire* by Anne Rice, published by Alfred A. Knopf, 1976; *Tangerine* by Colin Cheong, published by Raffles Editions, an imprint of SNP Publishing Pte Ltd, 1997. Copyright © 1997 Colin Cheong; "The Story of an Hour" by Kate Chopin, first published in 1894; "Dead Men's Path" from *Girls at War* by Chinua Achebe. Reprinted by permission of Harcourt Education; *Foreign Bodies* by Tan Hwee Hwee, copyright © 1997 by Tan Hwee Hwee. Reproduced with the kind permission of Tan Hwee Hwee; *Schindler's List* by Thomas Keneally, published by Simon & Schuster, copyright © 1982 by Serpentine Publishing Co Pty Ltd; *The No. 1 Ladies' Detective Agency* by Alexander McCall Smith, published by Abacus, 2003; *You Are Now Entering the Human Heart: Stories* by Janet Frame. Victoria University Press, Wellington, New Zealand (1983, reprinted 2005). Copyright © Janet Frame 1983. Reprinted by permission of Janet Frame Literary Trust; *The Iron Woman* by Ted Hughes; "The Pedestrian" by Ray Bradbury, from *Bradbury Stories: 100 of His Most Celebrated Tales*, published by HarperCollins Publishers, copyright © 2003 by Ray Bradbury; *Fire on the Mountain* by Anita Desai, published by Vintage, 2001; "The Landlady" from *Kiss Kiss* by Roald Dahl, published by Penguin, 1973; "The Blind Man" by Kate Chopin, first published 1891; *Fair Stood the Wind for France* by H.E. Bates, first published 1944. Reproduced by permission of Pollinger Limited and the proprietor.

Photographs and pictures: (p 6) "Loch Ness monster" from Susan Parman, the photograph is of a statue for tourists at Drumnadrochit, Scotland, Website: http://anthro.fullerton.edu/sparman; (p 13) Rolex advertisement from http://www.adclassix.com; (p 26) seascape (Photograph A) from www.bigfoto.com, and seascape (Photograph B) from Suzanne Choo; (p 38) "Animal Face Illusion" from http://www.coolopticalillusions.com; (p 68) three portraits from Suzanne Choo, taken at the Louvre Museum; (p 108) "Machine Gunning Squirrel" and "Toddler Mischief" from http://www.utahgeocachers.com/PhotoCaptions.php; (p 133) two screen shots from "Nailed", Episode 6 of *CSI: Miami* from CBS Television Network; (p 145) "Spiderman 3" and "Silent Hill" posters from Sony Pictures; (p 161) three photographs from www.bigfoto.com; (p 181) two cartoons from http://www.generalcomics.com; (p 193) photograph of street graffiti from www.bigfoto.com; (p 200) two pictures (cognitive illusions) from http://www.world-mysteries.com.

The GCE 'N' and 'O' level past examination questions are reproduced by permission of the Singapore Examinations and Assessment Board.

Every effort has been made to trace the copyright holders of material used in this book. If any copyright holder has been overlooked, we should be pleased to make any necessary arrangements at the first opportunity.

Chapter 1
SEEING THE UNSEEN

Trigger activity

Imagine this scenario: your teacher hands out the following poem and asks the class for an interpretation of it.

> My twin points are bound by an iron bar.
> I wrestle with wind, struggle with the sea.
> I probe deep waters—I bite the earth.
>
> *Symphosius*

Here are some things we could do:

(a) Find out who the writer is.

In this case, we know that the writer is a man named "Symphosius". Research on him tells us that he lived at the end of the 4th and beginning of the 5th century and specialized in writing Latin poetic riddles. We could then find out more about life in Europe in the 4th and 5th centuries and the tradition of Latin riddles.

OR

(b) Find out what other people have said about the poem.

We could browse the Internet, read articles on the poem and compile the opinions of their writers—researchers and scholars—regarding the poem and what it is about.

OR

(c) **Analyse the poem on our own.**
We could try to decipher the poem on our own, using our own wit and intellect. We might examine the structure of the poem, look for patterns and repeated ideas in the poem, and think about specific words that seem to stand out.

Discuss in a small group which of the above three options you would consider. As Literature students, what should your attitude be when you encounter a text you have not read before?

 Group work: Inference

Work in a group of four or five.

(1) In your group, do the following:
   (a) Discuss and agree on an interpretation of the poem given above.
   (b) Formulate a riddle poem and share this with other groups. The group which is able to solve the most riddles in the shortest time wins.

(2) Next, think about what went on in your minds when you interpreted the poem as well as when you constructed your own. Then complete the following table:

	What are some qualities of 'good' readers? (List three.)	What are some qualities of 'bad' readers? (List three.)
1		
2		
3		

(3) Finally, discuss some of the reading habits that would make each of you a better reader.

1.1 How should we approach the Unseen?

To do well in the Unseen, we need to be and do the following:

Be inquisitive	Texts contain meanings to be unravelled. For this reason, we need to get into the habit of questioning what we read.
Show initiative	Oftentimes, the meanings of texts are embedded or hidden. We thus need the drive, determination and patience to decipher them.
Develop independence	Deriving the answer to the above poem could be a lot quicker if we turned to the research or writings of scholars or referred to study guides. On the other hand, we would have gained less from the experience of learning to think on our own.

 Point to note

We rely on ourselves to solve the riddle/meaning of the text.

Through acquiring strategies in tackling the Unseen, we will learn how to approach the text on our own without resorting to the ideas or knowledge of others. In the process, we would gain an invaluable skill necessary for success in life—the ability to think critically for ourselves.

1.2 What is the Unseen?

 Definition—The Unseen

The **Unseen** is a **piece of writing,** or text, that you have **to analyse** or appreciate without having seen it before, particularly as part of an examination.

Dealing with the Unseen or Practical Criticism essentially refers to **a method of close reading** which developed during a movement in the 1940s and 50s known as New Criticism.

The New Critics, particularly Cambridge professor I.A. Richards, challenged traditional methods of studying literature which dealt with acquiring knowledge about the author's background, the historical period in which the text was written, scholarly opinions of the text and other areas extrinsic to the text. Instead, Richards proposed a new method of close reading in which attention is focused on the form and content of the text itself. This book uses mainly the theoretical approach of New Criticism as well as that of Reader-response, another movement that took place in the 1960s and 70s which emphasizes the role of the reader in responding to the text.

1.3 Approaching the Unseen

 Method—The macro to micro approach

The following is a diagrammatic representation of how you should approach the Unseen:

Stage 1: Understanding overall meaning

Question to ask: What is the text about?

- Obtain a basic understanding of the text's meaning.
- Identify the genre of the text and its subject matter.
- Identify the overall mood of the text.

Stage 2: Close reading

Question to ask: What devices does the writer use to convey meaning to the reader?

- Poetic devices—diction, word order, figurative language, rhythm, sound.
- Prose techniques—plot structure, narration, characterization, tension, repetition and development.

Stage 3: Philosophical insight and response

Questions to ask: What issues about the world and human nature does the text highlight? What is my response to them?

Point to note

The zoom-out and zoom-in effect

Think of yourself as someone operating a camera. Your task as a critic will be to zoom out and have an overview (what the text is about, what its underlying meaning is) and then to zoom in and analyse the text in detail (close analysis of form, language, content) before finally responding to it.

Application example

In a station of the metro

The apparition of these faces in the crowd;
Petals on a wet, black bough.

Ezra Pound

Stage 1: Understanding overall meaning

The speaker is standing at a train station and observing the crowds walking by. He describes them as "Petals on a wet, black bough". There is an overall sense of beauty and romance in the poem.

Stage 2: Close reading

The writing uses interesting words—for instance, "apparition", which conveys the idea of a passing illusion. The implied meaning is that the speaker is able to connect with these people for a moment. It is a connection that is beautiful and profound but temporary. This is emphasized in the metaphor of the petal, which symbolizes beauty as well as fragility.

Stage 3: Philosophical insight and response

The images in this short poem are powerful and vivid. The reader feels a sense of awe, especially through the writer's use of contrast. For example, the petals contrast with the black bough, which is a reference to the cold dark world we live in. Perhaps the implication is that human love and warmth are the only qualities which give life to the world.

1.4 How this book is organized

The first sections of this book are organized according to the diagram above. The remaining sections comprise exercises that will prepare you for the revised Literature in English GCE 'N' and 'O' level examinations.

SECTION I

Chapter 2

WHAT IS THE TEXT ABOUT?

The aim of this section is to help students make an accurate overview of the text, especially its mood and underlying truth. Students cannot properly proceed to a close analysis of the text unless they have first formed a clear understanding of what it is about.

Chapter outline

2.1 Two levels of meaning in the text

2.2 Questions to ask as we read the text

Trigger activity

Villagers from a small town in Scotland recently spotted a strange-looking monster in a nearby lake. Imagine you are a reporter covering the story. What questions would you ask?

The following are some questions you could ask as an investigative reporter. With a partner, rank the questions in order of complexity from 1 to 8 (1 = the question which is most unlikely to tell you more about the picture, while 8 = the question which is thought-provoking and most likely to lead to further insights and/or the truth about the picture).

	(a)	What do the people living nearby think about this picture?
	(b)	What kind of monster is this?
	(c)	Who saw the monster besides the photographer?
	(d)	Where was this picture taken?
	(e)	Why was the monster lying completely on top of the water? How was this possible?
	(f)	What time of day was the picture taken?
	(g)	Who took the picture?
	(h)	Why did the photographer send the picture to the newspaper and not the police?

2.1 Two levels of meaning in the text

When we read a text (any kind of text), it is important that, as we read, we **question** what we are reading. The advantage of doing this is that it enables us **to gain a basic understanding** of the text. It will also allow us to move from the basic, superficial understanding **to a deeper, more profound insight** into the text.

The first question you should ask when you read a text is: "What is it about?" It is another way of asking, "What does the text mean?"

The meaning of the text may be found at two levels:

(1) Surface meaning

When we read a text for its surface meaning, we are basically comprehending the ideas of the text such as what it is about, what has happened, and what the subject matter is.

(2) Implied meaning

When we read a text for its implied meaning, we apply analytical and inferential skills to understand the deeper meaning of the text such as what underlying message it conveys about life, what underlying reasons could motivate a character to behave in a certain way, and so on.

Application example

Read the following poem. Before looking at the suggested answers below it, try to write one paragraph each describing (1) the surface meaning and (2) the implied meaning of the poem.

The Road Not Taken

Two roads diverged in a yellow wood,
And sorry I could not travel both
And be one traveller, long I stood
And looked down one as far as I could
5   To where it bent in the undergrowth;

Then took the other, as just as fair,
And having perhaps the better claim,
Because it was grassy and wanted wear;
Though as for that, the passing there
10   Had worn them really about the same,

And both that morning equally lay
In leaves no step had trodden black.
Oh, I kept the first for another day!
Yet knowing how way leads on to way,
15   I doubted if I should ever come back.

I shall be telling this with a sigh
Somewhere ages and ages hence:
Two roads diverged in a wood, and I —
I took the one less travelled by,
20   And that has made all the difference.

Robert Frost

The suggested answers are:

(1) Surface meaning

As the poem indicates, a traveller makes a choice between two roads as one seems more appealing and he wants to save the other for "another day". He knows that he is unlikely to come back and, recollecting the event years later, he says that his choice has made "all the difference" but does not explain the difference.

(2) Implied meaning

Life is about making choices and it is important to make the right choices as we may not get another chance. In writing about the poem, you should take into account the poet's use of the idea of "roads" to suggest choice. A road often suggests a route, a way, and is an important symbol in the poem—that is, it refers to a crucial decision which has life-influencing consequences.

In stating that life is about making choices, as well as pinpointing the theme, you are expressing a widely-held philosophical truth. Poems, novels and plays often comment about the world we live in or about human nature and their perceptive general statements are called philosophical truths.

Point to note

When reading a text, always **aim to read beyond the surface meaning** of the text.

Think about the underlying issues and concerns the text raises, particularly what the text says about the world and about human nature.

2.2 Questions to ask as we read the text

Method—How do we access the two levels of meaning?

Surface meaning

Before reading the text, you should have these questions in mind:

1. Who?   — Who is the speaker in the poem or who are the key characters involved in the story/prose text?
2. What?   — What is the subject matter of the text? What is the text about?
3. Where? — Where does the story take place?
4. When?   — In what time period is the story set?

Implied meaning

After getting a clearer idea of the text's surface meaning, think about the following questions:

1. Why? — Does the writer have a reason for writing this text?
2. How is the text structured? What value or message is highlighted at the end and what does this tell us about the world we live in and/or about human nature?

 Group work: Inference—Poetic riddles

Work in a group to solve these poetic riddles.

Poem 1

The beginning of eternity,
The end of time and space,
The beginning of every end,
And the end of every place.

From The Guess Book *(c. 1820)*

Poem 2

There is one that has a head without an eye,
And there's one that has an eye without a head.
You may find the answer if you try;
And when all is said,
Half the answer hangs upon a thread.

Christina Rossetti

Poem 3

We are little airy Creatures,
All of diff'rent Voice and Features,
One of us in Glass is set,
One of us you'll find in Jet,
T'other you may see in Tin,
And the fourth a Box within,
If the fifth you should pursue
It can never fly from you.

Jonathan Swift

Poem 4

The deep sea suckled me, the waves sounded over me;
Rollers were my coverlet as I rested on my bed.
I have no feet and frequently open my mouth
To the flood. Sooner or later some man will
Consume me, who cares nothing for my shell.
With the point of his knife he will pierce me through,
Ripping the skin away from my side and straight away
Eat me uncooked as I am ...

K. Crossley-Holland

Poem 5

Voiceless it cries,
Wingless flutters,
Toothless bites,
Mouthless mutters.

J.R.R. Tolkien

Poem 6

Alive without breath,
As cold as death;
Never thirsty, ever drinking,
All in mail, never clinking.

J.R.R. Tolkien

 Exercise 2A – Poetry

The Secret Sits

We dance round in a ring and suppose,
But the Secret sits in the middle and knows.

Robert Frost

1   From the title, what do you think the poem is about?

2   What do you feel as you read the poem? Explain why you
feel the way you do.

3 Who or what do you think the "Secret" is? What does it know?

4 Why do you think the writer wrote this poem? What does he say about the world we live in?

Exercise 2B – Prose

The wind and the sun once had an argument as to which was the stronger of the two, and they agreed to settle the issue by holding a contest: whoever could make a traveller take off his coat first would be recognized as the more
5   powerful. The wind began and blew with all his might until he stirred up a blast, cold and fierce as an Alaskan storm. The stronger he blew, however, the tighter the traveller wrapped his coat around him and clasped it with his hands. Then the sun broke out, and with his welcome beams he
10   dispersed the clouds and the cold. The traveller felt the sudden warmth, and as the sun shone brighter and brighter, he sat down, overcome by the heat, and threw his coat on the ground.
    Thus the sun was declared the winner, and ever since
15   then, persuasion has been held in higher esteem than force. Indeed, sunshine of a kind and gentle manner will sooner open a poor man's heart than all the threats and force of blustering authority.

"The Wind and the Sun" from Aesop's Fables

1 Summarize in one sentence, the main idea in this passage.

2 Who are the main characters in this text? Where did the incident in the story take place?

3 Explain why the sun and not the wind was declared the winner in the end.

4 State the main theme of this passage in one sentence.

Chapter 3
WHAT IS THE GENRE
OF THE TEXT?

Trigger activity

Suppose you came across the following text in a newspaper. How would you respond to it?

Chapter outline

3.1 What is a genre?

3.2 Overview of genres in poetry

3.3 Overview of genres in prose

Wear perfection on your wrist

A perfect movement with perfect accuracy. Accuracy that's protected by the Oyster case, accuracy that can't be harmed by dust or dirt or damp or water, or any of a watch's natural enemies. A man's Rolex Oyster, of course.

Beauty in miniature, good-looks combined with good time-keeping. The skill of the Rolex designers gives you a watch that's as beautiful as fashion demands, as accurate as *you* demand.

TO OUR FRIENDS FROM OVERSEAS
The Rolex International Repair Department is at your service. Write, call or phone, from anywhere in the world to 1 Green Street, Mayfair.

TUDOR
Why not ask your jeweller to show you the Tudor watch, a distinguished member of the Rolex family ?

ROLEX
The World's first waterproof wrist-watch

THE ROLEX WATCH COMPANY LIMITED (H. WILSDORF, GOVERNING DIRECTOR)
1 GREEN STREET, MAYFAIR, W.1

Here are two things you could do:

(a) **Respond to the text.**
You would rush to a watch shop to purchase this attractive watch.

(b) **Recognize the text and respond to it accordingly.**
You would, of course, recognize that this text is different from other articles in the newspaper. It is an advertisement intended to entice people to buy watches. We know this because (1) it has pictures of two which exhibit certain 'special' features; (2) it is written in persuasive, exaggerated language, for example: "Wear perfection on your wrist"; and (3) the brand name is familiar to us.

Most of us would, no doubt, have recognized the text as an advertisement. On the other hand, imagine that you lived in another country with no access to newspapers, television or the outside world. If you stumbled on something like this, would you recognize this text as an advertisement? Terry Eagleton, a famous literary scholar, once said, "There is no such thing as an innocent reading." In other words, before we even read a text, we have already been conditioned to respond to it in a certain way. This is through our encounters with the genre.

3.1 What is a genre?

 Definition—Genre

The word **"genre"** is a French word meaning **"kind"** or **"type"**. To classify texts into genres is to classify them according to a **code of expectations**. In a broad sense, there are three main literary genres: poetry, prose and drama.

However, within each of these literary genres, there exist other forms of classification as well.

- In poetry, poems can be further classified according to form or style.
- In prose, texts can be classified according to theme or subject matter.

Note that there are many genres aside from the above. Also, the boundary between genres may often be blurred so that we may read a text that is part adventure and part fantasy at the same time. One example is a series of novels called "The Chronicles of Narnia" by C.S. Lewis.

Group work: Discussion

> Humpty Dumpty sat on a wall
> Humpty Dumpty had a great fall
> All the king's horses and all the king's men
> Couldn't put Humpty together again

Work in a group of four and discuss the following questions:

1   What genre does this poem belong to? How do you know this?

2   Give other examples of poems in this genre.

3   List five characteristics about this genre of poetry.

4   List other genres you are familiar with and state their characteristics.

The poem above no doubt seems very familiar to you—it is in the category of the nursery rhyme. The knowledge that this is a nursery rhyme would already have set up certain expectations about the text. Here, we are not expected to take the text too seriously since it seems light and happy-go-lucky and we know it is a poem for very young children. If we were to analyse this text further, we would then consider how the writer creates this jovial mood through the rhyme scheme.

Although it is unnecessary to have a detailed knowledge of the various genres, a basic knowledge of the common ones can help you to

- identify the sort of text you have in hand
- identify the theme(s) and the truth that it expresses
- develop an appropriate response to it.

 Point to note

Get exposed to different genres.

The more you are exposed to different genres, the more you will know what to expect and what the writer of the text expects of you when you read it.

3.2 Overview of genres in poetry

Type	Description—type of text	Key features	What to expect: How to respond to the genre
Petrarchan sonnet	A poem of 14 lines. The first eight lines (octave) have the following rhyme scheme: **abbaabba**. The remaining six lines (sestet) follow the rhyme scheme **cdecde** or **cdcdcd**.	Sonnets typically celebrate or idealize love.	Look at how the idea of love is developed by comparing the octave and the sestet.
English sonnet	A poem of 14 lines divided into three stanzas, each following this rhyme scheme: **abab**. The poem ends with a couplet.		Look at how the idea of love is developed in each stanza. What is the difference? What main point is emphasized in the final couplet?
Haiku	A poem consisting of three unrhymed lines and 17 Japanese syllables. This style originated in Japan.	Haikus are reflective and express a view of life in relation to nature.	Examine the images of nature used and think about the qualities they are associated with. What aspect of the natural or the spiritual world is described?
Ballad	A poem that is meant to be sung and which recounts a dramatic incident or a story. The poem usually has a strong emotional quality and is descriptive of the time, place and persons involved.	Ballads are narrative poems which tell a story and are written to celebrate or reflect on a particular period or person.	Pay attention to the tone of the speaker. How does he sound? Consider carefully the descriptive nature of the subject—what is valued about it and why. Note the language—is it simple, colloquial?
Ode	A meditative poem intended to be sung, or recited, which celebrates, elevates or draws attention to a particular person, object or event.	An ode is usually a poem of celebration in connection with an important event, or one in praise of a person, emphasizing certain worthy attributes.	Examine the tone of the speaker. How does he sound and why? What quality of the subject is repeated? What images are associated with the main subject and what pattern can we infer from this? Is the language elevated? Why?

Type	Description—type of text	Key features	What to expect: How to respond to the genre
Elegy	A poem that is characterized by its mournful, reflective nature. It laments the loss or death of something or someone.	An elegiac poem usually conveys feelings of love and loss.	Pick out details from the poem about what the speaker is lamenting and why he is doing so. Relate the idea of loss or death to the larger picture of the reality of life.
Pastoral poem	A poem with a rural setting which celebrates the rustic lifestyle.	Pastoral poems are descriptive and usually convey the beauty of nature and the poet's love of it.	Pick out language used to describe various aspects of nature in the poem. What overall impression do you have? What does the speaker say about nature and his land? How does this relate to his sense of identity or belonging?

Note that the above list is not exhaustive. There are many other genres in poetry.

 Exercise 3A – Identifying poetic genres

Read the following texts. Identify their genres and respond to them, keeping these questions in mind.

1 How would you classify Texts A, B, C and D? Explain your choice of genre for each text, referring to the table on genres in poetry if necessary. What features make this different from the other texts?

2 Analyse each text closely and make an appropriate response to it. What are your feelings as you read the text? What is the text's underlying message? Support your answer with reference to the text.

3 Imagine that you are an examiner. What kind of questions would you ask on each text? Why?

My native town
    And in a borrowed bed:
Migrating birds.

Kyorai

Tropics

here,
the red sun catches the world in its stare.
here the exploded seed of a tall parent tree
climbs its way between the damp humus
5   to the sun, to the beckoning redness.
the green world, dark and deep in the myriad leaves
stretches its tendrils, breathing the air.
under the straight trunks and umbrella of vegetation
see the quality of shade, more liquid and calm,
10   or the slanted rays of afternoon
cutting their way
drilling holes between the leaves
and changing the pattern of the shadows.

here,
15   brown bodies, laughing faces
still standing smiling on the long monsoon beaches
waiting for sampans, celebrating each catch.
the round sea, held by the ring of the horizon,
rushes in filling your eyes.
20   girls running in bateks
in the afternoon waves,
laughing
to reach the beach's end.

here,
25   the water will rush at your feet
playing around your ankles,
or the monsoon waves will leave foam on your face,
and flood your house, roaring its days and nights,
but the beach is the brown people's home,
30   their traditions engraved by every tide.
they speak the language of the sea
birds and earth, praying only to their own God.

here,
they still dance and sing graceful
35   with hands and voices that reach the heart.
they love life and neighbours
and share their love in the neighbourhood.
each tide washes the earth and
dead leaves from their backs.

Muhammad Haji Salleh

Text C

Remembering Grandma

When yellow deepened in the cheeks
of Mother's sharp, dry face, Grandma
knew. A canine instinct
nosed out all the soft parts
5   that death had slightly smudged.
How would she conduct herself?
Mother would leave her to herself
in the impending wildernesses of our house.
How then would she conduct herself?
10   She was but old flesh drying on the bone
and could not die.
A son-in-law, improbable, yet Chinese.
Off-accent. His Malacca sister regularly rose
to plague him out of the ashes
15   of a painful past. Grandma had no claim
on their intense, murky quarrels in Malay.

Wong Phui Nam

Text D

Barbara Allen's Cruelty

In Scarlet town, where I was born,
    There was a fair maid dwellin',
Made every youth cry *Well-a-way!*
    Her name was Barbara Allen.

5 All in the merry month of May,
   When green buds they were swellin',
 Young Jemmy Grove on his death-bed lay,
   For love of Barbara Allen.

 He sent his man in to her then,
10   To the town where she was dwellin',
 "O haste and come to my master dear,
   If your name be Barbara Allen."

 So slowly, slowly rase she up,
   And slowly she came nigh him,
15 And when she drew the curtain by —
   "Young man, I think you're dyin'."

 "O it's I am sick and very very sick,
   And it's all for Barbara Allen." —
 "O the better for me ye'se never be,
20   Tho' your heart's blood were a-spillin'!

 "O dinna ye mind, young man," says she,
   "When the red wine ye were fillin',
 That ye made the healths go round and round,
   And slighted Barbara Allen?"

25 He turn'd his face unto the wall,
   And death was with him dealin':
 "Adieu, adieu, my dear friends all,
   And be kind to Barbara Allen!"

 As she was walking o'er the fields,
30   She heard the dead-bell knellin';
 And every jow the dead-bell gave
   Cried "Woe to Barbara Allen."

 "O mother, mother, make my bed,
   O make it saft and narrow:
35 My love has died for me to-day,
   I'll die for him to-morrow.

 "Farewell," she said, "ye virgins all,
   And shun the fault I fell in:
 Henceforth take warning by the fall
40   Of cruel Barbara Allen."

Thomas Percy

3.3 Overview of genres in prose

Type	Description—type of text	Key features	Starting points: How to respond to the genre
Tragedy	The story often ends in disaster or tragedy and often involves death. The protagonist is often isolated and has a character flaw which leads to tragic consequences.	Tragedies often cause us to reflect on the meaning of life and fate. We are also led to sympathize with the protagonist.	Identify the central dilemma faced by the protagonist and how his flaws are revealed in the process of addressing this dilemma. Look at what universal truth of human nature or the world is exemplified.
Comedy	The character wants something and attains it at the end. Comedies are characterized by their happy endings: a resolution of problems posed at the beginning and often involving marriage or romance of some sort. Romantic comedies are a sub-category of this genre.	Comedies usually allow us to laugh at the flaws of human nature or of society. The purpose is either to entertain the audience or to criticize others (or society) in a light-hearted manner.	Identify the central problem posed at the beginning and how this is resolved at the end. Identify whether the intention of the writer is simply to entertain or to provoke criticism of human nature or society.
Adventure/ Detective	In an adventure/detective story, the protagonist needs to solve a problem or crime and a large part of the story involves his search for the answer.	These stories usually revolve round the theme of quest. There is a strong element of suspense and tension. The ending may also be unexpected or surprising.	Look at the process by which the protagonist goes about piecing the information together. What elements of suspense, tension and surprise are incorporated in this process?
Horror	Horror stories are often descriptive of the environment as well as the emotions of the characters trapped in that environment.	These stories revolve round the idea that life is unpredictable; they involve a gradual development of tension. At its climax, the sense of tension is intense.	Look at how tension is gradually developed. Pay attention to foreshadowing devices employed by the writer and how the sense of suspense and tension intensifies.

Type	Description—type of text	Key features	Starting points: How to respond to the genre
Science fiction/ Fantasy	Science fiction or fantasy often plays with the idea of a utopia or ideal world. It is descriptive and meant to immerse the reader in an alternate reality.	These stories often show how even in an ideal setting, human foibles and flaws remain the same. Thus these worlds are, ironically, not so ideal after all.	Compare the science fiction world with the real world. What are the similarities and differences? What does this fantastical world highlight about the real world we live in?

Note that the above list is not exhaustive. There are many other genres in prose. Also, some of these categories and themes apply in poetry and drama as well.

Links to real-world issues

The huge variety of genres is an indication of the range of themes and stylistic features of literature as a whole. Aside from this, genres may be categorized according to different cultures, for example, African-American writing, South-east Asian writing and Indian writing. Why do you think writers choose to write in a certain genre? As a reader, why is it important to be exposed to different genres and different issues?

Exercise 3B – Identifying genres of fiction

Take a look at the opening paragraphs of four stories below. Can you identify the genre of each? Read the texts with the following questions in mind.

1   How would you classify Texts A, B, C and D? Explain your choice of genre for each text, referring to the table on genres in prose if necessary. What features make this different from the other texts?

2   Analyse each text closely and make an appropriate response to it. What are your feelings as you read the text? What is

the text's underlying message? Support your answer with reference to the text.

3   Imagine that you are an examiner. What kind of questions would you ask on each text? Why?

Text A

As a mother sits at the bedside of her sick child, Death comes and snatches him from her. The woman follows, desperately questioning the Night, a rosebush and a lake and winning answers to her questions by sacrificing her songs, her blood and her eyes. She crosses to the other side where Death has a greenhouse of human souls and searches among the plants for her own child. When Death returns to interrogate her, she, in a frenzy, threatens to uproot two plants at her feet. Then Death gives her back her eyes and shows her a vision of two futures, one of them happy and one tragic, telling her that one of them is her child's own. She, frightened at the tragic possibilities, begs Death to save her child by taking him away from her.

Extract from "The Story of a Mother"
by Hans Christian Andersen

Text B

I am Gimpel the fool. I don't think myself a fool. On the contrary. But that's what folks call me. They gave me the name while I was still in school. I had seven names in all: imbecile, donkey, flax-head, dope, glump, ninny, and fool. The last name stuck. What did my foolishness consist of? I was easy to take in. They said, "Gimpel, you know the rabbi's wife has been brought to childbed?" So I skipped school. Well, it turned out to be a lie. How was I supposed to know? She hadn't had a big belly. But I never looked at her belly. Was that really so foolish? The gang laughed and hee-hawed, stomped and danced and chanted a good-night prayer. And instead of the raisins they give when a woman's lying in, they stuffed my hand full of goat turds. I was no weakling. If I slapped someone he'd see all the way to Cracow. But I'm really not a slugger by nature. I think to myself: Let it pass. So they take advantage of me.

Extract from "Gimpel the Fool" by Isaac Bashevis Singer

When the man came out onto the street, he found that night had already gathered and the town was prostrate beneath its dun lead, the streets composed flat: the latter so many cool, metallic ribbons. He walked along one, heading for the bus stop.

For some reason, and he felt this ambiguously, he was slightly uneasy, so much so that if someone were to ask him why he felt that way, he would not be able, such was his uncertainty, to give a coherent answer. He walked slowly, with even, easy pacing, pondering. There was strangeness, but this was a distant feeble feeling, something vague hovering on the boundary of consciousness and did not permit any clear analysis. Was it the night itself, investing the town with tremulous, tiny points of light, sourceless light that did not seem to arise from any particular place or object, but seemed to be in the air itself, gossamery and waftable by any wind, by a mere breath? Was the strangeness within himself?

Extract from "The Temple Bells" by Goh Poh Seng

Till now that she was threatened with its loss, Emma had never known how much of her happiness depended on being first with Mr Knightley, first in interest and affection. Satisfied that it was so, and feeling it her due, she had enjoyed it without reflection, and only in the dread of being supplanted found how inexpressibly important it had been. Long, very long, she felt she had been first … She had not deserved it; she had often been negligent or perverse, slighting his advice or even wilfully opposing him, insensible of half his merits and quarrelling with him because he would not acknowledge her false and insolent estimate of her own—but still, from family attachment and habit, and thorough excellence of mind, he had loved her and watched over her from a girl, with an endeavour to improve her and an anxiety for her doing right which no other creature had at all shared. In spite of all her faults, she knew she was dear to him; might she not say very dear?

Extract from Emma *by Jane Austen*

Group work: Research project

Work in a group of eight. Half your group should 'specialize' in poetry and the other half, in prose.

(1) Each sub-group of four is to select a generic form based on the tables given earlier (genres in poetry and genres in prose).

(2) Each sub-group must then do the following:
(a) Find at least three examples of texts in that genre.
(b) Identify specific features of that genre: What defines this genre? How is it different from other genres? What is unique about its theme, form or style of writing? And so on.

(3) Sub-group members must present their work or findings to the other half of their group. They could also present the same to the class or design an educational poster and put this up on the class's Literature noticeboard.

 Point to note

Genres overlap!

While it is good to be exposed to a wide variety of genres, you should not be unduly worried about not knowing every genre well. A knowledge of genres may only help you identify the category the unseen text belongs to and understand its broad structure. Also, sometimes writers can deliberately go against expectations of a genre in order to make a point or surprise the reader. In this case, the text would contain an element of irony.

Chapter **4**

WHAT IS THE MOOD
OF THE TEXT?

Chapter outline

4.1 Mood

4.2 Atmosphere

4.3 Feelings of the
speaker

Trigger activity

Look at Photograph A and Photograph B. What is
the difference?

Photograph A   *(Source: www.bigfoto.com)*

Photograph B

Both photographs deal with the same subject matter—the sea. However, we would respond to the two photographs differently. Our response is influenced by the mood expressed in each photograph. The mood in Photograph A is heavy and melancholic as indicated by the darker tones while the mood in Photograph B is light-hearted as expressed by the brighter tones.

 Point to note

What is the colour of the text?

One way to discern or get at the underlying meaning of a text is to ask ourselves: What is the overall colour of the writing? Is it light or dark?

When we think about the colour of a text, we are actually thinking about the kind of feelings or emotions the text evokes in the reader.

4.1 Mood

 Definition—Mood

The **mood** of a text refers to the **emotions it evokes**. Moods can range from heavy to light-hearted to exciting. Within these categories, there are also specific emotive qualities. Refer to the following table for a better idea.

Words to describe mood

Philosophical	Sad	Positive	Jovial	Unpredictable
Reflective	Melancholic	Joyous	Humorous	Tense
Nostalgic	Heavy	Light-hearted	Lively	Disturbing
Sympathetic	Depressing	Dreamy	Celebratory	Mysterious
Wistful	Sorrowful	Romantic	Delirious	Oppressive

Purpose—Why do we analyse mood?

Gauging the mood of a text allows us to formulate an accurate response to it, as shown in the following:

Examples of mood	Types of response
Nostalgic mood	• Stirs the reader's sympathy for a person • Causes the reader to reflect on an issue
Light-hearted mood	• Provokes amusement and laughter, thereby keeping the reader entertained
Oppressive/tense mood	• Arouses a sense of fear and anticipation in the reader, thereby keeping the reader motivated to read on

Without analysing the mood of the text, students may respond in inappropriate ways. For example, they may find a text comic when it is intended to be tragic; they may feel sympathy for a character when the text is meant to be read as ironic or critical of that character.

 Method—How do we analyse mood?

We can analyse mood by paying attention to the adjectives (descriptive words) in the text. This is especially important for words describing atmosphere (description of surroundings) and the feelings of the narrator.

4.2 Atmosphere

 Definition—Atmosphere

The **atmosphere** of a text refers to the **description of the surroundings**. To analyse the atmosphere, pick out adjectives which describe

(a) the climate/weather
(b) the natural environment
(c) the man-made environment.

Driving to Town Late to Mail a Letter

It is a <u>cold and snowy</u> night.
The main street is <u>deserted</u>.
The only things moving are <u>swirls of snow</u>.
As I lift the mailbox door, I feel its <u>cold</u> iron.
There is a privacy I love in this <u>snowy</u> night
Driving around, I will waste more time.

Robert Bly

From this poem, we can list the descriptive words as follows:

Atmosphere	Noun (Phrase)	Adjective (Phrase)
Weather	snow	swirling (swirls of snow)
Natural environment	night	cold and snowy snowy (night)
Man-made environment	mailbox door main street	cold (iron) deserted

Method—How do we analyse atmosphere?

To analyse atmosphere in a poem/text:

(1) Look at the adjectives describing the surroundings.

(2) Then pick out ideas that are repeated.

(3) Analyse the text by asking yourself what pattern or general impression comes to your mind.

In the poem above, the repetition of the words "snow" and "snowy" and the repetition of the word "cold" both contribute to the sense of isolation and chill. On the other hand, snow also conveys a vision of purity, whiteness—adding to the impression of the beauty of the natural landscape. This attention to the snow enables the reader to appreciate nature alongside the speaker.

1801—I have just returned from a visit to my landlord—
the solitary neighbour that I shall have trouble with. This is
certainly a beautiful country! In all England, I do not believe
that I could have fixed on a situation so completely removed
5 from the stir of society ... Wuthering Heights is the name of
Mr Heathcliff's dwelling. "Wuthering" being a significant
provincial adjective, descriptive of the atmospheric tumult
to which its station is exposed in stormy weather. Pure,
bracing ventilation they must have up there at all times,
10 indeed: one may guess the power of the north wind blowing
over the edge, by the excessive slant of a few stunted firs at
the end of the house; and by a range of gaunt thorns stretching
their limbs one way as if craving for sunlight. Happily, the
architect had foresight to build it strong: the narrow windows
15 are deeply set in the wall, and the corners defended with
jutting stones.

Extract from Wuthering Heights *by Emily Bronte*

1 Where is the story set and how does this contribute to the
mood and atmosphere of the story?

2 Underline all the adjectives and adjectival phrases in the text
describing the environment. What pattern emerges? State
how this contributes to the mood in the text.

3 Outward appearance often gives us a hint of the inner
qualities of a character. How does the physical description of
Wuthering Heights reflect on the owner? Support your
answer with reference to the text.

4.3 Feelings of the speaker

Analysing the atmosphere in a text is one way to gauge its mood.
Another way is to examine the feelings of the speaker (in poetry) or the
feelings of the narrator (in prose).

Definition—Feelings

This refers to the **emotion/s felt by the narrator** in the text **regarding the subject matter.**

Application example

In the extract from *Wuthering Heights*, the narrator's feelings towards Mr Heathcliff, his landlord, can be represented diagrammatically in this way:

Feelings	towards	subject
Discomfort, sense of of tension and fear		landlord

Method—How do we infer feelings?

To analyse feeling, you need to

(1) recognize the subject matter and use the most accurate adjectives to describe the feeling or attitude towards it. (Note that the title of a text can sometimes help you to recognize the text's subject matter.)

(2) Once you have come up with an adjective which you think applies, check it in a dictionary; next, refer to a book of synonyms (such as a thesaurus) for words that are close in meaning to your original one. Use the reference books so that it becomes a habit.

Method—How do we write about feelings?

Feeling (or attitude) is best expressed by using *adjectives*. If you want to use the noun form of an adjective, you may do so. Look at our list and note the changes.

Adjective	Noun form
Angry	Anger
Bitter	Bitterness
Believing	Belief
Doubtful	Doubt
Distrustful	Distrust
Disgusted	Disgust

Thus, you may write a sentence, for example, about the extract from *Wuthering Heights*, using

♦ **an adjective**

The narrator is *fearful* of his landlord, Mr Heathcliff.

But if you want to write a different sentence which expresses a similar meaning, you could use

♦ **a noun**

The narrator expresses his *fear* of his landlord, Mr Heathcliff.

On the whole, it is best to use adjectives as they are more direct in describing feeling.

 Group work: Analysis and discussion

mirror, mirror

until twelve
i could believe in you
believe i was part of you
miming. Dancing. funny or sad
5   i loved you every day

at sixteen, sixteen
i chose to make my character
eyes blue. Cheeks blushed. lips pink
i began to doubt you

10   twenty, twenty
i saw in others
what i couldn't find in you

mirror, mirror
you're a liar

Chung Yee Chong

1 The subject matter is the mirror that the growing child sees before her. What is her attitude to the mirror?

2   Compare the feelings of the speaker at the beginning of the poem and at the end. Is there a change? Give reasons.

Stages	Attitude (express this with adjectives)
At first	
Later	
At the end	

Links to real-world issues

This poem encapsulates some of the pressures of teenage life. What are some of these? For example, some teenagers have an inferiority complex and compare themselves unfavourably with their peers. What do you think is the root cause of this?

Point to note

Moods and feelings are never static.

Mood and feeling may change in a text. For example, the mood may shift from belief to doubt and to distrust, ending in disgust. The point to note is that mood and feeling need not be consistent but can develop and change.

Exercise 4B – Feelings of speaker

When you are old

When you are old and grey and full of sleep,
And nodding by the fire, take down this book,
And slowly read, and dream of the soft look
Your eyes had once, and of their shadows deep;

5

How many loved your moments of glad grace,
And loved your beauty with love false or true;
But one man loved the pilgrim soul in you,
And loved the sorrows of your changing face.

And bending down beside the glowing bars,
Murmur, a little sadly, how love fled
And paced upon the mountains overhead
And hid his face amid a crowd of stars.

W.B. Yeats

1 Who do you think the speaker is addressing in this poem? What is he saying?

2 Refer to section 4.3 and write down adjectives in the left column below that accurately reflect the speaker's feelings about old age.

Speaker's feelings	towards	subject
		old age

3 What adjectives would you use to describe the mood created?

4 Does the mood change as the poem progresses? Give evidence to support your points.

 Exercise 4C – More practice in gauging mood (poetry)

old house at ang siang hill

an unusual house this is
dreams are here before you sleep
tread softly

5   into the three storyed gloom
sit gently
on the straits-born furniture
imported from china
speak quietly
to the contemporary occupants

10   they are not afraid of you
waiting for you to go
before they dislocate your intentions
so what if this is
your grandfather's house

15   his ghost doesn't live here anymore
your family past is
superannuated grime
which increases with time
otherwise nothing adds or subtracts

20   the bricks and tiles
until re-development
which will greatly change
this house-that-was
dozens like it along the street

25   the next and the next as well

nothing much will be missed
eyes not tradition tell you this

Arthur Yap

1   Describe what the poem is about.

2   What adjectives would you use to describe the mood created?

3   What are your feelings as you read this poem? Does it change as the poem progresses?

4   How would you describe the tone of the speaker and the message conveyed at the end of the poem?

Links to real-world issues

The above poem by a well-known Singaporean writer conveys some of the conflicts and dilemmas brought about as a by-product of modernization in Singapore. What do you think some of these conflicts and dilemmas are and how we can achieve balance between modernization and the need to preserve history?

Exercise 4D – More practice in gauging mood (prose)

Thirty-seven nights later, I picked up my diary. "Meng Chuan," I wrote, "this morning the tide was right for us to go down to the South China Sea. We, that is Mei Yew, Meng Yew, Chong Yew and I, together with Kenneth Loke, who had
5 helped so much with the funeral and who made all the arrangements for this morning, we went out to where the Singapore waters join the South China Sea. We left the house at about four in the morning with the urn; Meng Yew, our elder boy, held on to it. The sea was rough. The journey took
10 us nearly an hour. As we neared the South China Sea, the motor launch came to a halt. Boisterous waves rocked the launch and Meng Yew took the Japanese urn into which your ashes had been put, and sat astride one of the main supports on deck, with help from Kenneth and our two other
15 children. I watched Meng Yew trying hard to stabilize himself so that he could pour the ashes slowly into the turbulent waters.

"We had also brought along red roses, and a tape of Beethoven's 9th. It was playing, trying hard to be heard
20 against the rush, to and fro, of the heaving waves. Meng Yew quietly and as steadily as he could scattered the ashes into the sea and then, as they were lost in solution and with increasing distance, we gently threw all the red roses we had brought with us into the dark-blue waters. That took us
25 nearly forty minutes. And all the time I could see you, me, through those years we spent together. When you first held my hand at the Alhambra on Beach Road during a re-run of *Limelight* with Claire Bloom and Charlie Chaplin. It was

30 such a moving film and you gave it more meaning and made it even more a memory to cherish: when you first kissed me and when you told me you loved me. That was nineteen years ago. So many remembered incidents ran through my mind. How you stayed with me right through the births of

35 our three children—how pleased, happy and proud you were with Mei Yew, our first born, and how your mother was so satisfied with the two boys who followed. So were we. I still have the pearl necklace you gave me on our first anniversary. It is still very special. Thousands of memories came flooding in, in quick succession.

40 "And then the strains of the 9th ended with the choral movement and brought me back to reality. Your ashes were drifting to Peking, as you desired. You had planned to go to China in the spring, but now, that would never be. Silently, tears streamed down my face, helplessly, heedlessly, as the

45 waters swept the last of your physical being away for always. Perhaps your ashes will seep through some small part of China's coast and as they reach mother earth again, perhaps a beautiful orange blossom tree will bloom there, but whether that happens is something I shall never know. You have

50 gone, but a part of you is still with me. Tonight as I write, I feel a sense of peace for you, and in me, because you went as you had wished to go, quickly; and because, this morning I did what you asked."

Extract from "What you asked"
by Nalla Tan

1   The woman in this passage is mourning her late husband and saying that she has done what he had asked her to do. What has she done?

2   In particular, describe her attitude to the events of the past in paragraph two.

3   Considering the passage as a whole, what other adjectives would you use to describe her feelings towards her late husband? Have her feelings changed? Support your answer with reference to the passage.

Chapter 5

INTRODUCTION TO CLOSE ANALYSIS OF POETRY

From Section I, students would have learned how to obtain an overall understanding of a piece of writing and its concerns. The aim of this section is to equip them with skills for more in-depth analysis. It deals with skills for close reading of poetry and an analysis of poetic devices.

Chapter outline

5.1 Introduction to poetry

5.2 A strategy for approaching poetry

 Trigger activity

Look at this picture and describe it closely.

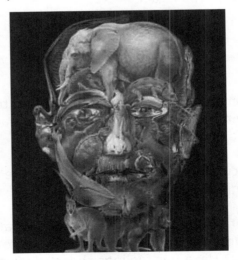

When we look at this picture from afar, we see a human face. However, on closer examination, we realize that there is more to the face—in fact, it is made up of 24 different animals. Can you make them out?

The point of this exercise is that analysing a poem or prose text often requires you to be able to zoom out of and zoom into it. In other words, to appreciate a text effectively, you need to grasp the big picture about what the text is about and then move to look at it closely for its details.

5.1 Introduction to poetry

In ancient times, the reading, as well as the creation, of a poem was regarded as a sacred act revered by many. Among ancient Celts, poets were regarded as magicians and priests and whoever insulted one was punishable by death. The reading of poetry as an art form has existed for centuries, long before novels and films became popular.

Definition—What is a poem?

In general, a **poem** is a **composition** or arrangement **of words in lines**. A poem can be identified by its

(a) form (poetic structure)
(b) language (diction, imagery, symbols, unusual word order)
(c) rhythm and sound (rhythm, metre, sound devices).

Group work: Compare and contrast

For a long time, people have tried to define what poetry is with very different results. However, most people would agree that poetry is most easily defined when compared with prose.

Look at the following texts. Identify which is a poem and which is from a prose text. Note that line divisions have been eliminated in this exercise.

Example A	Text 1	Text 2
	Jack and Jill went up a hill To fetch a pail of water Jack fell down and broke his crown and Jill followed shortly after.	Once upon a time, there were two children named Jack and Jill. One day, they went up a hill to get water when Jack slipped and fell, pulling Jill along with him.

Example B	Text 1	Text 2
	When my father was seventy-three he fell ill and the doctors gave him only a few weeks to live. My father was convinced that his illness had come on him because he'd hit a particularly bad losing streak at cards.	Sundays too my father got up early and put his clothes on in the blueblack cold, then with cracked hands that ached from labour in the weekday weather made banked fires blaze.

Example C	Text 1	Text 2
	I was waiting for you where the four lanes wander into a city street, listening to the freight train's whistle and thunder.	She glanced at the clock. He had probably gone past his own door, to drink before coming home. Then she took the potatoes to strain them in the yard.

Explain why you would consider one text a poem and another, prose. What distinct features define poetry and prose?

5.2 A strategy for approaching poetry

 Definition—Close analysis

The **close analysis** of a poem refers to an **in-depth examination of** the **form and language** of the poem as well as its **rhythm and sound**. You should do a close analysis of the poem only after you have made an overview of it.

 Purpose—Why do we need to do a close analysis of the poem?

(a) A poem is often much shorter than a prose text and its ideas and meaning are necessarily condensed in the lines and stanzas. Analysing the poem, therefore, requires an in-depth critical examination of its form, language, rhythm and sound.

(b) As the meaning of a poem is conveyed through its form, language and rhythm/sound, questions and answers on it will deal with these main characteristics or aspects.

Method—A strategy for approaching poetry

This is a step-by-step strategy for approaching and analysing a poem:

Steps	What you should do
Step 1: Understanding overall meaning	Aim: Get a clear overview of WHAT the text is about. Read the text once through to get an impression of what the poem is about: its subject matter, genre and mood. *(Refer to Section I of this book.)*
Step 2: Close reading	Aim: Look at HOW the central meaning is conveyed to the reader through language and rhythm and sound devices. (1) Read the poem more closely, paying attention to • diction (word choice) • word order (unusual punctuation, unusual word placement) • figurative language (simile, metaphor, personification) • rhythm (rhythm, rhyme, metre) • sound devices (alliteration, assonance, consonance, onomatopoeia) (2) Look at how these are used to convey the message and mood of the poem. *(Each of these techniques will be covered in the following chapters of this book.)*
Step 3: Philosophical insight and response	Aim: Respond to the poem. (1) Read the poem, paying attention to the underlying meaning and truth through • oppositional structure (What is the central tension or theme in the text?) • intention (What is the intention of the writer in writing the text?) (2) Summarize this as a statement about what philosophical insight about the world and about human nature the poem conveys to the reader. (3) As you reflect on these insights, note down your feelings at different parts of the poem. Then look at how your feelings change in the course of the poem. *(Refer to Section IV of this book.)*

Application example

Note: It is not expected that you would, at this stage, be able to analyse a poem in the manner given in this example. The point of this example is to give you an idea of how the strategy proposed can be used to analyse any poem.

The Secret Sits

We dance round in a ring and suppose,
But the Secret sits in the middle and knows.

Robert Frost

Stage 1: Understanding overall meaning

Subject matter: It is about a group of unknown figures dancing around an unknown entity.

Mood: The mood moves from a sense of innocence to an ominous feel. For example, the word "suppose" implies innocence and naiveté, whereas "knows" conveys the idea of omniscient power. What exactly is known is not clear, and this gives a sinister tone to the poem.

Genre: The two-line poem, structured like a riddle, creates a sense of mystery and awe about the poem.

Stage 2: Close reading

Diction—the name "Secret" implies that there is no clear identification of who or what the subject is. It cannot be known.

Word order—the two lines reflect each other in structure. We have the subject, its action/verb and finally its attitude. The structure of the parallel lines emphasizes connectedness ("We" and "Secret" are connected by knowledge—either the lack of or possession of it) and yet the distance between the two is indicated by their separation; they seem never to meet.

Figurative language—"dance round in a ring" could be taken literally, but metaphorically, it could also imply that they are going in circles, trying to find meaning and truth but not being able to.

Rhythm—regular rhythmic structure of two unstressed syllables followed by a stressed syllable conveys the impression of a chant.

Sound—the use of consonance in "suppose" and "knows" repeats the "s" consonant to create a hissing sound. This adds to the sinister feel of the poem.

Stage 3: Philosophical insight and response

The first line is in a light-hearted tone, conveyed by words like "dance" and "suppose", as if these people are playing a game or enjoying the bliss they live in. **However, the second line** causes us to feel afraid for these people, who may be ignorant of an important truth and who are not aware that they are watched.

Oppositional structure: "We" versus "the Secret"; "ring" versus "middle"—suggests that this is a poem about power—a group of people surround an entity that seems to be in control.

Intention: Why did the writer write this poem or frame the poem in the form of a riddle? The paradox in the poem is that a group of people are actively moving and trying hard to decipher the meaning but are unable to—could this be similar to the reader who is trying hard to decipher what the poem means? In that case, this poem could also be a reflection of the power of the poet. In a larger context, it could reflect the idea that human beings can never know anything for certain.

The following chapters of this book will go into more detail about how to conduct a close analysis of a poem and how to respond to it.

 Point to note

Be sensitive to details.

In poetry, it is particularly important to pay attention to details. These details will typically form the evidence supporting your answers about the message, mood, theme/truth and intention of the text.

With a partner, try analysing the following two poems. Write
your responses down.

Text A

letter from a youth to his prospective employer

sir: i refer to my interview & your salary offer:
you said i would be given a commensurate salary:
commensurate with what? the depth of the filing
cabinet or the old bag sitting 3 desks & one right-
5 hand corner away? i am reasonably qualified:
quite handsome: my lack of experience compensated
by my prodigal intelligence: i shall not expect
to marry the typewriter: it's decision-making
i am after: that's what i am: a leader of tomorrow:
10 so why don't you make it today? my personality
is personable: & all opportunities being equal:
i am equal to any most opportune moment:
any most momentous opportunity: so take me
to your highest superior: & spare nothing:
15 at my earliest convenience: yours faithfully

Arthur Yap

1 First, construct a general understanding of the poem.
  a What is the poem about? Who is speaking to whom and
     why?
  b What is the genre of this poem?
  c How would you describe the tone of the speaker?

2 Second, attempt a close reading of the poem.
  a Pick out five words or phrases that give you an
     impression of the attitude and character of the speaker.
  b Why is the poem written entirely in lower case? Look at
     any other interesting punctuation and comment on its
     use.

Links to real-world issues

Imagine you are the owner of a large company. Would you hire the above speaker? Why? How important do you think looking at things from other perspectives will be in your future career? Why? Provide examples.

Text B

The Death of the Ball Turret Gunner

From my mother's sleep I fell into the State,
And I hunched in its belly till my wet fur froze.
Six miles from earth, loosed from its dream of life,
I woke to black flak and the nightmare fighters.
When I died they washed me out of the turret with a hose.

Randall Jarrell

1   How can we tell that the gunner refers to an airman fighting in a war?

2   What is the overall message of the poem? Pick out any interesting words which substantiate this.

3   What does the poet mean to suggest when he writes that the airman is "from his mother's sleep"?

4   Look at the whole poem, specifically the last line, and answer this question: Is this a patriotic poem? Give reasons for your answer.

Chapter *6*
DICTION

Chapter outline

Trigger activity

Imagine that the boss of a company has written the following statements in a report on his employees. Can you list the ways each of these statements may be interpreted?

(a) "Mary is an efficient worker who is able to delegate her duties well."

(b) "Jerry submitted an interesting report last year which proposed many ideas, a few of which were applicable."

(c) "Thomas has an outspoken personality and he does not hesitate to contribute many opinions at meetings."

Point to note

In literature, meaning may not always be obvious.

Writers take pains to add complexity to their writing and the message they intend to convey may not be obvious to the reader. Hence, writers choose their words carefully. When we pay attention to specific words employed by writers, we are actually paying attention to diction.

Group work: Filling in the gaps

I wish I could remember the first day,

First hour, first moment of your meeting me;

The weather was like _____.

And I felt like _____

If only I could recollect it! Such

A day of days! I let it _____

It was like _____ to me.

It seemed to mean _____ to me.

If only now I could recall that _____

That first _____.

1 In a group, think of a purpose for this poem. For example, you could be writing this to someone you have a secret crush on, someone you have trouble working with, someone you respect and so on.

2 Now fill in the blanks. One rule: try to make the text sound and feel like a poem.

3 Share your answers with another group. Ask them to guess the intention behind the letter.

6.1 Analysing diction

Definition—Diction

Diction refers to the **selection of words** employed by poets to **convey ideas**. Another commonly used term for diction is "word choice".

Purpose—Why should we analyse diction?

Language or words are at the heart of poetry. The poet S.T. Coleridge says that poetry is the "best words in the best order". Because poets must often convey meaning within a small space, a poet must choose his/her words carefully. Therefore, in order to better appreciate a poem, we need to look at why the poet uses one word instead of another.

Method—How do we analyse diction?

In looking at language, it is often useful to imagine yourself as an interviewer. Imagine that the poet is seated right in front of you and you are about to have a conversation with him. Then imagine yourself asking the poet why he chose a certain word, why he used this image or this specific allusion and not another. In other words, when you are analysing the language of a poem, your role is to question the use of specific words or phrases. This involves three steps:

(1) Read the poem, highlighting interesting words or phrases that attract your attention.

(2) Think about why a particular word is used instead of another. For example, you could phrase it in this manner, "Why X and not Y?"

(3) Examine what the word/phrase **denotes** (its literal meaning) and, more importantly, what it **connotes** (its implied meaning).

(4) Examine the word in the larger context, that is, how it elaborates the underlying meaning or theme of the poem.

Application example

For example, read this poem and analyse diction.

Those Winter Sundays

<u>Sundays</u> too <u>my</u> father got up early
and put his clothes on in the blueblack cold,
then with cracked hands that ached
from labour in the weekday weather made
5   banked fires blaze. No one ever thanked him.

I'd wake and hear the cold splintering, breaking.
When the rooms were warm, he'd call,
and slowly I would rise and dress,
fearing the chronic angers of that house,

10   speaking indifferently to him,
who had driven out the cold
and polished my good shoes as well.
What did I know, what did I know
of love's austere and lonely offices?

Robert Hayden

(1) Highlight interesting words/phrases.
We have underlined the word "Sundays" in the first line of the poem as we consider it interesting.

(2) Why X and not Y?
We begin to question the choice of this word and ask ourselves why the poet chose Sunday rather than any other day of the week to begin his description of the topic of his poem.

(3) Analyse denotation and connotation of the word.
We now analyse the denotation and connotation of the word "Sundays". At a literal (denotative) level, Sunday, in Western society, is a day of rest. At an implied (connotative) level, this reveals that the father is someone who cares very much for his family. Instead of taking time to rest on a Sunday, he chooses to wake up early and get his house in order for the rest of his family members.

(4) Relate to a larger theme of the poem.
One of the themes of the poem is about appearance versus reality. Appearance-wise, the father seems hard and tough. However, in reality, he displays great love and sacrifice for his family.

This is a step-by-step strategy of analysing diction. We could apply this strategy to other interesting words in the poem. Another interesting word is "my". The speaker could have simply said, "Sundays too father got up early". Why does he add the word "my"? At a literal level, the word "my" is a possessive term indicating that the speaker is the son. However, at an implied level, "my" conveys the sense of pride he has for his father. Once again, the theme of appearance versus reality is exemplified—the son fears his father but at the same time, he respects and admires him.

Group work: Application and analysis

With a partner, or in a small group, read the poem "Those Winter Sundays" again. As you read, underline any interesting words or phrases in the text. Next, think about why the writer chose to use those words/phrases instead of others and then state how his choices contribute to the meaning of the poem. Apply the strategy outlined above to your analysis and then discuss your conclusions in class.

 Exercise 6A – Word choice

The First Day

I wish I could remember the first day,
First hour, first moment of your meeting me;
If bright or dim the season, it might be
Summer or winter for aught I can say.
5   So unrecorded did it slip away,
So blind was I to see and to foresee,
So dull to mark the budding of my tree
That would not blossom yet for many a May.
If only I could recollect it! Such
10   A day of days! I let it come and go
As traceless as a thaw of bygone snow.
It seemed to mean so little, meant so much!
If only now I could recall that touch,
First touch of hand in hand!—Did one but know!

Christina Rossetti

1   Recall the group gap-filling task at the beginning of this chapter. How is this poem similar to or different from the text your group completed?

2   What is this poem about? Support your answer with relevant examples.

3   Explain why the writer pays a lot of attention to describing the season and the weather. What does she want to bring to our notice?

4 Pick out other interesting words, phrases and imagery in the poem and decide what they imply and how they contribute to the larger meaning of the text.

5 How does the writer show that the speaker has feelings of regret? Support your answer with reference to the poem.

 Exercise 6B – Word choice

in Just-

in Just-
spring   when the world is mud-
luscious the little
lame balloonman

5   whistles   far   and wee

and eddieandbill come
running from marbles and
piracies and it's
spring

10   when the world is puddle-wonderful

the queer
old balloonman whistles
far   and   wee
and bettyandisbel come dancing

15   from hop-scotch and jump-rope and

it's
spring
and
       the

20   goat-footed

balloonMan   whistles
far
and
wee

E.E. Cummings

51

1   Why is spring important in this poem?

2   The poet is fond of joining words like "eddieandbill". Can you explain why? Point to other examples of interesting words employed by the writer. Explain why the writer does this.

3   How does the way the poem is arranged give you a clue about reading it?

6.2 Symbolism

Definition—Symbol

Sometimes, specific words in a poem may have a larger significance. They may be representative of an idea, an issue or a value. A **symbol** is something that **represents a larger idea or value**.

Purpose—Why are symbols used?

Symbols are often used to concretize abstract qualities such as human emotions. For example, giving someone a rose on Valentine's Day is a visible act of affection because the rose symbolizes love.

Here are some examples of symbolism.

Details	Symbolic of
Seasons	The seasons are associated with the stages of life: birth, growth, maturity and death. • Spring – associated with birth: rejuvenation, revival, new life and new beginnings. Spring is also a symbol of motherhood. • Summer – associated with growth: happiness, joy, carefree living • Autumn – associated with maturity: wisdom, learning or development, and fulfilment in life • Winter – associated with death: old age, alienation, isolation, despair

Details	Symbolic of
Flowers and trees	• Sunflower – brightness, joy • Roses – romance, love • White lilies – purity, beauty • Yew tree – old age, sickness, death
Other aspects of nature	• The river – symbolic of life and energy. Water is associated with fertility or prosperity. • Fire – passion, anger or fury • Sky – heaven, bliss • Star – symbol of light, peace, universal harmony • Rain – cleansing and purification. In another context, rain may be associated with sadness and loss. • Sun – happiness, life, freedom, energy
Animals	• Birds – freedom • Owl – foreshadows something ominous to come • Snake – presence of evil, associated with deceit • Black cat – bad luck, witchcraft
Objects	• Key – authority, power to achieve something • Ring – commitment, marriage, faithfulness • School badge – loyalty, belonging to a community
Actions	• Waving – friendliness, welcome • Hug – reconciliation, acceptance
People	• Mother Theresa – courage, sacrifice

Work with a partner and think of more symbols. Try to think of symbols from both the Eastern and Western cultures.

 Method—How do we analyse symbols?

Analysing symbols is similar to analysing word choice.

(1) Look for words (especially for objects or actions) that are emphasized (that is, they are repeated several times in the text or they may be in the title or first stanza of the text).

(2) Look at their denotative (literal) and connotative (implied) meanings.

(3) Think about how the connotative meanings can represent larger truths about the world or human nature.

Singapore River

The operation was massive;
Designed to give new life
To the old lady.
We have cleaned out
5   Her arteries, removed
Detritus and silt,
Created a by-pass
For the old blood.
Now you can hardly tell
10   Her history.

We have become
So health conscious
The heart
Can sometimes be troublesome.

Lee Tzu Pheng

(1) **Emphasized words (for objects or actions)**
The name "Singapore River" is emphasized as it appears in the title.

(2) **Denotation and connotation**
The title tells us that the poem is literally about the Singapore River. On the other hand, the river could also be representative of the country that existed long before Singapore as a nation was established.

(3) **Larger universal value or truth**
Thus, we can say that in this poem, the river is symbolic of Singaporean society, and that its reconstruction is symbolic of how Singapore's history and culture may be gradually eroded by modernization.

Point to note

Have a "what if" question in your mind.

Every time you read a text, it is useful to have a "what if" question in your mind. Ask yourself: "What if the writer had used another word? What if the writer had not included this word?" And, with regard to object/symbol: "How would the text have been different?" When you start thinking like this, you are essentially thinking about the power of language and images in influencing the reader's understanding of the text

Exercise 6C – Symbolism

1   Now analyse the poem "Singapore River" on your own, identifying other symbols in it.

2   How do these symbols contribute to a larger truth about the world or human nature?

3   What is the speaker's attitude to what has happened? How can you tell?

Exercise 6D – More practice on symbolism

A Poison Tree

I was angry with my friend:
I told my wrath, my wrath did end.
I was angry with my foe:
I told it not, my wrath did grow.

5   And I watered it in fears,
Night and morning with my tears;
And I sunned it with smiles,
And with soft deceitful wiles.

And it grew both day and night,
10 Till it bore an apple bright.
And my foe beheld it shine,
And he knew that it was mine,

And into my garden stole,
When the night had veil'd the pole;
15 In the morning glad I see
My foe outstretched beneath the tree.

William Blake

Note the features of the poem, namely, (1) it tells a story; (2) it makes reference to an apple and a tree; and (3) it has a moral.

The story is about a person who does not tell his foe of his anger but instead nurses it. As a result, their relationship leads to the injury or death of the foe. The moral is: do not keep negative feelings towards another person or else they will develop and endanger your relationship. It is better to confess the hurt and release the feelings. The question to ask is: How is the story told through reference or allusion to the apple and the tree?

Now answer these questions on the poem.

1 What does the apple symbolize?

2 What does the tree symbolize?

3 Where do the references to both apple and tree come from?

4 How do the references enlarge the moral of the story?

5 RESPONSE: Write freely about a real situation in which you concealed your anger and describe what happened as a result.

Links to real-world issues

Sometime in 2002, in Singapore, the newspapers reported an incident in which a man, driven by his anger against a woman, tried to poison her. He ended up poisoning three other people, but not his intended victim, and was jailed for it.

How does this example illustrate the truth of the poem "A Poison Tree"? Even though other people were hurt and not the intended victim, does this change or alter the moral of the poem?

List ten moral or ethical principles you believe you and your classmates should abide by.

Chapter 7
WORD ORDER

Trigger activity

An English professor asked his class to punctuate the following sentence correctly:

"A woman without her man is nothing."

Before reading on, discuss, in a small group, the different ways this statement may be punctuated.

After the session, the professor collated the answers. As expected, all the males in the class wrote: "A woman, without her man, is nothing." However, all the female students wrote: "A woman: without her, man is nothing."

From this example, we see that the way words are punctuated can affect their meaning. Hence, in addition to paying attention to diction, writers also pay attention to the arrangement of their words and punctuation on a page. When analysing word order, we should look out for unusual word placement and unusual punctuation marks.

7.1 Unusual punctuation

Definition—How do we identify unusual punctuation?

Unusual punctuation usually stands out because it is

- unusually placed
- repeated too often
- missing altogether from the text.

Purpose—Why do writers employ unusual punctuation?

Writers employ unusual punctuation for several reasons:

(a) to make the reader pay attention to the unusual punctuation so as to emphasize a certain word or meaning in the text

(b) to convey a certain tone or emotion through drawing the reader's attention to a form of punctuation or the lack of it in the text.

Method—How do we analyse unusual punctuation?

(1) Identify any punctuation marks that are unusually placed.

(2) Think about the effect these punctuation marks have on you, the reader. For example, if a punctuation mark were removed or replaced by another, how would your reaction be different? Why is your attention drawn to it? Does the punctuation mark encourage you to respond in a certain way?

(3) Explain how this contributes to the larger meaning of the text.

Application example

King Lear makes this statement after two of his daughters, Regan and Goneril, abandon him:

> Blow, winds, and crack your cheeks! rage! blow!
> You cataracts and hurricanes, spout
> Till you have drench'd our steeples, drown'd the cocks!
> You sulphurous and thought-executing fires,
> Vaunt-couriers to oak-cleaving thunderbolts,
> Singe my white head!

Without analysing the rich imagery in this speech we can already sense the anger and energy in his tone simply by the repetition of the exclamation mark, which expresses great emotional frustration. Here, King Lear invokes the heavens and all of nature to kill him and this expresses the intensity of the hurt in him.

Examples of common types of unusual punctuation:
Run-on lines

Another common example of unusual punctuation in poems is the use of **run-on lines** in poems. *Run-on lines are lines which do not end with a grammatical break; the meaning must be completed by reading the next* *line.* Another term often used to describe this technique is "**enjambment**". Run-on lines often force us to pay attention to the words or phrases before the pause.

Application example

Marina Bay

This was not
new, we made it new,
stole from the sea what
the sea does not need
5   We are doing
it, again and again
Sixties, seventies,
eighties, nineties
Not dinosaurs
10   we are raptors of time,
ruthless users, dis-
respectful movers
The best renewers after
the Dutch
15   Scorning the
sea, loving the sea

Robert Yeo

This poem is only punctuated with commas and capital letters. It is deliberately written with run-on lines to suggest the flow of the meaning from one line to the next. At the same time, however, there is an attempt to interrupt the flow of the grammatical unit in the first two lines by writing thus: "This was not / new, we made it new," and not as is usual: "This was not new, / we made it new". So, the reader is forced to pause at the end of the line at "not", before going on to the next line, where he meets "new". Thus, the significance of the word "new", which is positioned at both the beginning and the end of the second line, is emphasized. The reference to the first "new" is to the fact that the reclamation of land is *not* a new enterprise; in Marina Bay, however, the process is renewed, that is, "made new".

Study the poem closely for other effects of the use of run-on lines. One of the things you can do is to try to punctuate the poem by adding full stops and regular stanza divisions. For instance, the first four lines could be arranged as follows:

This was not new, we made it new.
Stole from the sea what the sea does not need.

Rearrange the lines like this all the way and then compare the two versions. Which makes for more interesting reading, the original with run-on lines or the more regularly aligned version?

Exercise 7A – Unusual punctuation

Child on Top of a Greenhouse

The wind billowing out the seat of my britches,
My feet crackling splinters of glass and dried putty,
The half-grown chrysanthemums staring up like
    accusers,
Up through the streaked glass, flashing with sunlight,
5   A few white clouds all rushing eastward,
A line of elms plunging and tossing like horses,
And everyone, everyone pointing up and shouting!

Theodore Roethke

1 What is the situation described in the poem? What is the overall mood in the poem? Give evidence to support your views.

2 Every line ends in a comma, causing the reader to pause. What effect does the poet try to achieve?

3 Note that none of the lines have a proper verb; the verb "be" is missing from most of the sentences/lines, for example:

The wind [is] billowing out the seat of my britches,
My feet [are] crackling splinters of glass and dried putty ...

Explain why you think the writer deliberately does this. What effect does he want to produce?

7.2 Unusual word placement

Besides unusual punctuation marks, we should look out for unusual word order. Words may stand out because they are not how we would normally write or say them; sometimes they are placed next to another word that does not seem to fit.

Purpose—Why do writers employ unusual word placement?

Writers employ unusual word placement for reasons such these:

(a) to make the reader pay attention to the unusual word. This may be to emphasize a certain point the writer is making.

(b) to show contradictions in the character or in society through contrasting words

(c) to create richness and even humour in the text through clever wordplay.

Method—How do we analyse unusual word placement?

(1) Look out for words or phrases which sound awkward or ungrammatical (not what we would commonly write or say).

(2) Look out for words that are awkwardly placed next to other words.

(3) Think about the effect this has on you, the reader: if the words were reordered in the right way, how would your response be different? Ask yourself why the writer wants to draw your attention to these words. Do they encourage you to respond in a certain way?

(4) Explain how this contributes to the larger meaning of the text.

Common types of unusual placement: Oxymoron, antithesis and parallelism

♦ **Oxymoron**

When two contradictory words are placed next to each other, we say that the writer employs an **oxymoron**. Common examples of oxymorons are: "they had a *love-hate* relationship", "Let me tell you a *bitter-sweet* story".

Application example

Read these opening lines of Epistle II in the poem "An Essay on Man" by the eighteenth century poet Alexander Pope.

> Know then thyself, presume not God to scan,
> The proper study of mankind is man.
> Placed on this isthmus of a middle state,
> A being darkly wise and rudely great: ...

In the last line are two examples of oxymorons: "darkly wise" and "rudely great". Pope uses them very effectively to illustrate the contradictory aspects of the nature of humanity.

♦ Antithesis

We say a statement is **antithetical** when a word, phrase or idea is placed near or next to another word, phrase or idea that is in contrast to it. The oxymoron and antithesis are similar. The difference is that an oxymoron is an expression comprising two opposite words while an antithesis is the placing together of contrasting words, phrases or ideas in a sentence or a paragraph. The purpose of both is to draw attention to the paradoxical nature of the issue or character.

Application example

Read this poem by W.B. Yeats:

An Irish Airman Foresees His Death

I KNOW that I shall meet my fate
Somewhere among the clouds above;
Those that I fight I do not hate,
Those that I guard I do not love;
5   My country is Kiltartan Cross,
My countrymen Kiltartan's poor,
No likely end could bring them loss
Or leave them happier than before.
Nor law, nor duty bade me fight,
10   Nor public men, nor cheering crowds,
A lonely impulse of delight
Drove to this tumult in the clouds;
I balanced all, brought all to mind,
The years to come seemed waste of breath,
15   A waste of breath the years behind
In balance with this life, this death.

In the poem, Yeats expresses the airman's deep resignation to his own death. In a series of antithetical lines, the speaker weighs his feelings about life and death, and concludes that they are well balanced.

♦ Parallelism

This occurs when words, phrases or lines are deliberately constructed to parallel each other. The purpose is to draw attention to the words, phrases or lines so as to highlight or emphasize a point. Parallelism may also be used to invite readers to compare and contrast the ideas in these lines.

Application example

In "An Essay on Man", Alexander Pope brings his long poem to a close by urging humanity to accept the universal Order ordained by God. He uses words, phrases and lines which are deliberately constructed to parallel each other; in particular, starting from the line "Secure to be as blest as thou canst bear:".

> Cease then, nor Order imperfection name:
> Our proper bliss depends on what we blame.
> Know thy own point: this kind, this due degree
> Of blindness, weakness, Heaven bestows on thee.
> Submit. — In this, or any other sphere,
> Secure to be as blest as thou canst bear:
> Safe in the hand of one disposing Power,
> Or, in the natal, or the mortal hour.
> All nature is but art, unknown to thee;
> All chance, direction, which thou canst not see;
> All discord, harmony not understood;
> All partial evil, universal good:
> And, spite of pride, in erring reason's spite,
> One truth is clear, WHATEVER IS, IS RIGHT.

Line numbers: 5 (line 5), 10 (line 10)

Exercise 7B – Unusual word placement

Look at the above text again. Can you identify any other unusual punctuation or unusual word placement? Comment on their function and effectiveness.

Point to note

Don't just identify; you must explain the *purpose* and *effect*!

When commenting on literary devices such as diction, word order and imagery, do not simply identify and throw in literary terms. It is more important to explain their purpose (why they are used) and effect (the effect these devices have on the reader).

Group work: Inference (Word order)

1   Look at the texts in the following table and identify unusual word order, punctuation and/or word placement. Try to use some of the terms explained in this unit.

2   Comment on their purpose as well as thier effect on the reader.

Text	What is unusual?	Purpose	Effect on the reader

A Brief History of China
(through the eyes of a third-generation immigrant)
 	
Greater China
China great,
denigrate—
     ingrate:
     decimate!
greater good
 	
demigod
 	
                               Daren Shiau			

Death, be not proud, though some have called thee Mighty and dreadful, for thou art not so; For those whom thou think'st thou dost overthrow, Die not, poor Death, nor yet canst thou kill me; *Extract from "Death, be not proud" by John Donne*			
How did the party go in Portman Square? I cannot tell you; Juliet was not there. And how did Lady Gaster's party go? Juliet was next to me and I do not know. *"Juliet" by Hilaire Belloc*			
—I am a gentleman in a dustcoat trying To make you hear. Your ears are soft and small And listen to an old man not at all, They want the young men's whispering and sighing. But see the roses on your trellis dying And hear the spectral singing of the moon; For I must have my lovely lady soon, I am a gentleman in a dustcoat trying. *Extract from "Piazza Piece" by John Crowe Ransom*			

The Shroud

The little childish happiness
Is taken off, together
With the old school uniform.
Never will I be in that uniform again.
5   And who will remember
The little girl with her two pigtails
With her petticoats always too long
And her thousand naughty and silly ways?

The old school uniform
10   With the childish delights and giggles
Is folded and locked up in the top drawer
Forever.

Shall I cry?
I am no longer a child
15   My eyes so dry
It's not easy to cry.

Yet I hear somebody weeping —
Crying louder and louder—howling
I feel her tears —
20   She is the girl locked up in the top drawer.

Wong May

1   Why has the writer chosen "The Shroud" as the title of the poem? How does the title help you to better understand the poem?

2   The poem contains several pauses. Can you explain why they are used? How do they contribute to your understanding of how the speaker feels?

3   Pick out other examples of unusual word or punctuation order in the text and explain why they are used and how effective they are in conveying the message and tone of the speaker.

4 Considering the poem as a whole, can you say that the speaker's attitude changes from stanza to stanza?

 Links to real-world issues

What does the speaker mean in the last line of the poem? Growing up and letting go of the past are part and parcel of life. What were some of the major transitions in your life? What are some strategies we can employ to adjust to new changes and challenges in life?

Chapter *8*

FIGURATIVE LANGUAGE

Chapter outline

8.1 What is figurative language and why do we use it?

8.2 Similes and metaphors

8.3 Personification

Trigger activity

Below are three female portraits. Pick one of the pictures and describe the woman's or girl's face and the emotions shown there. Then show your description to a classmate and ask him or her to point out the picture you have described.

Picture A

Picture B

Picture C

As you described the picture, how many times did you use the words "like", "as" and "as if" and when did you use them?

For example, one could describe the girl in Picture B as follows:

Facial features	Although she does not show much expression on her face, she displays a satisfied smile.
Emotion	Her eyes have an almost dreamlike quality about them. She looks to be posing for the picture but there are other thoughts on her mind.

It is often easier to describe physical appearance and qualities than to describe emotional qualities. Whenever we read a description, however brief, an image or picture is automatically created in our minds. For example, when you read the sentence: "Her eyes have an almost dreamlike quality about them", an image would naturally form in your mind. On the other hand, if you read the words "She felt troubled", any number of different images could arise in your mind because the description is ambiguous. Hence, to describe more abstract, intangible qualities, writers make use of figurative language.

8.1 What is figurative language and why do we use it?

Definition—Figurative language

Figurative language is language that employs a **figure of speech** (simile, metaphor, personification) to **create an image in the mind** of the reader.

Purpose—Why do writers employ figurative language?

The purpose of using figurative language is

(a) to create an accurate mental picture (image) in the reader.

(b) to supplement literal meanings of words with complexity and richness through the use of connotations.

Application example

Figurative language may be used in both poetry and prose. For example, compare the following two short passages:

Text A	Text B
I followed the path down towards the village. It was a difficult journey because the wind was strong and the sea was violent. I was grateful that the weather distracted me from the thoughts that were troubling me. Was life so unpredictable?	The path from our house followed the edge of the sea cliffs before turning inland towards the village. Walking it on a day like this was difficult, but I remember feeling grateful that the fierce wind drew my mind from the things troubling me. The sea was violent, with waves like stones chipped into blades, sharp enough to cut. It seemed to me the world itself was feeling just as I felt. Was life nothing more than a storm that constantly washed away what had been there only a moment before, and left behind something barren and unrecognizable? *Extract from* Memoirs of a Geisha *by Arthur Golden*

Text A contains a direct description of what the main character was doing. However, some aspects of the description are vague. For example, "the wind was strong and the sea was violent" is rather vague. How violent was the sea? One reader's idea of a violent sea could be different from another's. Also, other than our knowledge that the protagonist was troubled, we have no other clue about how she felt.

Text B, on the other hand, can evoke a clearer mental picture and the verbal descriptions are full of richer, connotative meanings.

The path from our house followed the edge of the sea cliffs before turning inland towards the village. Walking it on a day like this was difficult, but I remember feeling grateful that the **fierce wind** drew my mind from the things troubling me. **The sea was violent, with waves like stones chipped into blades, sharp enough to cut.** It seemed to me the world itself was feeling just as I felt. **Was life nothing more than a storm that constantly washed away what had been there only a moment before, and left behind something barren and unrecognizable?**

Personification—the literal meaning of the wind is supplemented by the connotative implications that it is violent and aggressive, battling hard with the protagonist and showing no mercy.

Simile—now we have a clear image of the sea. Its violence is made concrete by comparing its strong waves with stones that are solid, hard and sharp enough to hurt. The implication is that nature is cruel and hurtful. In a larger context, nature is symbolic of the world and here shows its powerful capacity to destroy lives.

Metaphor—now we also have a clearer idea of the emotions of the speaker. The metaphor conveys her view of the futility of life, that nothing lasts forever. It brings out her nihilistic, pessimistic view of life.

Point to note

The easiest way to convey what writers feel is through comparison.

Writers need to communicate the image they see in their minds or what they feel in and about a situation to the reader. One powerful tool is **comparison**. Writers can convey their personal thoughts and feelings clearly by comparing them with things that the reader is familiar with. For example, we can empathize with the writer when he says "the weather felt like a thousand knives cutting into my skin", rather than when he makes a statement like "the weather was really hot".

8.2 Similes and metaphors

Definitions—Simile and metaphor

Both similes and metaphors are figures of speech in which a comparison is made between two things.

A **simile compares one aspect of an object** or action **with that of another**. The comparison is usually made explicit by words such as "as" and "like". For example, the simile in "John eats like a pig" compares John's eating habits with those of a pig to emphasize greed.

A **metaphor**, on the other hand, **makes a total connection between two objects**. The comparison is so strong that one thing embraces all the qualities of the thing it is compared to. For example, the metaphor in "John is a pig" compares every aspect of John, not just his eating habits but his total behaviour, to that of a pig! In other words, we can say that a metaphor is often richer in meaning compared with a simile because more than one aspect of the other object is compared. There has been a transformation, that is, John is not just compared to a pig, he has become one!

Group work: Research project

Work in a group of four or five.

(1) Select an advertisement from a newspaper or popular magazine that contains at least three similes and metaphors.

(2) Comment on their purpose and effect.

Method—How do we analyse similes and metaphors?

Analysing similes

Steps of analysis	Example
(1) A comparison between one thing and another is made. Look out for the words "like" and "as".	"I wandered lonely <u>as</u> a cloud".
(2) Identify what is being compared. Phrase it in the following manner: "A (the subject) is compared to B (the thing compared to)."	The speaker's wandering is compared to that of a lone cloud.
(3) Look at the implied meaning of B and say what it implies of A.	The comparison implies that the speaker feels free yet aimless like the cloud.

Analysing metaphors

Analysing a metaphor is similar to analysing a simile. However, a metaphor is often harder to recognize.

Steps of analysis	Example
(1) Something is defined as another. Metaphors often contain an "is" or "was".	"Her face <u>is</u> a garden".
(2) Identify what is being compared. Phrase it in the following manner: "A (the subject) is compared to B (the thing compared to)."	The subject's face is compared to a garden.
(3) Look at the implied meaning of B and say what it implies of A.	A garden implies variety, colour and life, all of which convey the impression of the attractive beauty of the subject.

Note: Metaphors which are more difficult to recognize are those in which the comparison is implied. For example, instead of saying "Her face is a garden", where the comparison between the subject's face and a garden is obvious, an implied metaphor does not show the link as clearly. For example, the sentence "I looked at the garden in her face" contains an implied metaphor. Here, the reader needs to infer that there is a comparison between her face and a garden.

 Group work: Analysis and discussion

Look at each of the following extracts; then state whether a simile or a metaphor is used and why.

No	Phrase	Metaphor or simile?	What is being compared to what?	Implied meaning?
1	I wandered lonely as a cloud *William Wordsworth*			
2	There is a garden in her face / Where roses and white lilies blow *Thomas Campion*			
3	The moon is a ghostly galleon tossed upon cloudy seas *Alfred Noyes*			
4	Hold fast to dreams / For if dreams die / Life is a broken-winged bird / That cannot fly. *Langston Hughes*			
5	The moon, impure as ever, like tea-leaves / Coffee dregs, on a cup of cream, cleaves / On to drooping leaves of rubber trees / Scatters bright thieves to steal the keys / That open to mem'ries of home. *Wang Gungwu*			

Read the following poems and analyse the similes and metaphors in them.

Text A

Road-works

(i)
Sometimes it is hard
to believe that creatures of flesh and bone
may tear up the roads like paper,
peeling the rind of the earth
5   as carelessly as eating an orange.
When they fall to the ground and devour it,
the scenario is one
of blasted sand, harsh talk
and machinery.

Aaron Lee

1   How many similes and metaphors can you identify in this poem? State what they imply.

2   What is the writer suggesting about road-works? How do the images in the poem contribute to his tone and attitude?

Text B

Metaphors

I'm a riddle in nine syllables,
An elephant, a ponderous house,
A melon strolling on two tendrils.
O red fruit, ivory, fine timbers!
5   This loaf's big with its yeasty rising.
Money's new-minted in this fat purse.
I'm a means, a stage, a cow in calf.
I've eaten a bag of green apples,
Boarded the train there's no getting off.

Sylvia Plath

1 What is the significance of the reference to "nine" in line 1? Pick out all the metaphors present in the text and state what they refer to.

2 How do all the images connect? What is this poem about?

8.3 Personification

 Definition—Personification

Personification is a figure of speech in which **an object** or **concept is given a human attribute**. For example, a common expression using personification is, "Time stole my youth away". Here, time, an abstract concept, is given a human attribute. It is compared to a thief robbing another individual of his/her youth.

 Purpose—Why do writers use personification?

Writers use personification to exaggerate and emphasize a point. For example, in the phrase "Time stole my youth away", time is given a human attribute to make its act of depriving someone of youth even more cruel.

 Method—How do we analyse personification?

The analysis of a personification is similar to the analysis of a simile or a metaphor.

Steps of analysis	Example
(1) Look out for areas where a comparison is made. Identify the abstract quality and the quality associated with a human attribute.	"<u>Love</u> <u>waits</u> at her door every morning."
(2) Identify what is being compared to what. Phrase it in the following manner: "A (the subject) is compared to B (the thing compared to)."	In this sentence, the concept of love is given a human attribute and compared to someone faithfully waiting at the door of his or her loved one.

Steps of analysis	Example
(3) Look at the implied meaning of B and say what it implies of A.	The idea of faithfully waiting implies that the speaker's love is not just one of passion but is one of commitment, sacrifice and faithfulness as well.

 Exercise 8B – Personification

Look at the following poem, "Morwenstow", by the English poet Charles Causley, who comes from the south-west of England.

Morwenstow

Where do you come from, sea,
To the sharp Cornish shore,
Leaping up to the raven's crag?
  From Labrador.

5 Do you grow tired, sea?
Are you weary ever
When the storms burst over your head?
  Never.

Are you hard as a diamond, sea,
10 As iron, as oak?
Are you stronger than flint or steel?
  And the lightning stroke.

Ten thousand years and more, sea,
You have gobbled your fill,
15 Swallowing stone and slate!
  I am hungry still.

When will you rest, sea?
  When moon and sun
  Ride only fields of salt water
20 *And the land is gone.*

        Charles Causley

1 In stanza three, similes are used to describe the 'hardness' of the sea. What qualities of hardness are suggested by these lines?
   a "Are you hard as a diamond, sea,"
   b "As iron, as oak?"

2 Discuss with a partner or in a group whether the reference to hardness is literal as well as figurative.

3 The sea is addressed as a person from the beginning of this poem. Look at stanza four:

> Ten thousand years and more, sea,
> You have gobbled your fill,
> Swallowing stone and slate!
> *I am hungry still.*

Write your response to the image of the sea as gobbling and swallowing and the sea's reply that it is still hungry.

4 Do you think, by the time you have finished reading the poem, the sea has become a symbol? If so, a symbol of what?

 Exercise 8C – More practice on imagery

Text A

Courage

It is in the small things we see it.
The child's first step,
as awesome as an earthquake.
The first time you rode a bike,
5   wallowing up the sidewalk.
The first spanking when your heart
went on a journey all alone.
When they called you crybaby
or poor or fatty or crazy
10   and made you into an alien,
you drank their acid
and concealed it.

Later,
if you faced the death of bombs and bullets
15   you did not do it with a banner,
you did it with only a hat to
cover your heart.
You did not fondle the weakness inside you
though it was there.
20   Your courage was a small coal
that you kept swallowing.
If your buddy saved you
and died himself in so doing,
then his courage was not courage,
25   it was love; love as simple as shaving soap.

Later,
if you have endured a great despair,
then you did it alone,
getting a transfusion from the fire,
30   picking the scabs off your heart,
then wringing it out like a sock.
Next, my kinsman, you powdered your sorrow,
you gave it a back rub
and then you covered it with a blanket
35   and after it had slept a while
it woke to the wings of the roses
and was transformed.

Later,
when you face old age and its natural conclusion
40   your courage will still be shown in the little ways,
each spring will be a sword you'll sharpen,
those you love will live in a fever of love,
and you'll bargain with the calendar
and at the last moment
45   when death opens the back door
you'll put on your carpet slippers
and stride out.

Anne Sexton

1   According to Anne Sexton, what are the four phases of courage?

2 Examine each phase of life described by the writer. Identify as many similes, metaphors and personifications as you can in the extract and show how they illustrate the importance of courage in life.

3 Explain what the writer means in the last two lines of the poem. What attitude does she suggest we adopt in the face of death?

Text B

Landing

What death may be: a slow, close-to-weightless
tilt, like a burgeoning foetus turning
slightly in the womb. The engine starts a low
growl like a stomach, the aircraft hungry to
5   land, to devour the space between its
falling body and the ground, followed by
the slow lick of its wheels against the runway's
belly: pressing down, then skating forward,
only to decelerate, a sensual slow-mo,
10   and the plane makes a sound
like the hugest sigh of relief.

The seatbelt sign blinks off for the final time.
We rise up from our seats like souls
from bodies, leaving bulky hand luggage
15   in the overhead compartments, then
begin a tense line down the aisle, awkwardly
smiling at each other, remaining few minutes
alive with all kinds of ambivalences,
or simply relief at having arrived, at long last,
20   in that no-time zone of a country
without a name except the ones we give it;
weeping, laughing, both at once.

Cyril Wong

1 The writer uses an extended metaphor to describe his impression of death. *An extended metaphor essentially refers to a **metaphor that is elaborated** in subsequent lines* *of the poem*. Analyse the main metaphor of death in this poem and show how the writer extends this metaphor. How effective is this and what does he imply about death?

2   Look at the last two lines of the poem. Explain what you think the writer's view of death is. Refer to any other part of the poem to support your point.

 Links to real-world issues

Films, music and popular culture sometimes promote the belief that everything is acceptable and permissible. This may cause us to compromise our own values. How important is moral courage in today's world? Think about other aspects of courage that we need in the face of globalization and constant changes in society.

Chapter 9
RHYTHM

Trigger activity

Read the lyrics of these two songs. Can you identify which lyric belongs to one of these categories: a rap or a slow love song?

Text A

If i feel off tomorrow would you still love me?
If i didn't smell so good would you still hug me?
If i got locked up and sentenced to a quarter
  century,
Could i count on you to be there to support me
  mentally?
If i went back to a hoopty from a benz, would
  you poof and disappear like some of my
  friends?
If i were hit and i were hurt would you be by my
  side
If it was time to put in work would you be down
  to ride?

Text B

Deep in the stillness
I can hear you speak
You're still an inspiration
Can it be?
That you are my
Forever love
And you are watching over me from up above
Fly me up to where you are
Beyond the distant star

I wish upon tonight
To see you smile
If only for a while to know you're there
A breath away's not far
To where you are.

It may be easy to identify the meaning of the song from the words. But what if you didn't understand English?

 Group work: Creative inference and construction

Try reading these lyrics out aloud and see if you can fit them into one of these categories: love song, pop song, national anthem.

Text A

Einigkeit und Recht und Freiheit,
fuer das deutsche Vaterland!
Danach lasst uns alle streben,
bruederlich mit Herz und Hand!
Einigkeit und Recht und Freiheit,
sind des Glueckes Unterpfand.
Blueh im Glanze dieses Gluekkes,
bluehe deutsches Vaterland!

Text B

Para bailar la bamba (x2)
Se necesita una poca de gracia
a Una poca de gracia para mi para ti
ya Arriba y arriba
ay arriba y arriba por ti sere
Por ti sere
Yo no soy marinero (x2)
Soy capitan (x3)
Bamba la bamba
Bamba la bamba
Bamba la bamba.

Text C

> Amore scusami
> se sto piangendo
> Amore scusami,
> ma ho capito che lasciandoti
> io soffriro,
> Amore baciami,
> arrivederci amore baciami,
> e se mi penserai ricordati
> che amo te.

Now, work in a group of four or five. Imagine you are from a different culture or tribe. Invent your own language and then construct a message to be sent to another group. The rules are as follows:

1. The message cannot be in any known language. It is in a language made up by the group.

2. The message can be in any form such as a news broadcast, a song, or a poem.

3. The message must contain a request to obtain something from the other group (such as a pen, an eraser, etc). No gestures or actions are allowed.

4. The message should contain one or two hints through its rhythm, form, punctuation—be creative!

5. The message may be delivered verbally by a member or more from the group.

6. The group wins if it manages to get what it wants from the other group.

 Definition—Rhythm

The meaning of a text is formed by an interplay between language, rhythm and sound. **Rhythm** basically refers to the **flow of words and movement** in a poem. The rhythm in a poem is created through the stresses and pauses within it. Rhythm can be **conveyed through metre, pace, rhyme** and **repetition**.

9.1 Rhythm and metre

Poetry has either rhythm in which stanzas have regular metrical patterns, as in much of traditional verse, or it may have irregular rhythm with lines of unequal lengths, as in most free verse.

Take this example from a Shakespearean sonnet:

> That time of year thou mayst in me behold
> When yellow leaves, or none, or few do hang
> Upon the boughs which shake against the cold,
> Bare, ruined choirs, where late the sweet birds sing.

If we scan the lines, that is, make out the rhythm by tapping the stresses in each line, we will come up with this pattern:

$$\cup \; / \quad \cup \; / \quad \cup \quad / \quad \cup \; / \; \cup \; /$$
> That time of year thou mayst in me behold

$$\cup \quad / \; \cup \quad / \quad \cup \; / \quad \cup \; / \; \cup \; /$$
> When yellow leaves, or none, or few do hang ...

This metrical pattern is **iambic**, $\cup /$, consisting of an unstressed syllable (indicated by $\cup$) followed by a stressed one (indicated by /). Each line has five beats and one runs on to the next regularly like a trotting horse, creating what is called a **pentameter**.

English poetry has many metrical forms and poets often use more than one metre in a line or stanza to create variation for a variety of purposes. The four most common metres are the **iambic**, the **trochaic**, the **anapaestic** and the **dactylic**. These are illustrated as follows:

iambic: $\cup \; /$
trochaic: $/ \; \cup$
anapaestic: $\cup \; \cup \; /$
dactylic: $/ \; \cup \; \cup$

 Purpose—What is the writer's purpose in employing metre?

(a) To convey the speaker's tone

Look at this first stanza from Alfred Tennyson's poem "Break, Break, Break". The three stressed syllables (words) in the opening lines clearly convey the impact of waves breaking upon the shore:

      /   /   /

Break, break, break,
    On thy cold, grey stones, O Sea!
And I would that my tongue could utter
    The thoughts that arise in me.

(b) To complement the mood of the poem

Read aloud this poem by Robert Browning. Hear how he creates the jaunty mood of spring when it breaks at the beginning of the seasonal year. The first line is scanned as shown:

   ∪   /   ∪ ∪   /

The year's at the spring
And day's at the morn;
Morning's at seven,
The hill-side's dew-pearled;
The lark's on the wing;
The snail's on the thorn:
God's in his heaven —
All's right with the world!

(c) To emphasize a particular word or phrase

Rhythm and metre may also draw the reader's attention to certain words or phrases in the text. For example:

The Ship of Death

VII
We are dying, we are dying, so all we can do
is now to be willing to die, and to build the ship
of death to carry the soul on the longest journey ...

There is no port, there is nowhere to go
5   only the deepening blackness darkening still
blacker upon the soundless, ungurgling flood
darkness at one with darkness, up and down
and sideways utterly dark, so there is no direction
     any more,
and the little ship is there; yet she is gone.
10   She is not seen, for there is nothing to see her by.

> She is gone! gone! And yet
> somewhere she is there.
>
> Nowhere!
>
> *D.H. Lawrence*

Try to read the poem aloud in your mind. Without analysing the poem in detail, which words are your eyes drawn to?

Most likely it would be the phrases "We are dying" and "There is no port" and the words "gone! gone!" and "Nowhere!". These stand out because the poem when read begins in a slow, depressing manner. At the end, words are stressed, as indicated by the exclamation marks. The writer clearly wants to draw our attention to them to emphasize the extent of hopelessness at the end of the poem.

9.2 Rhythm and pace

 Definition—Pace

Pace refers to the **speed** at which a poem is read. The pace of the poem may be fast or slow, light or heavy, monotonous or varying. Pace can contribute to the tone or mood of the poem by the choice or variation of metre.

 Method—How do we analyse pace?

Pace may be affected by:

(a) **Pauses**

The pace of a poem may slow down if there are many pauses in the lines. This creates a sad, mournful mood.

For example, look at D.H. Lawrence's poem "The Ship of Death" again. Note the first few lines contain many pauses, indicated by []:

> We are dying, [] we are dying, [] so all we can do []
> is now [] to be willing to die, [] and to build the ship []
> of death [] to carry the soul on the longest journey [] ...

The pauses cause the poem to slow down, thus complementing its mournful tone. Also, the many pauses reflect the speaker's attitude— it is as if he is sighing as he says these words.

(b) Number of syllables in a line

The pace of a poem may quicken if there are short, monosyllabic words. However, the pace may also slow down if most of the words in a line contain three or more syllables.

For example, look at Lawrence's poem again. The three-syllable words in the lines "only the deepening blackness darkening still / blacker upon the soundless, ungurgling flood" force us to slow down as we read. Once again, the pace complements the heavy mood of the poem.

 Group work: Metre and pace

The best way to illustrate rhythm and metre is by reading a poem aloud. Try analysing the rhythm in the following poem.

The Band

Solo 1: Hey, there! Listen awhile! Listen awhile, and
     come.
  Down in the street there are marching feet,
    And I hear the beat of a drum.

Solo 2: Bim! Boom!! Out of the room! Pick up your
     hat and fly!
  Isn't it grand? The band! The band! The band
    is marching by!

Chorus: Oh, the clarinet is the finest yet, and the
     uniforms are gay.
  Tah, rah! We don't go home —
  Oom, pah! We won't go home —
  Oh, we shan't go home, and we can't go home
    when the band begins to play.

Solo 3: Oh, see them swinging along, swinging along
     the street!
  Left, right! Buttons so bright, jackets and
    caps so neat!

> Solo 4: Ho, the Fire Brigade, or a dress parade of the
>   soldier-man is grand;
>   But everyone, for regular fun, wants a Big —
>   Brass — Band.
>
> Chorus: The slide-trombone is a joy alone, and the
>   drummer! He's a treat!
>   So Rackety-rumph! We don't go home —
>   Boom, Bumph! We won't go home —
>   Oh, we shan't go home, and we can't go home
>   While the band is in the street.
>   Tooral-ooral, Oom — pah!
>   The band is in the street!
>
> C.J. Dennis

To appreciate the extent to which the sound echoes the sense, this poem must be read out loud, with a combination of solo and choral voices. The poet has indicated how this is done; there are four solo voices and two choruses. Your teacher should assign reading parts and orchestrate the reading.

Reading aloud
Solo 1 will be read by student A.
Solo 2 will be read by student B.
Chorus will be read by the whole class.
Solo 3 will be read by student C.
Solo 4 will be read by student D.
Chorus will be read by the whole class.

Scanning
To scan is to make out, through reading aloud or beating time with our hands, the rhythm of a poem. The rhythm of a poem is usually established in the opening lines and this provides a guide to reading the rest of the poem.

Now, if we scan the first stanza of "The Band", we will see that line one has six units or beats, line two has four and line three has three. The poet, C.J. Dennis, has used these different kinds of metre, namely, iambic ($\cup$ /), trochaic (/ $\cup$) and anapaestic ($\cup \cup$ /), and combined them in a poem. He has skilfully mixed his metres to produce the effect of a marching band.

Hey, there! | Listen | awhile! | Listen | awhile | and come. (6)

Down in | the street | there are mar | ching feet, (4)

And I hear | the beat | of a drum. (3)

Now trying scanning stanza two in this space.

Bim! Boom! Out of the room! Pick up your hat and fly!

Isn't it grand? The band! The band! The band is marching by!

Once the principle of scanning is understood, the whole class can read the poem aloud.

9.3 Rhythm and rhyme

 Definition—Rhyme

Rhyme refers to the **repetition** of a final sound of a word by that of another word, at the end of lines or within the lines of a poem. Some modern poems are written in free verse, which means that there is no particular rhyming structure. The reason for some poets adopting free verse in their writing is to have the freedom to express their thoughts without the constraints of a rhyming structure. Most poems, however, have a definite rhyme scheme. Rhymes tend to make a poem sound more lyrical and, thus, more memorable.

There are two types of rhyme:

(a) **End rhyme**

This refers to the rhyming of words at the end of lines in a poem. For example, in the Humpty Dumpty nursery rhyme, the words at the end of every two lines rhyme, for example: "wall—fall"; "men—again".

(b) **Internal rhyme**

This refers to the rhyming of words within the lines of a poem. For example, in the phrase "The long light shakes across the lakes", the word "shakes" rhymes with "lakes" in the same line of the poem.

Purpose—What is the purpose of analysing rhyme?

What is more important than identifying the type of rhyme poets use is the ability to state the purpose for which it is used. Usually rhymes have several purposes:

(a) **Rhymes link words/ideas together to complement or emphasize the meaning, mood or attitude in a poem.**

For example in the poem "Sea Fever" by John Masefield, we find the following rhyme-scheme:

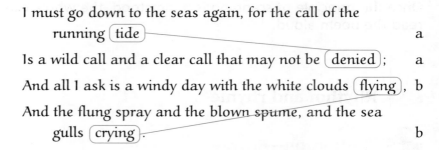

> I must go down to the seas again, for the call of the
> running (tide)   a
> Is a wild call and a clear call that may not be (denied);   a
> And all I ask is a windy day with the white clouds (flying), b
> And the flung spray and the blown spume, and the sea
> gulls (crying).   b

A close analysis shows how the poet uses rhyme to link ideas together. For example, the 'a'-rhyme-scheme links the idea that the tide's call is something he cannot deny or avoid. This creates the impression that the longing for the sea is a persuasive and urgent one. The 'b'-rhyme-scheme links images of nature together, for example, the visual image of the flying clouds and the sound effect of the sea gulls crying combine to create a sense of beauty within the poem.

(b) **Rhymes create a harmonious sound so as to make the poem more memorable.**

For example, the first stanza of the same poem contains the following:

> I must go down to the seas again, to the lonely sea and
> the <u>sky</u>,
> And all I ask is a tall ship and a star to steer her <u>by</u>,

These two lines are beautifully expressed and will stay in the mind of the reader. This is not only because of the imagery used but also because of the harmonious sounds of the rhyming words which complement the soothing and serene atmosphere in the text.

Blow, Bugle, Blow

The splendour falls on castle walls
    And snowy summits old in story;
The long light shakes across the lakes
    And the wild cataract[1] leaps in glory.
5   Blow, bugle[2], blow, set the wild echoes flying,
Blow, bugle; answer, echoes, dying, dying, dying.

O hark, O hear! how thin and clear,
    And thinner, clearer, farther going!
O sweet and far from cliff and scar[3]
10   The horns of Elfland faintly blowing!
Blow, let us hear the purple glens replying:
Blow, bugle; answer, echoes, dying, dying, dying.

O love, they die in yon rich sky,
    They faint on hill or field or river;
15   Our echoes roll from soul to soul,
    And grow for ever and for ever.
Blow, bugle, blow, set the wild echoes flying,
And answer, echoes, answer, dying, dying, dying.

Alfred Tennyson

1. Underline the rhymes you find in this poem. State whether they are end rhymes or internal rhymes. Then state what their purposes are and how they contribute to the meaning of the poem.

2. Look at the rhyming couplet (two lines which rhyme) at the end of the first stanza. Explain how the end rhymes link and the poet's intention in linking these words.

3. The poet uses a lot of repetition in the poem, for example, "blow" and "dying". Explain why repetition is used and what effect it has on the reader.

---

[1] cataract: waterfall.
[2] bugle: horn.
[3] scar: jutting rock.

Rhythm and repetition

Another way in which rhythm is created is through the use of repetition. Repetition can create an internal rhythm or beat in the poem. In addition, repetition is used to emphasize certain words so that we can give more thought to them.

Application example

Leisure

What is this life if, full of care,
We have no time to stand and stare?

No time to stand beneath the boughs
And stare as long as sheep or cows.

5   No time to see, when woods we pass,
Where squirrels hide their nuts in grass.

No time to see, in broad daylight,
Streams full of stars, like skies at night.

No time to turn at Beauty's glance,
10   And watch her feet, how they can dance.

No time to wait till her mouth can
Enrich that smile her eyes began.

A poor life this if, full of care,
We have no time to stand and stare.

W.H. Davies

The repetition of "No time" at the beginning of each stanza (except the first and last) emphasizes the speaker's point that often in our hectic, modern-day living, we lose the ability to reflect and appreciate nature and other more meaningful aspects of life.

Exercise 9B – Repetition

Analyse the rest of the poem "Leisure" and pick out other words that are repeated. How does this contribute to the rhythm of the poem? What is emphasized in the repetition?

9.5 How to analyse rhythm

Method—How do we analyse rhythm?

In general, rhythm is often used together with other sound devices (see Chapter 10) to convey the underlying meaning of the poem as well as to convey the overall mood and tone of the poem.

When you are analysing rhythm, you should ask yourself these seven questions:

Metre	1. Is there a regular or irregular rhythm? If so, why? 2. Are there consecutively stressed syllables? If so, what is stressed?
Pace	3. Is the pace fast or slow? Light or heavy? How does the pace contribute to the mood? 4. Are there frequent pauses? If so, why? 5. Are there many monosyllabic or polysyllabic words? If so, why?
Rhyme	6. Is there a regular rhyme-scheme? How do the rhymed words connect?
Repetition	7. What word is repeated? What idea is emphasized?

Examples of words to describe rhythm:

Light	*versus*	Heavy
Regular	*versus*	Irregular
Lively	*versus*	Ponderous
Quick	*versus*	Slow

Point to note

Rhythm is closely related to mood.

Remember it is not enough to simply describe the rhythm. You must show HOW the writer creates this rhythm, for instance, through the use of metre, pace, rhyme or repetition. More importantly, you must show WHY he uses it (purpose) and the effect it has on the reader.

Group work: Cooperative learning

Work in a group of four or five.

(1) Analyse the poem below and specialize in one of the seven questions in the rhythm summary box on page 93. Each of the other groups in class should specialize in another different question.

(2) Group members should attempt to generate as many words as they can in answer to the question.

(3) The group should then share its answers with the other groups.

Palanquin-Bearers

Lightly, O lightly we bear her along,
She sways like a flower in the wind of our song;
She skims like a bird on the foam of a stream,
She floats like a laugh from the lips of a dream.
5   Gaily, O gaily we glide and we sing,
We bear her along like a pearl on a string.
Softly, O softly we bear her along,
She hangs like a star in the dew of our song;
She springs like a beam on the brow of the tide,
10   She falls like a tear from the eyes of a bride.
Lightly, O lightly we glide and we sing,
We bear her along like a pearl on a string.

Sarojini Naidu

Note: A palanquin is a covered coach used by one or two persons, suspended from poles on the shoulders of men. It is usually used for ceremonial reasons.

Further questions for discussion:

1   Read the poem aloud, discuss it with a partner or in a small group and answer these questions:

   a What is the sound effect the poet wishes to convey in this poem?

   b How is the sound conveyed through the rhythm?

2   Which words are stressed in the poem? What is the idea the poet wishes to convey to the listener?

3   Rhyme is another aspect of sound. This poem uses couplets, that is, two consecutive lines that rhyme. How does rhyme add to the mood?

 Exercise 9C – Rhythm

Moon Fall

Drunk on a boat
in the cool night
Li Po touched the moon
with a hand
5   and drowned
and became the maroon
of ink slab beneath
the ink, ripple
of the pre-word,
10   a great Chinese myth.

Armstrong, in a ship
in the night, spacedrunk,
touched the moon with a foot
and, returning,
15   became
renowned with his loot,

escaping the arrest
of a certain
mortality,
20   a myth for the West.

One moon and two reflexes,
one entity that teaches
us to celebrate different heroes —

So who coined the lame
25   notion that East
and West are the same
when colour is the least
of divides?

Gwee Li Sui

1   What is this poem about? What point is the speaker making?

2   Is there a regular rhyme structure in this poem? Why?

3   Describe the rhythm and pace of the poem. How do they contribute to the mood of the poem?

 Links to real-world issues

Do you agree with the poet that "colour is the least / of divides"? Give reasons for your answer. Apart from the East–West divide, what other divisions are there in the world? What do you think is the root cause of racial tension in society?

Chapter **10**
SOUND

Trigger activity

In the film "Four Weddings and a Funeral", there is a scene where an elegiac poem by W.H. Auden is read. It begins in this way:

> Stop all the clocks, cut off the telephone
> Prevent the dog from barking with a juicy bone
> Silence the pianos and with a muffled drum
> Bring out the coffin, let the mourners come

In the background, a soft classical tune is played which conveys the mood of pain even more powerfully. Now try this activity on your own.

(1) Listen to a few classical or contemporary instrumental tunes.

(2) For each tune, write down three words describing the mood of the piece.

(3) Then compose a short poem to fit the tune.

(4) Read the short composition with the tune played in the background to see if it fits.

Chapter outline

10.1 Use of words to convey sound: alliteration, assonance and consonance

10.2 Use of words to imitate sound: onomatopoeia

Definition—Sound

The eighteenth century English poet Alexander Pope had this to say about poetry: "The sound must seem an echo of the sense." To put it simply, the **sound** of what is said **should reinforce** its **meaning**. Sound may be conveyed through words using devices such as **alliteration, assonance** and **consonance**, or through words imitating real sound (**onomatopoeia**).

10.1 Use of words to convey sound: alliteration, assonance and consonance

This is the idea that the sense of a poem is conveyed through individual words that sound close to the meaning they are intended to convey. Words like these fall into the categories of alliteration, assonance and onomatopoeia.

 Definitions—Alliteration, assonance, consonance

Alliteration is defined by *The Oxford Advanced Learner's Dictionary* as "**the use of the same letter or sound at the beginning of words that are close together**". For example, the phrase "sing a song of sixpence" is alliterative since it repeats the "s" consonant sound at the beginning of most of the words.

Assonance is defined as the **repetition of identical or similar vowel sounds in words which are close together**. For example, assonance is present in the phrase "So we'll go no more a-roving" where the "o" vowel sound is repeated.

Consonance is defined as the **repetition of consonant sounds** (letters that are not vowels) **at the beginning, middle or at the end of words in a line**. For example, the phrase, "Pike, three inches long, perfect / Pike in all parts, green tigering the gold" contains an alliteration of the "p" consonant in the first line. However, the poet also employs consonance in the second line by repeating the sound of the "g" consonant in "tigering the gold".

 Purpose—Why do writers employ sound devices?

Here are some reasons why writers employ these techniques:

(a) **To emphasize a point**

For example, the alliteration of the heavy "d" consonant sound in "It was a dull, dreary day" emphasizes the dreariness of the moment.

(b) To complement a mood

For example, the alliteration of the "s" consonant sound in the line "She sells seashells on the seashore" creates a soft sound echoing the sound of the sea. This gives rise to a peaceful, serene mood.

Examples of types of sound and their contribution to mood:

Repetition of vowel/ consonant sounds	Sample words/ phrases	Sound quality produced	Contribution to mood (Many such words are examples of onomatopoeia.)
b, d	break, dark	Heavy, hard	Depressing, heavy
c, g, k, p, t	crack, grate, kerb, pressure, tough	Harsh, grating	Tense, suggestive of impending violence
c, g, k, p, t	call, groove, kind, pine, time	Calm, cool	Softer mood, suggestive of a low-pressure situation

 Point to note

Sound must be in context.

Note that you will need to refer to the context of the poem when discussing or analysing sound effects. For example, the alliteration of the "s" consonant sound may convey a sinister effect in a poem about a snake while in another poem about the sea, it may contribute to a peaceful, harmonious mood. Likewise, as the above table shows, the same letters "c", "g", "k", "p" and "t", used in different combinations with other letters, can produce a contrasting sound quality and contribute to an alternative mood.

 Method—How do we analyse sound devices?

Here are the steps involved in analysing alliteration and assonance:

(1) Identify the *technique* used. For example: Is it alliteration, assonance, or consonance?

(2) State which consonant or vowel is repeated and state the sound *quality* produced. For example: Is it a hard sound, a soft sound, or is the sound soothing or harsh?

(3) State the poet's *intention* in creating this sound effect; that is, how does the sound contribute to the meaning of the poem? Does it complement the mood?

Application example

One poet who uses sound very effectively is Alfred Tennyson, who lived in the Victorian era. Here is an example:

Blow, Bugle, Blow

     The splendour falls on castle walls
        And snowy summits old in story;
     The long light shakes across the lakes,
        And the wild cataract leaps in glory.
5   Blow, bugle, blow, set the wild echoes flying,
     Blow, bugle; answer, echoes, dying, dying, dying.

     O hark, O hear! How thin and clear,
        And thinner, clearer, farther going!
     O sweet and far from cliff and scar
10   The horns of Elfland faintly blowing!
     Blow, let us hear the purple glens replying:
     Blow, bugle; answer, echoes, dying, dying, dying.

     O love, they die in yon rich sky,
        They faint on hill or field or river;
15   Our echoes roll from soul to soul,
        And grow for ever and for ever.
     Blow, bugle, blow, set the wild echoes flying,
     And answer, echoes, answer, dying, dying, dying.

Alfred Tennyson

Example	Sound technique	Sound quality	Purpose
The splendour falls on castle walls / And snowy summits old in story;	The alliteration is on the letter "s".	This produces a soft, soothing sound, complementing the sound of the wind.	The intention is to create a nostalgic, even mournful mood.

Example	Sound technique	Sound quality	Purpose
The long light shakes across the lakes,	Use of assonance, repeating the "a" vowel	A slow echo-effect	This complements the reflective mood of the scene. It creates a drawn-out effect which slows down the pace of the poem and adds to its mournful tone.

 Exercise 10A – Alliteration, assonance and consonance

1   In stanzas two and three of the poem "Blow, Bugle, Blow", pick out a line in which alliterative words are found. Read the lines aloud and say what effect is created by the alliteration.

2   Pick out examples of assonance and consonance in the poem and state the sound quality and its contribution to the poem's tone and mood.

10.2 Use of words to imitate sound: onomatopoeia

 Definition—Onomatopoeia

Onomatopoeia is a device using **"words containing sounds similar to the noises they describe"** (*The Oxford Advanced Learner's Dictionary*); for example, "hiss", "bang", "clang" or "thud". The sound/sense correspondence is more direct than that of alliteration or assonance and the intention is obviously to reinforce the meaning with the sound.

Pleasant Sounds

The rustling of leaves under the feet in woods and under
hedges.
The crumpling of cat-ice and snow down wood rides, narrow
lanes and every street causeways.
Rustling through a wood, or rather rushing while the wind
halloos in the oak tops like thunder.
The rustles of birds' wings startled from their nests, or flying
unseen into the bushes.
The whizzing of larger birds overhead in a wood, such as
crows, puddocks, buzzards etc.
The trample of robust wood larks on the brown leaves, and
the patter of squirrels on the green moss.
The fall of an acorn on the ground, the pattering of nuts on
the hazel branches ere they fall from ripeness.
The flirt of the ground-lark's wing from the stubbles, how
sweet such pictures on dewy mornings when the dew
flashes from its brown feathers.

John Clare

The phrase "while the wind halloos in the oak-top like thunder" is an example of onomatopoeia. Here, the poet uses the word "halloos" to imitate the sound of the echoing wind.

 Exercise 10B – Onomatopoeia

1   Read John Clare's poem again. Can you find another example of onomatopoeia?

2   What other sound devices are used in this poem? Why do you think they are used?

Group work: Analysis and discussion

Work in a small group to identify the various sound devices (alliteration, assonance, consonance, onomatopoeia) in these lines and analyse them.

Text A

> Over the cobbles he clattered and clashed in the dark
>   inn-yard,
> And he tapped with his whip on the shutters, but all was
>   locked and barred ...
>
> *From "The Highwayman" by Alfred Noyes*

Sound device?	Sound produced and sound quality?	What is the poet's purpose in using this device? What is the effect on the reader?

Text B

> What passing-bells for these who die as cattle?
> Only the monstrous anger of the guns.
> Only the stuttering rifles' rapid rattle
> Can patter out their hasty orisons.
>
> *From "Anthem for Doomed Youth" by Wilfred Owen*

Sound device?	Sound produced and sound quality?	What is the poet's purpose in using this device?

Text C

> Out of the night that covers me,
>   Black as the Pit from pole to pole,
> I thank whatever gods may be
>   For my unconquerable soul.
>
> *From "Invictus" by William Ernest Henley*

Sound device?	Sound produced and sound quality?	What is the poet's purpose in using this device?

Text D

I must go down to the seas again, to the lonely sea and
    the sky,
And all I ask is a tall ship and a star to steer her by,
And the wheel's kick and the wind's song and the white
    sail's shaking,
And a grey mist on the sea's face, and a grey dawn
    breaking.

I must go down to the seas again, for the call of the
    running tide
Is a wild call and a clear call that may not be denied;
And all I ask is a windy day with the white clouds flying,
And the flung spray and the blown spume, and the sea
    gulls crying.

From "Sea Fever" by John Masefield

Sound device?	Sound produced and sound quality?	What is the poet's purpose in using this device?

Text E

Whenever silence, like satin, falls
On the clamour of conversation;
When noiselessness from pre-creation
Bounces off the walls;

And suddenly, something is left unsaid
Some say angels are passing overhead.

And I give wordless thanks
For the reminder to listen
To pockets of the divine;
For the poetry of the unspoken.

For silences, quiets
All pulsing. Whole. All
Still. Perfect. Unbroken.

"angels overhead" by Aaron Maniam

Sound device?	Sound produced and sound quality?	What is the poet's purpose in using this device?

Exercise 10C – Sound

Text A

Fly-Fishing

A soft flick, vague as memory,
And then the straight plunge

Of weight, laying out a line from
Life to life, a morse-code of motion;

5   You listen for the slips, the signal,
The tentative nudge, and count

Each wink in flaked sunlight
A trout for every thought. One

Slapped the river in a frenzy of thrashing
10   Then flashed away, lure and not

Steel in its dark maws. But
The joy is in the tense tremble,

The reining in with the reel
Held close to your ear, watching

15   The vague wake burst
Into rich silvery form. Later,

Stooped to scale it and oblivious
To the wet slime slick on my skin,

I might remember leaping gurgle oracles,
Bubbles babbled like words, recalling

20

Men back to the bait
With caution and exuberance:

Immerse yourself and play by the rules.

Alvin Pang

1 Briefly describe the experience of fly-fishing in the poem.

2 How would you describe the mood in the poem? Pick out sound devices in the poem and show how they contribute to the mood.

3 How does the poet develop the sense of excitement in the poem? Show examples of this.

4 Explain the last line of this poem. What is the point the poet is making?

Text B

Auto wreck

Its quick soft silver bell beating, beating
And down the dark one ruby flare
Pulsing out red light like an artery,
The ambulance at top speed floating down

5   Past beacons and illuminated clocks
Wings in a heavy curve, dips down,
And brakes speed, entering the crowd.
The doors leap open, emptying light;
Stretchers are laid out, the mangled lifted

10   And stowed into the little hospital.
Then the bell, breaking the hush, tolls once,
And the ambulance with its terrible cargo
Rocking, slightly rocking, moves away,

As the doors, an afterthought, are closed.
15   We are deranged, walking among the cops
Who sweep glass and are large and composed.
One is still making notes under the light.
One with a bucket douches ponds of blood
Into the street and gutter.
20   One hangs lanterns on the wrecks that cling,
Empty husks of locusts, to iron poles.

Karl Shapiro

1   How many types of sound device can you find in the first
line of the poem? State their purposes in the poem.

2   How does the poet increase the tension of the scene
through the use of sound devices? Identify them and
comment on their effect on the reader.

3   "Its quick soft silver bell beating, beating … / Pulsing out
red light like an artery" What type of image is this? What is
being compared and what is the effect of this? Identify
other images used by the poet and state their effect on the
reader.

4   How does the poet's description of the police officers differ
from the description of the accident? What do you think the
poet is implying?

 ## Links to real-world issues

In "Fly-Fishing", the poet talks about an uncommon sport in
modern-day Singapore. What other uncommon activities do some
Singaporeans indulge in? How important is it to connect with
nature? The last line can also be seen as a reference to the real
world of office politics, in which case the poem is a metaphor
about survival in modern society. Where do we draw the line
between creativity and caution?

Chapter 11

INTRODUCTION TO CLOSE ANALYSIS OF PROSE

As students would have learned how to obtain an overall understanding of a piece of writing and its concerns, the aim of this section is to equip them with skills for more in-depth analysis. It deals with skills for close reading of prose and the analysis of techniques used in prose.

Chapter outline

11.1 The importance of sustaining the reader's attention

11.2 A strategy for analysing prose

 Trigger activity

What do these pictures suggest to you? Which caption would fit each best?

Picture A

Picture B

1 Which is the best caption for Picture A?
　(a) Go ahead, cat; make my day!
　(b) Shh … I'm hunting rabbits!
　(c) It's time we animals took control!
　(d) *Write your own original caption.*

2 Which is the best caption for Picture B?
- (a) Creativity without limits …
- (b) Hand over the candy, Dad, or I'll pull the plug!
- (c) This is why you need to buy a videocam and not a webcam.
- (d) *Write your own original caption.*

Point to note

Subtlety is key!

It is ingrained in us, human beings, that when we read a text, watch a film, look at a photograph or a painting, we enjoy a piece of work even more if it is clever, subtle and complex.

11.1 The importance of sustaining the reader's attention

Novels, even short stories, are not usually written overnight; instead, much time and effort may be taken to ensure that the plot progresses, characters develop and mature, and suspense is kept at a consistent pace. Perhaps what most good writers try to achieve is to make the reader unaware of what they set out to achieve. For example, we say an actor has poor acting skills if, while watching the programme, we are aware he is trying to act the role; this distracts us from the story and spoils our enjoyment of the programme. Similarly, good writers always attempt to create a realistic scenario so that the reader is comfortable in whatever world he or she is transported to. Techniques are used subtly to develop the story while maintaining the reader's absorption in that fictional world.

Purpose—Why do writers need to add complexity to the text?

A story that is explicitly told to the reader does not allow the reader to become involved and keep guessing what is going to happen next. There would be no motivation for the reader to read on. Hence, stories explicitly told do not sustain or develop the reader's interest in what is going on.

Method—How do writers sustain the reader's attention?

One of the main techniques writers use is the "Show—don't tell" method:

(1) Writers begin with a message that they want to convey about the world and/or about human nature.

(2) They do this by giving hints and clues in the text, that is, by showing the reader what to pay attention to and think about.

Therefore, our job as readers and critics is to look at what the writer shows us and then to infer what he may tell us about life and/or human nature.

 Group work: Construction and inference

Work in a group of four or five.

(1) As a group, come up with a specific philosophical statement such as "Good triumphs over evil". This statement must be a truth about human nature or the world.

(2) Next, design an art piece that communicates the philosophical statement indirectly. You can use pictures and texts from magazines and newspapers and paste these onto a blank piece of paper. The pictures and texts should combine to form the final art piece and should give clues about the philosophical statement.

(3) At the end of twenty minutes, exchange your art work with another group and guess what the other group's philosophical statement is by using the "Show—don't tell" method described above. Share your insights with the class.

11.2 A strategy for analysing prose

 Method—The "Show—don't tell" strategy for approaching prose

How do we infer what the writer is telling us? Here is a strategy for approaching and analysing prose from start to finish.

Steps	What you should do
Step 1: **Understanding overall meaning**	Aim: Get a clear overview of WHAT the text is about. Read the text once through to get an impression of what the text is about: its subject matter, genre and mood. *(Refer to Section I of this book.)*
Step 2: **Close reading**	Aim: Look at HOW the central meaning is conveyed to the reader through what the writer SHOWS. (a) Start by paying attention to specific concrete details in the text. If a writer spends a lot of time describing something or someone to you, he is probably hinting to you that you need to pay attention to that description and you should think about what the detailed description implies. (b) Look specifically at these five techniques writers may use: • Narrative features • Characterization • Tension and suspense • Humour and irony • Language features *(These techniques will be covered in the following chapters of this book.)*
Step 3: **Philosophical insight and response**	Aim: Respond to the text by thinking about what the writer is telling us through showing. Don't just focus on what the story is about. Learn to step out of the text as a critic and think about the philosophical insight about the world or the human condition that the writer is revealing through the text. (a) Read the text, paying attention to the underlying meaning and truth through examining • oppositional structure (What is the central tension or theme in the text?) • intention (What is the intention of the writer in writing the text?) (b) Summarize this in a statement about what philosophical insight about the world and/or about human nature the text conveys to the reader. (c) As you reflect on these insights, note down your feelings at different parts of the text. Then look at how your feelings change in the course of the text. *(Refer to Section IV of this book.)*

Application example

Now we will apply this methodology to an analysis of a prose text. Read the extract below regarding the life of a housewife set in Africa in the 1960s.

> There came an end to embroidery; again she was left empty-handed. Again she looked about for something to do. The walls, she decided, were filthy. She would whitewash them all, herself, to save money. So, for two weeks, Dick
> 5 came back to the house to find furniture stacked in the middle of rooms and pails of thick white stuff standing on the floor.
>
> *Extract from "The Grass Is Singing" by Doris Lessing*

Domain	Evidence	What the writer shows
Specific concrete details	The writer describes in chronological order the way in which the protagonist attempts to occupy herself with things to do in the house. Lessing describes how she thought of whitewashing the walls and then proceeded to do so. There is also the repetition of "again" in the second sentence.	The writer is hinting at the protagonist's repressed energy and creativity. She is bored with the routine in her life and feels a need to change things. The repetition of "again" emphasizes the emptiness of her life; she yearns to do something more fulfilling.

Conclusion—What is the writer telling us about human nature or life?

Perhaps Doris Lessing is telling us about how some women who are confined to their homes may not always be truly free or happy but may, instead, be feeling repressed because of their mundane existence.

Read the following paragraphs, which are a continuation of Lessing's story.

But she was very methodical. One room was finished before another was begun; and while he admired her for her capability and self-assurance, undertaking this work she had no experience or knowledge of, he was alarmed too.

5 What was she going to do with all this energy and efficiency? It undermined his own self-assurance even further, seeing her like this, for he knew, deep down, that this quality was one he lacked. Soon, the walls were dazzling blue-white, every inch of them painted by Mary herself, standing on a

10 rough ladder for days at a time.

And now she found she was tired. She found it pleasant to let go a little, and to spend her time sitting with her hands folded, on the big sofa. But not for long. She was restless, so restless she did not know what to do with herself. She

15 unpacked the novels she had brought with her, and turned them over. These were the books she had collected over years from the mass that had come her way. She had read each one a dozen times, knowing it by heart, following the familiar tales as a child listens to his mother telling him a

20 well-known fairy tale. It had been a drug, a soporific, in the past, reading them; now, as she turned them over listlessly, she wondered why they had lost their flavour. Her mind wandered as she determinedly turned the pages; and she realized, after she had been reading for perhaps an hour,

25 that she had not taken in a word. She threw the book aside and tried another, but with the same result. For a few days the house was littered with books in faded dust covers. Dick was pleased: it flattered him to think he had married a woman who read books.

Extract from "The Grass Is Singing" by Doris Lessing

With a partner, pick out specific concrete details in the text. Then make inferences about what the writer may be telling us (the readers).

Exercise 11A

The following are the opening paragraphs of short stories. Can you make inferences about what the writer is showing and indirectly telling us in each extract?

Text A

On the twenty-eighth of February, 1936 (on the third day, that is, of the February 26 Incident), Lieutenant Shinji Takeyama of the Konoe Transport Battalion—profoundly disturbed by the knowledge that his closest colleagues had been with the mutineers from the beginning, and indignant at the imminent prospect of Imperial troops attacking Imperial troops—took his officer's sword and ceremonially disembowelled himself in the eight-mat room of his private residence in the sixth block of Aoba-cho in Yotsuya Ward. His wife, Reiko, followed him, stabbing herself to death. The lieutenant's farewell note consisted of one sentence: "Long live the Imperial Forces." His wife's, after apologies for her unfilial conduct in thus preceding her parents to the grave, concluded: "The day which, for a soldier's wife, had to come, has come ..." The last moments of this heroic and dedicated couple were such as to make the gods themselves weep. The lieutenant's age, it should be noted, was thirty-one, his wife's twenty-three; and it was not half a year since the celebration of their marriage.

Extract from "Patriotism" by Yukio Mishima

What is the writer showing us? (Look at the specific concrete details.)	What is the writer telling us about human nature and/or the world?

Text B

It was on the eve of August Bank Holiday that the latest recruit became the leader of the Wormsley Common Gang. No one was surprised except Mike, but Mike at the age of nine was surprised by everything. "If you don't shut your mouth," somebody once said to him, "you'll get a frog down

it." After that Mike kept his teeth tightly clamped except when the surprise was too great.

The new recruit had been with the gang since the beginning of the summer holidays, and there were
10 possibilities about his brooding silence that all recognized. He never wasted a word even to tell his name until that was required of him by the rules. When he said "Trevor" it was a statement of fact, not as it would have been with the others a statement of shame or defiance. Nor did anyone laugh
15 except Mike, who, finding himself without support and meeting the dark gaze of the newcomer, opened his mouth and was quiet again. There was every reason why T, as he was afterwards referred to, should have been an object of mockery—there was his name (and they substituted the initial
20 because otherwise they had no excuse not to laugh at it), the fact that his father, a former architect and present clerk, had "come down in the world" and that his mother considered herself better than the neighbours. What but an odd quality of danger, of the unpredictable, established him in the gang
25 without any ignoble ceremony of initiation?

Extract from "The Destructors" by Graham Greene

What is the writer showing us? (Look at the specific concrete details.)	What is the writer telling us about human nature and/or the world?

Text C

The crowd was full of men.

They came in their sandals and, sitting in one dollar seats, stared hard at the performers. Overhead, the ceiling fans whirred, glistening like spinning white flowers in the
5 lights. On the floor were pieces of newspaper carrying the news of guerilla warfare. But in the theatre, the men stared at the stage, lit up like an aquarium tank. It was a Revue show newly come to town.

Sometimes, three or four girls, ... did their turn on the
10 stage and the men followed each gesture they made, silently. ... At 11.30 pm sharp, the Revue closed. Every night the men went away and came back the following night. As usual they were without their wives and daughters. They walked up the

15   aisle with swift silent strides, feeling a bit ashamed, and when they recognized their friends, laughed a little to hide their embarrassment. When the curtain fell, they shuffled off, more lonely than ever, back to their worries and their squalid little rooms.

Extract from "The Glittering Game" by Lee Kok Liang

What is the writer showing us? (Look at the specific concrete details.)	What is the writer telling us about human nature and/or the world?

Exercise 11B

Read this passage and answer the questions that follow.

     The day's heat, soaring to previously unheard of heights for a Malaysian October, had increasingly given way to humid storm clouds. Incandescent streaks of forked lightning were swiftly followed by deafening cracks of thunder, as if
5   mischievous stagehands battled behind a Chinese opera stage. Outside, the caged kitten mewed in chorus with a puppy's terrified yelps, appending vibrant theatrical effects to the fluctuations of Devi's anxious heart.

     Now married twenty-eight years, she had resided in her
10   house in Butterworth since her wedding reception. The growing clutter, gathered by an increasingly obsessive husband, threatened to consume the entire house. The walls badly needed painting.

     The toilet pipe needed fixing—water gushed onto the
15   floor every time the handle was flushed, and piles of ancient newspapers were obstacles that constantly impeded visitors' progress. Some years ago she had planned to divide the single storey house into an upper and lower level, but her husband, for reasons unknown, forbade her to execute the
20   already drawn-up plans.

Devi had forsaken a law career in favour of her arranged marriage to Chandran. One day her ageing father had presented her with a *fait accompli,* marry Chandran—a man fourteen years her senior, with good prospects—or wait and maybe never find such a good match again. She had little choice but to comply with her father's wishes. Her father was not a man to contradict. As the eldest daughter, Devi was compelled to marry first, for custom demanded that her sisters would be unable to wed if she did not. Or, at the very least, society would view Devi as suspect, were one of her sisters to be betrothed before she was. Devi might be considered unmarriageable in that eventuality. From the time of her father's request, it would appear her fate was sealed.

Lightning accented an enlargement of Devi's deceased father's photograph, hanging opposite her on the greying wall. The ceremonial ash, faint but still visible on the dusty glass over the figure's forehead, indicated that she still remembered and revered him. As the thunder cracked again, Devi recalled the early years of her marriage to Chandran, the beatings and his overbearing dominance of her. She remembered running home to her father and the urge she had to see Chandran again. Deep within her, a segment of her soul recalled the almost addictive nature of her relationship with him, and her inability to break free from his almost Rasputin-like mesmerizing effect upon her. Several times her brothers extracted her from Chandran's house, only for her to long for him and return within days. It was an anxious attachment she couldn't explain, but that was the force that kept her with him through the years, despite his treatment of her.

Extract from "The Orchid Wife" by Yusuf Martin A. Bradley

1 Look at the title of the story from which this extract is taken. Explain the metaphor used and say what you think the story is about.

2 Why do you think the writer pays so much attention to describing the weather in paragraph one? Where else in the text is the weather described? What do you think the writer is showing?

3 What is your impression of Devi and her relationship with Chandran? What specific concrete details are given to support this?

4 What are your feelings for Devi at the end of this passage? Support your answer with reference to the text.

 Links to real-world issues

Though uncommon in modern-day Singapore, the practice of arranged marriages continues to exist. What is your opinion of arranged marriages? Try to examine this issue from various perspectives: those of parents, the modern couple, the government and society.

Chapter **12**
PLOT STRUCTURE

Trigger activity

Compare Example A with Example B. Which one would likely end up on a best-seller list and why?

Chapter outline

12.1 Conflict

12.2 Climax

12.3 Conclusion

Example A

> Rose and Jon meet in college. Both are beautiful, intelligent, talented, popular and well-adjusted. They are of the same race, class, religion. Their parents are good friends. Jon loves Rose and Rose loves Jon. They marry and have three children, all of whom are beautiful, intelligent, popular, filial and well-behaved. All the children succeed in their career and marriage. Rose and Jon die peacefully of natural causes at the age of 99 and are buried in the same grave.

Example B

> Rose and Jon meet in college. Both are beautiful, intelligent, talented, popular and well-adjusted. They are of the same race, class, religion. Their parents are good friends. Jon loves Rose but Rose doesn't love Jon. They go on a cruise and Rose, in her depression, tries to jump off the ship. However, she is rescued by Jack and she falls in love with him. Jon finds out about this and becomes increasingly jealous. The ship hits an iceberg, killing many on board. Rose and Jack escape in the nick of time but Jack freezes to death in the icy-cold water.

Purpose—Why the need for plot?

Obviously, Example B has already been made into the blockbuster Hollywood movie *Titanic* whereas nobody has heard of or read about Example A. Most people pick up a good book in order to escape the mundane reality of their lives. Thus, a writer of prose fiction must create and develop an interesting plot rich in suspense and conflict, with issues which will engage the reader.

 ## Definition—Plot

Plot refers to **events arranged sequentially which involve characters in conflict**. Every story is told within a specific period of time. Most stories are told in a **chronological** order where events are told sequentially as they occur. Writers may also employ the **flashback** (in which the story moves to a past event). A typical plot structure contains three main areas: conflict, climax and resolution.

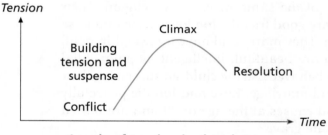

Levels of tension in the plot

12.1 Conflict

 ## Definition—Conflict

At the start of the story, the writer usually prepares the reader by providing background information, establishing the setting and introducing the main character. The writer also needs to introduce the central conflict of the story. **Conflict** refers to the **key problem or tension in the story**. Conflict may take two main forms.

(a) **External conflict**
   This occurs when the character struggles with an external situation. There are four types of external conflict which you may find in texts:

- conflict with another character such as a violent quarrel
- conflict with society, as when a person is up against certain laws or issues imposed by society
- conflict with nature, as when a person struggles with the weather
- conflict with God.

For example, Hemingway's *The Old Man and the Sea* tells the classic tale of an old man who struggles to catch a huge fish. In the process, he battles not just the weather but also his society, which sees him as useless and too old. The fact that the old man has to face not just one but many types of conflict (environmental, societal, relations with others, etc) increases our sympathy for him.

(b) Internal/Inner conflict

This refers to a conflict within the individual, such as a mental struggle over a certain issue. It may also involve a personal fear or paranoia. One way to tell whether a character is struggling with an inner conflict is to observe visible, physical signs. For example, a person who has an intense fear of exams may exhibit physical signs such as sweaty palms and the nervous swinging of the legs minutes before an exam begins.

Method—How do we analyse conflict?

(1) Read the text and identify aspects of external and internal conflict.

(2) More importantly, state how these various conflicts contribute to:
- the mood of the text
- the state of mind of the character concerned
- the feelings the reader experiences as he or she reads the text.

Exercise 12A – Conflict

Read this account of Odysseus' encounter with a Cyclops—a huge terrifying monster.

> "Strangers!" he cried. "And who are you? Where do you come from over the watery ways? Is yours a trading venture; or are you cruising the main on chance, like roving pirates, who risk their lives to ruin other people?"

5   Our hearts sank. The booming voice and the very sight of the monster filled us with panic. Still, I managed to find words to answer him. "We are Achaeans," I said, "on our way back from Troy—driven astray by contrary winds across a vast expanse of sea—we're making our way home but took

10   the wrong way—the wrong route—as Zeus, I suppose, intended that we should. We find ourselves here as suppliants* at your knees, in the hope that you may give us hospitality or even give us the kind of gifts that hosts customarily give their guests. Good sir, remember your duty to the gods; we are

15   your suppliants, and Zeus is the champion of suppliants and guests. He is the god of guests: guests are sacred to him and he goes alongside them."

That is what I said, and he answered me promptly out of his pitiless heart: "Stranger, you must be a fool or must

20   have come from very far afield, to order me to fear or reverence the gods. We Cyclops care nothing for Zeus with his aegis nor for the rest of the blessed gods, since we are much stronger than they are. I would never spare you or your men for fear of incurring Zeus' enmity, unless I felt like

25   it. But tell me where you moored your good ship when you came. Was it somewhere along the coast or nearby? I'd like to know."

His words were designed to get the better of me, but he could not outwit someone with my knowledge of the world.

30   I answered with plausible words: "As for my ship, it was wrecked by the Earthshaker Poseidon on the borders of your land. The wind had carried us on to a lee shore. He drove the ship up to a headland and hurled it on the rocks. But I and my friends here managed to escape with our lives." To this

35   the cruel brute made no reply. Instead, he jumped up, and reaching out towards my men, seized a couple and dashed their heads against the floor as though they had been puppies. Their brains ran out on the ground and soaked the earth. Limb by limb he tore them to pieces to make his meal, which

40   he devoured like a mountain lion, leaving nothing, neither entrails nor flesh, marrow nor bones, while we, weeping, lifted up our hands to Zeus in horror at the ghastly sight. We felt completely helpless.

Extract from The Odyssey *by Homer, translated by E.V. Rieu and Dominic Rieu*

---

* suppliants: beggars.

1 Contrast Odysseus with the Cyclops. How does this contribute to our understanding of the conflict in this situation? Are there elements in Odysseus' character which offer a glimmer of hope for him and his companions?

2 Pick out and identify other elements of conflict in this passage. Say how these elements contribute to the overall mood of the text.

 12.2 Climax

 Definition—Climax

The conflict, which is often introduced at the beginning of a story, must be gradually built up in order to sustain interest. **When the conflict has been developed to its highest point**, we term this the **climax** of the story.

 Method—How do we analyse climax?

(1) To establish the climax, first identify where the moment of greatest excitement or intensity in the story is.

(2) Next, examine how the writer develops the conflict towards the climax. What specific techniques does he use?

Note: One key technique writers often employ to drive the conflict towards the climax is the use of suspense. This will be covered in greater detail in Chapter 14.

Exercise 12B – Climax

Read the previous extract from *The Odyssey* again and try to predict what the outcome of the encounter will be. Before you read the passage that follows, try to write your own outcome and climax of the situation based on the problem posed to Odysseus by the Cyclops. Then share your work in class and discuss the ways in which you built your conflict towards the climax. What techniques did you use and how effective are they?

Now read Homer's account of how Odysseus responds to the Cyclops.

Then with an olive-wood bowl of my dark wine in my hands, I went up to him and said: "Here, Cyclops, have some wine to wash down that meal of human flesh, and find out for yourself what kind of vintage was stored away in our
5   ship's hold. I brought it for you as an offering in the hope that you would take pity on me and help me on my homeward way. But your savagery is more than we can bear."

The Cyclops took the wine and drank it up. And the delicious drink gave him such exquisite pleasure that he
10   asked me for another bowlful. "Give me more please, and tell me your name—I would like to make you a gift that will please you. We Cyclops have wine of our own made from the grapes that our rich soil and rains from Zeus produce. But this vintage of yours is a drop of the real nectar and
15   ambrosia."

So said the Cyclops, and I handed him another bowlful of the sparkling wine. Three times I filled it for him; and three times the fool drained the bowl to the dregs. At last, when the wine had fuddled his wits, I addressed him with soothing
20   words.

"Cyclops," I said, "you ask me my name. I'll tell it to you; and in return give me the gift you promised me. My name is Nobody. That is what I am called by my mother and father and by all my friends."

25   The Cyclops answered me from his cruel heart. "Of all his company I will eat Nobody last, and the rest before him. That shall be your gift."

He had hardly spoken before he toppled over and fell face upwards on the floor, where he lay with his great neck
30   twisted to one side, and the all-compelling sleep overpowered him. In his drunken stupor he vomited, and a stream of wine mixed with morsels of men's flesh poured from his throat. I went at once and thrust our pole deep under the ashes of the fire to make it hot, and meanwhile gave a word of
35   encouragement to all my men, to make sure that no one would hang back through fear. When the fierce glow from the live stake warned me that it was about to catch alight in the flames, green as it was, I withdrew it from the fire and my men gathered round. A god now inspired them with
40   tremendous courage. Seizing the olive pole, they drove its sharpened end into the Cyclops' eye while I used my weight from above to twist it home, like a man boring a ship's timber with a drill which his mates below him twirl with a

45 strap they hold at either end, so that it spins continuously. In much the same way we handled our pole with its red-hot point and twisted it in his eye till the blood boiled up round the burning wood. The scorching heat singed his lids and brow all round while his eyeball blazed and the very roots crackled in the flame. The Cyclops' eye hissed round the live
50 stake in the same way that an axe or adze hisses when a smith plunges it into cold water to quench and strengthen the iron. He gave a dreadful shriek, which echoed round the rocky walls, and we backed away from him in terror, while he pulled the stake from his eye, streaming with blood. Then
55 he hurled it away from him with frenzied hands and raised a great shout to the other Cyclops who lived in neighbouring caves along the windy heights. Hearing his screams, they came up from every quarter, and gathering outside the cave asked him what the matter was.
60 "What on earth is wrong with you, Polyphemus? Why must you disturb the peaceful night and spoil our sleep with all this shouting? Is someone trying by treachery or violence to kill you?"

Out of the cave came mighty Polyphemus' voice in reply:
65 "O my friends, it's Nobody's treachery, not violence, that is killing me."

"Well, then," came the immediate reply, "if you are alone and nobody is assaulting you, you must be sick and sickness comes from almighty Zeus and cannot be helped."
70 And off they went while I laughed to myself at the way in which my cunning notion of a false name had taken them in.

1 Examine the extract and try to locate the climax (moment of greatest tension and excitement) in the extract. Give reasons for your answer.

2 Notice one technique writers often employ to develop the conflict towards its climax is the use of a **complicating situation**. This occurs when an incident or event complicates or worsens the key conflict in the text. A complicating situation often increases the sense of excitement and suspense because the reader is left wondering whether what he expects to happen will actually take place. Now read the above extract again. Can you identify where the complicating situation is? Remember this usually takes place prior to the climax. Then try to state in detail how it contributes to the climax.

12.3 Conclusion

After building the conflict to a climax, writers **conclude the story with** some form of **resolution** in which the key issues are addressed.

 Definition—Resolution

A **resolution** may take one of several forms.

(a) **Complete resolution**
Here, the issue or conflict is resolved. This is typical of happy endings in many fairy tales.

(b) **Ironic resolution**
Here, the expected resolution is reversed and the opposite of what one expects occurs. For example, in Kate Chopin's "The Story of an Hour", the wife rejoices at news of her husband's death and makes plans for living a life of freedom. However, at the end, she discovers that her husband is still alive.

(c) **The twist**
This is similar to the ironic resolution. However, here, a new fact is introduced which resolves the problems posed in the story. This is common in many detective stories in which the detective who originally suspects one character is given a new lead at the end and discovers that the criminal is someone else.

(d) **The revelation**
A common form of ending is one in which the character gains a revelation or a new awareness of the situation or issue. In a sense, the character then matures and is able to step out of the situation to reflect on his experiences. Sometimes, it is not the character who attains that revelation but the reader.

(e) **The open ending**
This happens when the issue is not resolved or only partially resolved. At times, this creates a sense of realism because happy endings do not commonly occur in real life. Open endings (or cliffhangers, as they are known in films or television serials) are sometimes employed by writers to cause the reader to ponder further on the issues raised at the end and, at times, they invite the reader to imagine other possible outcomes.

Note that some stories end with a combination of these types. For example, a story may conclude happily through a twist and revelation.

Method—How do we analyse the resolution?

(1) Pay careful attention to the last few paragraphs of any unseen prose text you are given because these often provide important clues and information to the overall meaning and direction of the story.

(2) Compare the last paragraph of the text with the first paragraph. What has changed? What issues have been addressed and what have been left unresolved?

 Point to note

There may not be a conclusion.

An unseen prose text is often extracted from a larger story. Hence, there is the possibility that there may be no conclusion in the text you are reading.

 Group work: Prediction and dramatization

"Cinderella" is a popular fairy tale. The central conflict is that Cinderella is reduced in position to a servant and is bullied by her stepmother and three stepsisters. One day, the fairy godmother appears to her and gives her a chance to go to the annual ball where she meets Prince Charming. At the stroke of midnight, as instructed by the fairy godmother, she has to leave and in her hurry, she leaves behind one of her glass slippers.

Now, work in a group of four or five to do the following:

(1) Create an ending to this tale which is different from the traditional one. (Each group in class should focus on one of the five types of resolution given earlier.)

(2) The group must be prepared to present a three-minute performance of their conclusion.

(3) At the end of this exercise, the group, together with the others, should evaluate the effectiveness of the different endings presented.

1   Read the previous extract from *The Odyssey,* paying special attention to the last five paragraphs.

2   What are your feelings for Odysseus and for the Cyclops at the end of the text? Why?

3   How would you describe the type of resolution in the text? Do you think it is an effective ending? Why?

Exercise 12D – More practice on plot structure

Identify the elements of plot structure as you read the extract below.

My mother was a stranger to me when she first arrived at my uncle's house in Ningpo. I was nine years old and had not seen her for many years. But I knew she was my mother, because I could feel her pain.

5   "Do not look at that woman," warned my aunt. "She has thrown her face into the eastward-flowing stream. Her ancestral spirit is lost forever. The person you see is just decayed flesh, evil, rotted to the bone."

       And I would stare at my mother. She did not look evil.
10   I wanted to touch her face, the one that looked like mine.

       It is true, she wore strange foreign clothes. But she did not speak back when my aunt cursed her. Her head bowed even lower when my uncle slapped her for calling him Brother. She cried from her heart when Popo died, even
15   though Popo, her mother, had sent her away so many years before. And after Popo's funeral, she obeyed my uncle. She prepared herself to return to Tientsin, where she had dishonoured her widowhood by becoming the third concubine to a rich man.

20   How could she leave without me? This was a question I could not ask. I was a child. I could only watch and listen.

The night before she was to leave, she held my head against her body, as if to protect me from a danger I could not see. I was crying to bring her back before she was even gone. And as I lay in her lap, she told me a story.

"An-mei," she whispered, "have you seen the little turtle that lives in the pond?" I nodded. This was a pond in our courtyard and I often poked a stick in the still water to make the turtle swim out from underneath the rocks.

"I also knew that turtle when I was a small child," said my mother. "I used to sit by the pond and watch him swimming to the surface, biting the air with his little beak. He is a very old turtle."

I could see that turtle in my mind and I knew my mother was seeing the same one.

"This turtle feeds on our thoughts," said my mother. "I learned this one day, when I was your age, and Popo said I could no longer be a child. She said I could not shout, or run, or sit on the ground to catch crickets. I could not cry if I was disappointed. I had to be silent and listen to my elders. And if I did not do this, Popo said she would cut off my hair and send me to a place where Buddhist nuns lived.

"That night, after Popo told me this, I sat by the pond, looking into the water. And because I was weak, I began to cry. Then I saw this turtle swimming to the top and his beak was eating my tears as soon as they touched the water. He ate them quickly, five, six, seven tears, then climbed out of the pond, crawled onto a smooth rock and began to speak.

"The turtle said, 'I have eaten your tears, and this is why I know your misery. But I must warn you. If you cry, your life will always be sad.'

"Then the turtle opened his beak and out poured five, six, seven pearly eggs. The eggs broke open and from them emerged seven birds, who immediately began to chatter and sing. I knew from their snow-white bellies and pretty voices that they were magpies, birds of joy. These birds bent their beaks to the pond and began to drink greedily. And when I reached out my hand to capture one, they all rose up, beat their black wings in my face, and flew up into the air, laughing.

"'Now you see,' said the turtle, drifting back into the pond, 'why it is useless to cry. Your tears do not wash away your sorrows. They feed someone else's joy. And that is why you must learn to swallow your own tears.'"

65 　 But after my mother finished her story, I looked at her and saw she was crying. And I also began to cry again, that this was our fate, to live like two turtles seeing the watery world together from the bottom of the little pond.

Extract from The Joy Luck Club *by Amy Tan*

1 What is the main conflict the narrator and her mother face? What other areas of conflict do you observe?

2 Who or what would you say is the cause of the main conflict?

3 Read the text carefully. Identify the climax. How does this contribute to the mood?

4 What are your feelings for both mother and daughter at the end of the extract? Give reasons to support your answer.

Exercise 12E – More practice on plot structure

　 He had found his mother beside the swimming pool in the backyard. Dappled by shadows of the papaya tree, she was feeding her chickens. A thin figure, slightly stooped, she was tossing a shower of millet around her. Wisps of grey
5 hair, worked free from the bun at the nape of her neck, softened her high forehead and bony cheeks.

"Ah-Ma," he called.

She lifted her eyes and stared blankly at him. Cloudy with the pale thickness of accumulated years, her eyes stared
10 at everything the same way, calm and blank like skyscraper windows.

"Ah-Ma, I bought—today—one thing, for you." As always when he switched from a day's usage of English back to Cantonese, he felt tongue-tied, even shy.

15 She smiled at him. "Ah-Wah," she said, "things you can buy, I do not need." Her voice was low, almost guttural, but

with the tonal lilt particular to Cantonese when it is spoken gently.

"But you don't even know what it is."

20 "I know I have everything I need."

"Everything, Mother? What about eyesight? Wouldn't you like to see?"

"Who says I cannot see now?" she asked sharply. "Is it that young doctor? Just because I wouldn't tell him what
25 shapes were on that silly wall-poster of his?"

"You want to see better, don't you?" he amended quickly.

"I am not, Ah-Wah, having my eyes sliced open," she said.

"I'm not talking about the operation, Ah-Ma ..."

30 "Like a clove of garlic or what, talking about peeling my eyes!"

"This has nothing to do with the operation," he said, and thrust the binoculars into her free hand. "They're special glasses, big ones to help you see things faraway."

35 "See-far glasses? What do I want to look at faraway things for?" She tossed a handful of millet to the chickens, clucking softly to them.

He looked at her, this papaya-shaped old woman whose womb, like the seed cavity of the fruit, had held countless
40 seeds within it. Mother of nine, grandmother of thirty-four, great grandmother of seventeen, her seeds had burst out from her and planted themselves in ripples of concentric circles round her. And she, riveted at their centre, held them together. Now, in the backyard of her eldest son's house, she
45 spent her evenings scattering grain to a brood of chickens. What, after all, would she need these binoculars for? He kicked aside a hen which was scuffing at his shoe, and turned back towards the house.

Without even looking up, she sensed his retreat. "Wait,"
50 she called after him. "Those see-far glasses of yours, can they see Tanjong Rhu?"

He stopped. "Tanjong Rhu?" he hesitated, frowning. "I suppose so—depends where you're looking from, of course."

"If they can see as far away as Tanjong Rhu," she said,
55 "I will try them."

He walked back to her, the eagerness growing in him again. "From my office window, Ah-Ma," he said quickly, "if you stand right at the end of the room, you can see Tanjong Rhu very clearly." He tugged at her wide sleeve to stop her
60 from tossing her handfuls of grain. "I'll take you up there—

you've never even been to my office—and we'll look through the see-far glasses at Tanjong Rhu. Would you like that?"

"I would," she said. "I have not seen your father's shipyard for a long time."

65   "Father's shipyard?"

"The one at Tanjong Rhu. Don't you remember?"

Extract from "Tanjong Rhu" by Ho Minfong

1   Aside from the generation gap, what other elements of conflict do you find between the son and his mother?

2   Trace the changing emotions in the mother during her conversation with the son. What can you infer about the mother?

3   At the end of the text, do you sympathize more with the son or the mother? Explain your answer.

 Links to real-world issues

One common area of conflict present in texts by Singaporean writers concerns the tension between the younger generation and the older generation. Can you list some of the differences in perspective and practice between the two generations? How can we overcome the communication barrier caused by this age gap? Recall your visits to some homes for the elderly. What were some of the difficulties you faced and how did you address them?

Chapter 13
NARRATIVE FEATURES

Trigger activity

It is common in television series and films for directors to switch between a first person and a third person camera view. For example, take a look at these two screen shots from "Nailed", Episode 6 of *CSI (Miami)*:

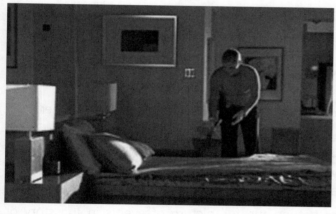

In this shot, the detective is dusting off evidence from the victim's bed. This is an example of a third person camera angle.

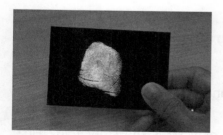

When the detective returns to the lab, she checks for fingerprints. However, the camera now moves to a first person perspective so that the camera represents her eyes as she examines the evidence.

Chapter outline

Discuss with your partner the advantages of both the first and the third person perspective. Pick any other episode in the *CSI* series and examine this switch between first and third person camera angles. Can you give reasons for the director's choice?

13.1 What is narration?

 Definition—Narration

Narration refers to the process of **telling the story**. When we analyse narrative features in texts, we ask ourselves these questions: From what point of view is the story told? Are there limitations to this viewpoint? Who is telling the story and why?

 Purpose—Why do we analyse narration?

We analyse a point of view and limitations to this point of view because the exercise can tell us:

(a) whether the story is told in an objective or subjective manner.

(b) whether the person telling the story is credible and whether we should believe everything he tells us; whether the narrator (or even the writer) may be influencing us (the reader) to adopt a particular position or to agree or sympathize with him and his cause.

(c) whether we are getting the full picture of events in the story or whether some of the information is deliberately withheld so that we may need to make our own inferences.

 Method—How do we analyse narrative features in texts?

We analyse narrative features by looking at three areas (which will be covered in the following sections):

(a) Point of view—from what point of view is the story told? First, second or third, and why?

(b) Degree of limitation in the point of view—how much information is given, and how much is withheld?

(c)   Characteristics and motives of the narrator—how credible or believable is the narrator? Does he have a motive for telling the story (especially if it is told in the first person)?

13.2 Point of view

Definition—Point of view

Point of view refers to the **perspective from which a story is told**. The two most common forms of perspective are the first person and the third person point of view.

(a)   First person narration

Definition
A story is told in the first person if the character who tells the story is involved in the story. Usually, this is indicated by the use of the word "I". Often in short stories, the first person narrator plays the central role in the story. However, there may be times when he may play a more minor role as an observer. For example, the novel *The Great Gatsby* by F. Scott Fitzgerald is told in the first person by the character Nick. However, the story revolves round the pretentious lifestyle of the main character, Gatsby. Nick plays a minor role as a commentator on the events he witnesses.

Advantages of the first person perspective
The first person point of view is effective because it enables the reader to see things from the point of view of the narrator. It is as if we are listening to an actual person recounting his experiences. This makes the story seem more personal and realistic. Because the story is more personal, we become more engaged, thus allowing the text to move us in a more powerful way. Telling a story in the first person is especially effective for evoking feelings of empathy or sympathy for the narrator on the part of the reader.

Disadvantages of the first person perspective
The first person point of view is limited in the sense that the reader cannot know everything that is going on. This is obvious because the story is told only from one person's point of view or perspective. For example, in *Jane Eyre* by Charlotte Bronte, Jane recounts her love for Rochester at the beginning, assuming that Rochester has ceased to notice her. It is only later in the text that we realize that it is Jane whom Rochester truly loves. Thus, the reader, together with Jane, is kept ignorant of what other characters feel. This subjective perspective

is helpful in creating a sense of suspense and allowing the reader, together with the narrator, to become engaged in piecing together the truth of the events.

(b) **Third person narration**

Definition
In the third person perspective, the events and characters are told by an implied narrator who is outside the text but who appears to have knowledge of the events and the characters in the story. For example, in the classic tale *Animal Farm*, the events at the farm are told from the third person perspective. The first sentence of the story reads: "Mr Jones, of the Manor Farm, had locked the hen-houses for the night, but was too drunk to remember to shut the pop-holes." In addition, the amount of information provided to the reader depends on whether the narrator is omniscient or not.

An **omniscient narrator** is one who **is all-knowing** and **able to read the minds of all the other characters** in the novel. He/She is able to relate an event and describe how the other characters feel about it. For example, read the following text: "Casey had a feeling that what they were doing, sneaking out in the middle of the night, was wrong, but Jay was insistent that the task be completed that night. Jay knew Mr Roberts would be upset if he could not find the boat in the morning and, thus, his sense of responsibility compelled him to retrieve the lost boat." The narrator of this text is obviously omniscient because he is able to tell the reader how both Casey and Jay feel about the retrieval of the boat.

A **partially omniscient narrator**, on the other hand, only **sees things through the eyes of a single character** (usually the main character of the text). For example, compare this next extract with the previous one: "Casey had a feeling that what they were doing, sneaking out in the middle of the night, was wrong. He could not understand why Jay was so insistent on sneaking out that night to get the boat." The narrator of this text is limited because the story is told only from the point of view of the main character, Casey.

Advantages of the third person perspective
Telling a story in the third person provides a more objective account of events because it enables the reader to look at events from the perspectives of various characters, and this allows the reader to make his own judgement.

Disadvantages of the third person perspective

One disadvantage of the third person perspective is that the story is told to the reader indirectly through a narrator. This makes the story less personal. Although the third person perspective lends a tone of objectivity to the narration, it can also create a sense of detachment in the reader.

 Group work: Compare and contrast

1. Can you think of more advantages and limitations to each perspective?

2. Look at a magazine or newspaper and pick out one example of a text written in the first person and one example written in the third person. Say what the effects of adopting such points of view are.

3. Attempt to rewrite the text from a different perspective and get other groups to assess it.

 Exercise 13A – Point of view

Both the following texts revolve around the lives of girls who are reduced to serving their family members. Compare and contrast the two texts.

Text A

>   Wash the white clothes on Monday and put them on the stone heap; wash the colour clothes on Tuesday and put them on the clothesline to dry; don't walk barehead in the hot sun; cook pumpkin fritters in very hot sweet oil; soak
> 5   your little cloths right after you take them off; when buying cotton to make yourself a nice blouse, be sure that it doesn't have gum on it, because that way it won't hold up well after a wash; soak salt fish overnight before you cook it; is it true that you sing benna in Sunday school?; always eat your food
> 10 in such a way that it won't turn someone else's stomach; on Sundays try to walk like a lady and not like the slut you are so bent on becoming; don't sing benna in Sunday school;

you mustn't speak to wharf-rat boys, not even to give
directions; don't eat fruits on the street—flies will follow you;
but I don't sing benna on Sundays at all and never in Sunday
15 *school;* this is how to sew on a button; this is how to make a
buttonhole for the button you have just sewed on; this is
how to hem a dress when you see the hem coming down and
so to prevent yourself from looking like the slut I know you
20 are so bent on becoming; this is how you iron your father's
khaki shirt so that it doesn't have a crease; this is how you
iron your father's khaki pants so that they don't have a
crease, ...

Extract from "Girl" by Jamaica Kincaid

Text B

And she remembered the time when she was in the
kitchen, taking the shells off a plate of prawns. It was a cold
wet day and she was feeling very tired and sleepy.
Mechanically, her fingers plucked off the head of each prawn,
5 then the tail, then the shell around the body. She must have
fallen asleep, for when she opened her eyes, she saw the cat
jumping off the table, and the plate bereft of half of its
contents. Chuan chuan, who had seen what had happened,
brought Aunt into the kitchen. Aunt's thin frame quivered
10 with fury, her pinched face took on an expression of
concentrated loathing as her hand shot out to pick up the
plate and bring it down resoundingly upon her head.
Fortunately it was a tin plate. Her head hurt and she began
to cry, whereupon Aunt pinched her arm, crying out, "What?
15 What? You dare to cry?" She hoped Auntie Siew Thong would
come in and comfort her but the neighbour had gone away
for a few days, visiting relatives in a nearby town.

Extract from "Durian" by Catherine Lim

1 Both texts explore the same theme. However, the
perspectives used differ. Can you think of some reasons why
the writers have adopted these perspectives?

2 What are your feelings for the main character in each of
these texts? Are your feelings different because of the
difference in perspective? Which character do you feel more
sympathy for? Can you say why?

I was glad to hear from my Japanese teacher but his letter also worried me. It was 1945: the British had just returned to Singapore. Sensei and the other Japanese had been interned as POWs and young Singaporeans (including
5 teenagers like me) were anxious, confused, feeling our way about under colonial rule—phasing from one subjugation to another.

I was surprised that Sensei had not yet been repatriated to Japan, but happy to learn that he was well treated, as he
10 was classified as civilian, not armed forces, or possible war crime suspect. My worry was for myself: I had received a letter from the enemy openly posted to me! Although the enemy was detained, still the letter could have attracted the attention of our new rulers—in particular some clandestine
15 police department responsible for keeping dossiers on subject people in their colony? I could be marked down, barred from education and jobs ... Surely they were now watching me—to see how I would respond to Sensei's letter? Indeed the envelope looked as though it had been opened and resealed.
20 Sensei's letter mentioned a pair of shoes that he had given me. The last time I saw him was at his home in Cavanagh Road (that seemingly long-ago time when Singapore was still Syonanto!). He had said, "Take these shoes. They're new. They look too big for you but you're still
25 growing and some day they'll fit. I don't mind going into the POW camp in these old shoes."

Extract from "The Shoes of My Sensei" by Goh Sin Tub

1 From which point of view is this story told? Why do you think the writer has chosen this point of view?

2 With reference to the second paragraph, do you think the narrator has a reason to be worried?

3 Rewrite the first paragraph using the third person point of view, beginning with "He was glad ..." What changes do you have to make? How would this make the story different? Explain your answer.

13.3 **Characteristics of the narrator**

Purpose—Why do we need to consider the characteristics of the narrator?

All stories are in some sense 'manipulative'. In other words, all texts attempt to persuade the reader to feel a certain way or to understand the cause the narrator is attempting to promote. When we start to consider the character of the narrator and his motives (as well as the writer's motive) in telling the story, we are essentially stepping outside of the story and thinking about how it has been written to persuade us to see things from a particular perspective. For example, we could say that Charles Dickens's story *Oliver Twist* attempts to persuade us to empathize with the poor.

 Method—What questions do we ask when we analyse characteristics of the narrator?

When analysing characteristics of the narrator, ask the following questions:

(a) Who is the narrator and how is he involved in the events of the story? Is he part of the story or merely an observer of what happens?

(b) What is your impression of the character of the narrator? Does he tell the story in an objective or emotional manner? Is he believable or does he lack credibility? Do we trust him or view him with suspicion?

(c) Why is the narrator telling you the story? Is he trying to influence you to sympathize with him and his cause?

 Group work: Analysing the narrator

Work with a partner, or in a small group, and read this first paragraph from a short story, "The Sandman" by Donald Barthelme.

> Dear Dr Hodder, I realize that it is probably wrong to write a letter to one's girlfriend's shrink but there are several things going on here that I think ought to be pointed out to you. I thought of making a personal visit but the situation then, as I'm sure you understand, would be completely untenable—I would be visiting a psychiatrist.

Discuss the following questions:

1   Who do you think the narrator is addressing?

2   Read the first sentence of the extract again carefully and think about what the narrator's intentions may be. Try to find evidence to support what you say.

3   From the second sentence, what do you think the narrator's attitude to his addressee may be?

Application example

How reliable is the narrator?

Reliability refers to the **extent to which you believe in** what **the speaker** says. A narrator is reliable if his story is believable and realistic. On the other hand, a narrator may be considered unreliable if you suspect that he is lying, is misled or is mentally unsound. For example, the story "The Tell-Tale Heart" by Edgar Allan Poe is told in the first person by a murderer who is obsessed and disturbed by his master's eye!

The first paragraph of the story reads:

> True!—nervous—very, very dreadfully nervous I had been and am; but why *will* you say that I am mad? The disease had sharpened my senses—not destroyed—not dulled them. Above all was the sense of hearing acute. I heard all things
> 5   in the heaven and in the earth. I heard many things in hell. How, then, am I mad? Hearken! And observe how healthily— how calmly I can tell you the whole story.

In this text, the narrator is obviously mentally unsound as proven by the fact that he keeps insisting that he is not mad! The more he attempts to persuade us that he has logical reasons for killing the old man, the less likely we are to believe him.

 Exercise 13C – Reliability of the narrator

In the following exercise, examine the perspective from which the story is told as well as the characteristics of the narrator. Be prepared to explain your answer.

I have told you, reader, that I had learnt to love Mr Rochester: I could not unlove him now, merely because I found that he had ceased to notice me—because I might pass hours in his presence and he would never once turn his eyes in my direction—because I saw all his attentions appropriated by a great lady, who scorned to touch me with the hem of her robes as she passed; who, if ever her dark and imperious eye fell on me by chance, would withdraw it instantly as from an object too mean to merit observation. I could not unlove him, because I felt sure he would soon marry this very lady—because I read daily in her proud security in his intentions respecting her—because I witnessed hourly in him a style of courtship which, if careless and choosing rather to be sought than to seek, was yet, in its very carelessness, captivating and in its very pride, irresistible.

Extract from Jane Eyre *by Charlotte Bronte*

1 From what perspective is the story told and why? What are the benefits or drawbacks of telling the tale from this perspective?

2 How reliable is the narrator? Explain why you say this. What other impression do you have of her?

Exercise 13D – Narrative features

In the following extract, examine the style of narration employed.

As Gregor Samsa awoke one morning from uneasy dreams he found himself transformed in his bed into a gigantic insect. He was lying on his hard, as it were armour-plated, back and when he lifted his head a little he could see his dome-like brown belly divided into stiff arched segments on top of which the bed quilt could hardly stay in place and was about to slide off completely. His numerous legs, which were pitifully thin compared to the rest of his bulk, waved helplessly before his eyes.

What has happened to me? he thought. It was no dream. ... Gregor's eyes turned next to the window, and the overcast sky—one could hear raindrops beating on the window gutter—made him quite melancholy. ...

"Gregor," said his father now from the room on the left, "the chief clerk has come and wants to know why you didn't catch the early train. We don't know what to say to him. Besides, he wants to talk to you in person. So open the door, please. He will be good enough to excuse the mess in your room." "Good morning, Mr Samsa," the chief clerk was calling amiably meanwhile. "He's not well," said his mother to the visitor, while his father was still speaking through the door, "he's not well, sir, believe me. What else would make him miss a train! The boy thinks about nothing but his work. It makes me almost cross the way he never goes out in the evening; he's been here all last week and has stayed at home every single evening. I must say I'm glad you've come, sir; we should never have gotten him to unlock the door by ourselves; he's so obstinate; and I'm sure he's unwell, even if he denied it earlier this morning." "Well, can the chief clerk come in now?" asked Gregor's father impatiently, again knocking on the door. "No," said Gregor. In the left-hand room a painful silence followed this refusal; in the right-hand room his sister began to sob.

"Mr Samsa," the chief clerk called now in a louder voice, "what's the matter with you? Here you are, barricading yourself in your room, giving only 'yes' and 'no' for answers, causing your parents a lot of unnecessary trouble and neglecting—I mention this only in passing—neglecting your business duties in an incredible fashion. I am speaking here in the name of your parents and of your employer, and I beg you quite seriously to give me an immediate and precise explanation. You amaze me, you amaze me. Now I see how incredibly obstinate you are. And your position in the firm is not exactly unassailable. I came with the intention of telling you all this in private, but since you are wasting my time so needlessly I don't see why your parents shouldn't hear it too. For some time now your work has been most unsatisfactory; this is not the best time of the year for business, of course, we admit that, but a time of the year for doing no business at all, that does not exist, Mr Samsa, must not exist."

"But, sir," cried Gregor, beside himself and in his agitation forgetting everything else, "I'm just about to open the door this very minute." Slowly Gregor pushed the chair toward the door, then let go of it, caught hold of the door for support—the pads at the ends of his little legs were somewhat sticky—and rested against it for a moment after his efforts.

Then he set himself to turning the key in the lock with his mouth. It seemed, unfortunately, that he didn't really have any teeth—what was he supposed to grip the key with?—but on the other hand his jaws were certainly very strong; with their help he did manage to get the key turning, heedless of the fact that he was undoubtedly damaging himself, since a brown fluid issued from his mouth, flowed over the key, and dripped onto the floor. Since he had to pull the door toward him, he was still invisible even when it was really wide open. He had to edge himself slowly around the near half of the double door, and to do it very carefully if he was not to fall flat on his back before he even got inside. He was still carrying out this difficult manoeuvre, with no time to observe anything else, when he heard the chief clerk utter a loud "Oh!"—it sounded like a gust of wind—and now he could see the man, standing as he was nearest to the door, clapping one hand over his open mouth and slowly backing away as if he were being repelled by some unseen but inexorable force. His mother—in spite of the chief clerk's presence her hair was still undone and sticking out in all directions—first clasped her hands and looked at his father, then took two steps toward Gregor and fell on the floor among her outspread skirts, her face completely hidden on her breast. His father clenched one fist with a fierce expression on his face as if he meant to knock Gregor back into his room, then looked uncertainly around the living room, covered his eyes with his hands, and wept until his great chest heaved.

Adapted from "The Metamorphosis" by Franz Kafka

1   What is the perspective from which this story is told—first or third person? State why you think the writer chose to tell the story from this perspective.

2   What would have been different if the story were told from a different perspective? How credible would the story be if told from that perspective and why?

3   What is bizarre about this tale besides the fact that Gregor has changed into an insect? What do you think Kafka is trying to convey through the bizarre elements of this story?

4   Is the story told by an omniscient narrator? Is the account completely objective or are there subjective elements present in the narrative? Support your answer with reference to the text.

Chapter **14**

TENSION AND SUSPENSE

Trigger activity

Look at these two posters of popular adventure and horror films. What makes these films so popular?

Poster A

Poster B

Examine each poster in detail by looking at the layout, fonts, visuals, etc. Say how these contribute to creating a sense of excitement and fear the producers may wish to have associated with the film.

Chapter outline

14.1 Tension

Definitions—Tension and suspense

The analysis of tension and suspense is a common requirement of questions on unseen prose. **Tension** refers to the **element of excitement** in the text while **suspense** refers to the **reader's expectation of what may happen** in the text as he reads.

Purpose—Why do writers employ tension and suspense?

Both tension and suspense are important elements in any story, especially horror or detective fiction, for the following reasons:

- they add to a sense of excitement in the text
- they cause a sense of anticipation in the reader and thus keep him eager to read on.

Application example

Horror films are popular with teenagers. What are the various ingredients necessary to create tension in such films? In the famous shower scene in the film *Psycho* (1956), we witness the murder of a woman as she is stabbed to death by the psychopath Norman Bates. The film utilizes elements of tension and suspense typical of many horror films. Here are some examples:

- the murder scene takes place at night (lighting)
- the scene is set in an old dilapidated house; the bathroom is dimly lit and creepy (setting)
- there is the usual creaking of the stairs and the slight opening of the door (sound effects) as Norman makes his way into the bathroom.
- the sense of suspense builds up as the camera shifts from Norman walking towards the bathroom to the woman in the shower. The increasing frequency of the shifts in perspective suggests the woman is about to meet her death (foreshadowing device).
- we are aware of a key difference between the two characters. Norman is the psychopath who is keenly aware of what he wants to do, that is, murder the woman, while the woman is simply ignorant, alone, unguarded and, hence, very vulnerable at this moment (external conflict).

Group work: Connecting with popular film

(1) Watch the opening sequence of a film (in one of these genres: horror, adventure, science fiction/fantasy). One film to use could be *Jaws*. Watch up to the point when people are attacked and killed by a shark.

(2) Work in a group and put yourselves in the position of a director. As a group, work out how you would shoot the next sequence, paying attention to lighting, sound, dialogue, storyline and so on. The objective is to build up the sense of excitement.

(3) Share your ideas with other groups. (Groups may also choose to enact their scenes.)

(4) After the sharing, the teacher will show the later part of the film and the class will discuss ways in which film directors convey tension. They will then think about how similar methods can be employed in literary texts.

 Method—How do we analyse tension?

Using films such as *Psycho* as examples, we see that there are mainly five devices which may be used to create tension:

(a) lighting
(b) setting
(c) sound effects
(d) character conflict
(e) language.

We can apply these five film devices to our study of tension in prose fiction.

(a) Lighting

The lack of **lighting** and even the colour of the lighting often **create a certain mood** which may enhance the sense of tension in the text.

Read the following paragraph and note the number of times the writer mentions the lack of lighting. What is the effect of this?

> 5 May—I must have been asleep, for certainly if I had been fully awake I would have noticed the approach of such a remarkable place. In the gloom the courtyard looked of considerable size, and as several dark ways led from it under
> 5   great round arches, it perhaps seemed bigger than it really is. I have not yet been able to see it by daylight.
>
> *Extract from* Dracula *by Bram Stoker*

(b) Setting

Setting refers to the **description of** the **time** as well as the **place** or environment. Sometimes the choice of environment complements the kind of mood and tension the writer is attempting to create.

The following text is a continuation of the previous passage. As you read, highlight words or phrases which describe both the time as well as the place and then think about how these contribute to the sense of tension in the scene.

>   When the caleche stopped, the driver jumped down and held out his hand to assist me to alight. Again I could not but notice his prodigious strength. His hand actually seemed
> 10   like a steel vice that could have crushed mine if he had chosen. Then he took my traps, and placed them on the ground beside me as I stood close to a great door, old and studded with large iron nails, and set in a projecting doorway of massive stone. I could see even in the dim light that the
> 15   stone was massively carved, but that the carving had been much worn by time and weather. As I stood, the driver jumped again into his seat and shook the reins. The horses started forward, and trap and all disappeared down one of the dark openings.

(c) Character conflict—internal and external conflict

A character's feelings and the struggles he faces often contribute to the sense of tension. **Internal conflict** refers to a **sense of conflict within a character** such as the character's struggle with a particular issue or his feelings of fear in a specific situation. **External conflict**, on the other hand, deals with the **character's visible, outer struggle with another character**. External conflict may range from a mild disagreement with another character to a more intense or violent argument. While internal conflict occurs within a character and may not be visible to others, external conflict is visible since it deals with the character's relationship with another character.

Exercise 14C – Character conflict

The next paragraph is a continuation of the above extract from *Dracula* by Bram Stoker. As you read it, analyse elements of internal and external conflict the main character experiences in this segment of the story.

20   I stood in silence where I was, for I did not know what to do. Of bell or knocker there was no sign. Through these frowning walls and dark window openings it was not likely that my voice could penetrate. The time I waited seemed endless, and I felt doubts and fears crowding upon me.
25   What sort of place had I come to, and among what kind of people? What sort of grim adventure was it on which I had embarked? Was this a customary incident in the life of a solicitor's clerk sent out to explain the purchase of a London estate to a foreigner? Solicitor's clerk! Mina would not like
30   that. Solicitor, for just before leaving London I got word that my examination was successful, and I am now a full-blown solicitor! I began to rub my eyes and pinch myself to see if I were awake. It all seemed like a horrible nightmare to me, and I expected that I should suddenly awake, and find myself
35   at home, with the dawn struggling in through the windows, as I had now and again felt in the morning after a day of overwork. But my flesh answered the pinching test, and my eyes were not to be deceived. I was indeed awake and among the Carpathians. All I could do now was to be patient, and to
40   wait the coming of morning

(d) Sound effects

In a film, we can literally hear **sound effects** such as the howling of the wolves, and so on. However, when we read, **sound is created in our minds through our impression of the setting and** by **the writer's choice of words**. For example, in the second extract from *Dracula*, when the narrator arrived at Dracula's mansion, after he had alighted from the caleche, "The horses started forward, and trap and all disappeared down one of the dark openings." Here, Stoker uses alliteration, repeating the "d" consonant to create an ominous mood.

 Exercise 14D – Sound effects

Read this further continuation of *Dracula* and pick out words describing sound or identify sound devices used in the text and state how they contribute to the mood and to tension.

> Just as I had come to this conclusion I heard a heavy step approaching behind the great door, and saw through the chinks the gleam of a coming light. Then there was the sound of rattling chains and the clanking of massive bolts
> 45   drawn back. A key was turned with the loud grating noise of long disuse, and the great door swung back.

(e) Language

The repetition of words or ideas may also help develop the sense of tension in the text. For example, if the word "dark" and words associated with it are repeated frequently in the text, we, the readers, are likely to start feeling some tension and discomfort. If the words or ideas become stronger as we read on, we can say that this contributes to the increasing sense of tension.

Exercise 14E – Language

Continue reading the story in the following extract. As you read, pay attention to the words used to describe the character, Dracula. The writer uses a simile to describe Dracula's handshake—"cold as ice". What does this simile imply? What other interesting words or images are used to describe Dracula? What idea is repeated in the text about the personality of Dracula?

Within, stood a tall old man, clean shaven save for a long white moustache, and clad in black from head to foot, without a single speck of other colour about him anywhere.
50 He held in his hand an antique silver lamp, in which the flame burned without a chimney or globe of any kind, throwing long quivering shadows as it flickered in the draught of the open door. The old man motioned me in with his right hand with a courtly gesture, saying in excellent English, but
55 with a strange intonation. "Welcome to my house! Enter freely and of your own free will!" He made no motion of stepping to meet me, but stood like a statue, as though his gesture of welcome had fixed him into stone. The instant, however, that I had stepped over the threshold, he moved
60 impulsively forward, and holding out his hand grasped mine with a strength which made me wince, an effect which was not lessened by the fact that it seemed cold as ice, more like the hand of a dead than a living man. Again he said, "Welcome to my house! Enter freely. Go safely, and leave
65 something of the happiness you bring!" The strength of the handshake was so much akin to that which I had noticed in the driver, whose face I had not seen, that for a moment I doubted if it were not the same person to whom I was speaking. So to make sure, I said interrogatively, "Count
70 Dracula?"

He bowed in a courtly way as he replied, "I am Dracula, and I bid you welcome, Mr Harker, to my house. Come in, the night air is chill, and you must need to eat and rest."

When you have done the above exercise, read all five extracts from Bram Stoker's *Dracula* together. What are your feelings as you read the story? At which point do you feel most disturbed? Identify any other devices used to develop tension.

The Company of the Ring stood silent beside the tomb of Balin. ... At length they stirred and looked up, and began to search for anything that would give them tidings of Balin's fate, or show what had become of his folk. There was another

5 smaller door on the other side of the chamber, under the shaft. By both the doors they could now see that many bones were lying, among them were broken swords and axe-heads, and cloven shields and helms. Some of the swords were crooked: orc-scimitars with blackened blades.

10 There were many recesses cut in the rock of the walls, and in them were large iron-bound chests of wood. All had been broken and plundered; but beside the shattered lid of one there lay the remains of a book. It had been slashed and stabbed and partly burned, and it was so stained with black

15 and other dark marks like old blood that little of it could be read. ...

"It seems to be a record of the fortunes of Balin's folk," Gandalf said. "I guess that it began with their coming to Dimrill Dale nigh on thirty years ago." ...

20 Gandalf paused and set a few leaves aside. "There are several pages of the same sort, rather hastily written and much damaged," he said; "but I can make little of them in this light. Now there must be a number of leaves missing, because they begin to be numbered *five*, the fifth year of the

25 colony, I suppose. Let me see! No, they are too cut and stained; I cannot read them. We might do better in the sunlight. Wait! Here is something: a large bold hand using an Elvish script."

"That would be Ori's hand," said Gimli, looking over

30 the wizard's arm. "He could write well and speedily, and often used the Elvish characters."

"I fear he had ill tidings to record in a fair hand," said Gandalf. "The first clear word is *sorrow*, but the rest of the line is lost, unless it ends in *estre*. Yes, it must be *yestre*

35 followed by *day being the tenth of novembre Balin lord of Moria fell in Dimrill Dale. He went alone to look in Mirror mere. An orc shot him from behind a stone. We slew the orc, but many more ... up from east up the Silverlode*. The remainder of the page is so blurred that I can hardly make

40 anything out, but I think I can read *we have barred the gates*,

and then *can hold them long if*, and then perhaps *horrible and suffer.* Poor Balin! He seems to have kept the title that he took for less than five years. I wonder what happened afterwards; but there is no time to puzzle out the last few pages. Here is the last page of all." He paused and sighed.

"It is grim reading," he said. "I fear their end was cruel. Listen! *We cannot get out. We cannot get out. They have taken the Bridge and second hall. Frar and Loni and Nali fell there.* Then there are four lines smeared so that I can read *went 5 days ago.* The last lines run *the pool is up to the wall at Westgate. The Watcher in the Water took Oin. We cannot get out. The end comes*, and then *drums, drums in the deep.* I wonder what that means. The last thing written is in a trailing scrawl of elf-letters: *they are coming.* There is nothing more." Gandalf paused and stood in silent thought.

A sudden dread and a horror of the chamber fell on the Company. "*We cannot get out*," muttered Gimli. "It was well for us that the pool had sunk a little, and that the Watcher was sleeping down at the southern end."

Gandalf raised his head and looked round. "They seem to have made a last stand by both doors," he said; "but there were not many left by that time. So ended the attempt to retake Moria! It was valiant but foolish. The time is not come yet. Now, I fear, we must say farewell to Balin, son of Fundin. Here he must lie in the halls of his fathers. We will take this book, the Book of Mazarbul, and look at it more closely later. You had better keep it, Gimli, and take it back to Dain, if you get a chance. It will interest him, though it will grieve him deeply. Come, let us go! The morning is passing."

"Which way shall we go?" asked Boromir.

"Back to the hall," answered Gandalf. "But our visit to this room has not been in vain. I now know where we are. This must be, as Gimli says, the Chamber of Mazarbul; and the hall must be the twenty-first of the North-end. Therefore we should leave by the eastern arch of the hall, and bear right and south, and go downwards. The Twenty-first Hall should be on the Seventh Level, that is six above the level of the Gates. Come now! Back to the hall!"

Gandalf had hardly spoken these words, when there came a great noise: a rolling *Boom* that seemed to come from depths far below, and to tremble in the stone at their feet. They sprang towards the door in alarm. *Doom, doom* it rolled again, as if huge hands were turning the very caverns of Moria into a vast drum. Then there came an echoing

85   blast: a great horn was blown in the hall, and answering horns and harsh cries were heard further off. There was a hurrying sound of many feet.

"They are coming!" cried Legolas.

"We cannot get out," said Gimli.

Extract from The Lord of the Rings: The Fellowship of the Ring *by J.R.R. Tolkien*

1   What are your feelings as you read the text? At which point is your sense of excitement and suspense the greatest? Give reasons for your answer.

2   Analyse how the writer uses setting, lighting, character conflict, sound effects and language to create tension and suspense in this text. What other devices are used to contribute to tension and suspense?

 Links to real-world issues

The Lord of the Rings was a blockbuster for three years from 2002 to 2004. Like many of today's popular films, it revolves round the idea of the common person who feels small and insignificant in the world and who then rises to the status of hero. Examples of such filmic characters are Frodo, Harry Potter and Spiderman. Watch excerpts from these shows and think about why audiences throughout the world admire them. What does the popularity of such themes suggest about modern society? Have you yourself admired some of these heroes? If you could be one of the characters from the *X-men* or *The Incredibles*, who would you be? What power would you want to have? What does this suggest about yourself? In what way can we find the hero within ourselves rather than search for external sources of power and approval?

14.2 Foreshadowing devices

Besides creating tension using the five devices (setting, lighting, character conflict, sound effects and language), writers need to sustain this sense of excitement and tension in the text. This is done by using foreshadowing devices.

Definition—Foreshadowing

Foreshadowing refers to **our anticipation of what is going to happen** before it does happen. In most crime or horror fiction, this anticipation (such as the anticipation of the coming death of a character) is often disturbing and ominous.

 ## Purpose—Why do writers employ foreshadowing?

Foreshadowing helps to create suspense and anticipation in the text. If the writer tells the reader everything in the beginning, there would be no incentive for the reader to read on and there would also be no element of surprise.

Symbols can also be used as foreshadowing devices. Examples of these are:
- the presence of an owl
- the howling of wolves
- a black cat crossing the street
- the breaking of a mirror.

For example, in *The Lord of the Rings* extract above, members of the Company, on arrival at the tomb of Balin, observe many bones lying around the place. Through this, the writer conveys an eerie feeling about the place. The bones foreshadow the danger and death to come. The purpose of using foreshadowing devices like this is to create suspense, encouraging the reader to read on in order to discover whether what he anticipates really does come true later.

 ## Group work: Urban legends

Work in a group of four.

(1) Select a specific country, for example, Ghana, Brazil, Singapore or England.

(2) Carry out research on two or three urban legends of the country your group has chosen. According to the *Oxford Dictionary*, urban legends or myths are stories of events that are supposed to have happened and these stories have been repeated so often that people believe them to be true.

(3) In addition to finding out about the urban legends of your chosen country, you should identify any symbols used in these stories and think about what they represent. Share and discuss your group's findings with the other groups in class.

 Method—How do we identify foreshadowing devices?

(1) Read the text and use your instincts. Identify areas where you feel most excited and disturbed. Differentiate between what the writer is saying and what he is not saying.

(2) Identify any references to objects or ideas and infer what the writer may be hinting at.

(3) Pay attention to the setting, especially changes in the external environment, and think about what these changes hint at regarding the future outcome of the characters.

(4) Anticipate what may happen later. Pay special attention to the endings of paragraphs and texts because these areas usually contain a higher degree of suspense.

 Exercise 14G – Foreshadowing devices

The use of foreshadowing is an important element in building tension in the extract from *The Lord of the Rings*. As you read the text again, you get the sense that something is about to happen to the Company. At which point in the text are you made aware that something dangerous is about to occur to them? How does the writer prepare you for this? Highlight the areas where you feel most disturbed and uncomfortable.

 Exercise 14H – More practice on tension and suspense

Read the following text and pick out elements of tension and suspense.

A patrol has to be sent out to discover just how strongly the enemy position is manned. Since my leave I feel a certain strange attachment to the other fellows, and so I volunteer to go with them. We agree on a plan, slip out through the wire and then divide and creep forward separately. After a while I find a shallow shell-hole and crawl into it. From here I peer forward.

There is moderate machine gun-fire. It sweeps across from all directions, not very heavy, but always sufficient to make one keep down.

A parachute star-shell opens out. The ground lies stark in the pale light, and then the darkness shuts down again blacker than ever. In the trenches we were told there were black troops in front of us. That is nasty, it is hard to see them; they are very good at patrolling too. And oddly enough they are often quite stupid; for instance, both Kat and Kropp were once able to shoot down a black enemy patrol because the fellows in their enthusiasm for cigarettes smoked while they were creeping about. Kat and Kropp had simply to aim at the glowing ends of the cigarettes.

A bomb or something lands close beside me. I have not heard it coming and am terrified. At the same moment a senseless fear takes hold of me. Here I am alone and almost helpless in the dark—perhaps two other eyes have been watching me for a long while from another shell-hole in front of me, and a bomb lies ready to blow me to pieces. I try to pull myself together. It is not my first patrol and not a particularly risky one. But it is the first since my leave, and, besides, the lie of the land is still rather strange to me.

I tell myself that my alarm is absurd, that there is probably nothing at all in the darkness watching me, otherwise they would not be firing so low.

It is in vain. In whirling confusion my thoughts hum in my brain—I hear the warning voice of my mother, I see the Russians with flowing beards leaning against the wire fence, I have a bright picture of a canteen with stools, of a cinema in Valenciennes; tormented, terrified, in my imagination I see the grey, implacable muzzle of a rifle which moves noiselessly before me whichever way I try to turn my head. The sweat breaks out from every pore.

I still continue to lie in the shallow bowl. I look at the time; only a few minutes have passed. My forehead is wet, the sockets of my eyes are damp, my hands tremble, and I am panting softly. It is nothing but an awful spasm of fear,

45   a simple animal fear poking at my head and crawling on farther.

All my efforts subside like froth into the one desire to be able just to stay lying there. My limbs are glued to the earth. I make a vain attempt; they refuse to come away. I press
50   myself down on the earth. I cannot go forward, I make up my mind to stay lying there.

Extract from All Quiet on the Western Front *by Erich Maria Remarque*

1 Describe the setting of this extract in detail and state how this contributes to a sense of tension in the text. Pick out other elements of tension such as lighting, sound, conflict and language and show how they heighten the sense of tension in the text.

2 What is the effect of employing both the present tense and the first person form of narration in the text? State how they contribute to the sense of suspense. How else is suspense maintained and developed? Which aspects of the text encourage you to read on? Explain your answer.

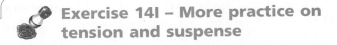

Exercise 14I – More practice on tension and suspense

Santinathan gripped the pillion seat tightly with his knees as Sabran swung his borrowed Norton Dominator in and out of the late evening traffic. They hurtled over Anderson Bridge and down Collyer Quay, past the glinting carbibe
5   lights of the hawkers' stalls at Clifford Pier and on to Pasir Panjang Road. Neat suburban brick houses swished past them like whips. Overhead a mass of brown cloud obscured the last light of the sun. The air was dry and charged; it looked as if it wanted to rain but could not. Soon after Haw
10   Par Villa, Sabran swung into a *lorong* on the left and they bumped over the rough surface till they reached the concrete embankment against which the sea lapped. Here they turned

left again, riding easily on the sandy promenade lined with casuarina trees. At last they entered the grounds of a house with two stone eagles at each gate.

Leaving the engine running, Sabran put a foot down and looked around with a frown. "They must be swimming still." They rode out to the embankment in front of the house and peered out over the sea. "Do you see anybody?"

"No."

Re-entering the grounds, Sabran parked the Norton and unzipped his jacket. "I suppose they've gone for a walk. Might as well make ourselves comfortable."

They sat on wicker chairs in the open verandah wonderingly. Out at sea, the *kelongs* ranged round them in a wide arc, their paraffin lights staring neutrally out of the deepening grey like some nearer stars, enclosing them. The slap-slap of water against the sea-wall somehow merged with the silence that pressed more closely upon the house and its grounds. Santinathan had just begun a tuneless whistle when a voice behind them said, "Sabran, Santi, come in quickly." They got up and entered the central corridor of the house.

"I think you'd better bring your bike into the verandah," Guan Kheng said. "No, don't ask any questions now, just bring it in." Sabran left them. "Come into this room, Santi."

In the gloom Santinathan could make out a figure lying inert on the bed. Sally half-knelt by it, her arm resting protectively on the pillow. Striding forward, Santinathan said, "Peter, what's happened?"

"He was beaten up."

"Peter, are you all right?"

Peter turned and looked at him with wild eyes. His face was discoloured with bruises, part of his scalp was matted with dried blood, his underlip was swollen. Sally sponged his forehead with a wet handkerchief. "I'm getting out of this place," he said, and turned his head away.

"Why haven't you taken him to a doctor?"

"We can't."

"What do you mean 'can't'? You've got a car."

"They're still around, hiding in the *lorong*, waiting for us."

"Who are? Why, what's he done?"

Guan Kheng looked at the night sky through the window and said, "I don't know. I don't understand anything. I don't know why it happened."

Sabran came in and crouched beside Peter, looking at him silently. "We thought it better to wait till morning before trying to get out. You see, there's Sally as well."

Extract from Scorpion Orchid *by Lloyd Fernando*

1   Describe the setting in detail and state how it contributes to the tension. Apart from setting, how else is suspense created and developed in this extract? Support your answer with reference to the text.

2   Which is more effective in maintaining tension in this extract—description or dialogue—or do they support one another? Give reasons for your answer.

Chapter **15**
CHARACTERIZATION

Trigger activity

We can tell a lot about a person by what he or she wears. Take a look at these pictures. What can you tell about the personality of each individual just by looking at his/her clothes and accessories?

Picture A

Picture B

Picture C

15.1 Character types and roles

Definitions—Types of characters in texts

Generally, stories comprise:

- A **main character**—this is the central character in the text. He/She is responsible for driving the plot forward; and
- **minor character/s**—these do not play as significant a role in the plot as the main character or other major characters. Often their role is to complement those of others in the main plot.

One way to distinguish whether a character is major or minor is to examine whether the plot would be significantly affected should the character be taken out of the text. If the effect is great, that character plays a major part.

Purpose—Why is good characterization central to the success of any story?

Good characterization is important because:

- we only understand the storyline and issues through the characters. This implies that if a character's speech is unclear or he/she is not consistent in his/her role or behaviour, the reader will be confused.
- the extent to which the reader is emotionally connected to the text parallels the extent to which the reader feels for the main characters. This implies that if the main character is unbelievable or unrealistic, the reader will not be engaged with the text. Therefore, writers take great pains to create strong, complex and believable characters.

Aside from identifying the main and minor characters, we should also look at the **role and function** of these characters. Note that characters may not fall neatly into any of the following categories but may, instead, be a combination of several of them.

Examples of character types and their respective roles

Type	Description
Protagonist	• The **main character** of the narrative, who may have either positive or negative values or even both. For example, if a story is told from the point of view of a serial killer, that criminal is known as the **protagonist**. • If the protagonist has very apparent positive values such as in a text which revolves round a knight rescuing a lady, we call that protagonist a **hero**.

Type	Description
Antagonist or character foil	<ul><li>For any protagonist or hero in a story, there is almost always an opposing character. This character may be called the **antagonist**. In some cases, the antagonist, though in opposition to the protagonist, may possess positive values. For example, in the story told from the point of the view of a serial killer, the antagonist could be a detective who courageously strives for justice. However, if he is portrayed negatively and has evil intentions, we term him the **villain**.</li><li>**Note:** We say one character is a **foil** of another if his personality or values are *in contrast* to the other character's. The result of that contrast is that it emphasizes or highlights the qualities of the first character. For example, the contrasting characteristics of the self-centred antagonist Lex Luther may serve to highlight the noble and sacrificial qualities of the protagonist Superman.</li></ul>
Round characters	These characters are:<ul><li>**complex**—they cannot be neatly classified. They represent a range of both positive and negative personality traits. In most cases, the main characters of stories are complex. They may evoke ambivalence in readers.</li><li>**changing**—they also mature and change with time so that their actions are often unpredictable.</li></ul>
Flat characters	These characters are:<ul><li>**predictable**—they are stable and do not change (for example, comic-book superheroes and villains). Their actions are often predictable.</li><li>**neatly classifiable**—they are two-dimensional and can be classified as one side in an oppositional structure, eg, either good or evil.</li><li>If every text consisted of realistic, complex characters, the reader may be confused and not know which character they should focus on, or the text will be extremely lengthy because it will need a lot of time to develop and build each of these characters. One way out of this situation is to have *stereotypical* characters. The advantage of stereotypical characters is that the audience recognizes them immediately and so they can focus their attention more on the main character. Another advantage is that sometimes these characters provide some comic relief, especially if the story is heavy-going.</li></ul>

Type	Description
The narrator	• The **narrator** is the person who is telling the story. If he is not involved in the events of the plot and is merely an observer and teller, we can say that the story is told in the third person. • If the main character himself is the narrator and is telling us the story of his life, then we are hearing a first person account of the story. • **Note:** In some texts, it is not necessary to have a narrator. The characters can tell the story for themselves.

Examples of character types and their respective roles

Type	Description
The troublemaker	• In all stories, there is usually a problem. This problem is often caused by one person or a group of individuals. They may intentionally or unintentionally be the cause of the problems for the main character. Whatever it is, these are termed the **troublemakers**. • If they cause problems intentionally, we call them villains, bullies, scheming or cunning individuals. Sometimes, they may not intend to cause problems but their ignorance often results in conflicts. One example is the irritating stepmother who constantly nags her children.
The catalyst	• This character helps **accelerate a process** or **event** in the narrative. For example, in Jane Austen's *Pride and Prejudice*, we can say that Mr Wickham is a minor character who functions as a catalyst. His sudden elopement with Lydia leads to Mr Darcy's involvement with the Bennet family and subsequent marriage to Elizabeth Bennet.
The mentor or advisor	• Often, the main character is someone who is lost and in search of something (either trying to find something like a clue to his past or family or trying to find out more about himself and his identity). • In stories, there are often characters whose main role is to help the main character along the way. These could be friends, parents or even strangers (for example, Gandalf in *The Lord of the Rings* or Peter Parker's uncle in *Spiderman*). • The role of the **advisor** is to direct the main character towards his goal or to provide more clarity as to how to solve his problems.

Point to note

Complexity = condition with many features or aspects

When you examine a character who displays great complexity, aim to identify both the strengths as well as the flaws of that character.

Exercise 15A – Types of characters and their roles

Read the following extract and comment on the characters and the roles they play.

An old ritual, Saturday morning shopping. Mother and daughter. Mrs Dietrich and Nola. Shops in the village, stores and boutiques at the splendid Livingstone Mall on Route 12: Bloomingdale's, Saks, Lord & Taylor, Bonwit's, Neiman-
5   Marcus, and the rest. Mrs Dietrich would know her way around the stores blindfolded but there is always the surprise of lavish seasonal displays, extraordinary holiday sales, the openings of new stores at the mall like Laura Ashley, Paraphernalia. On one of their mall days, Mrs Dietrich and
10   Nola would try to get there at midmorning, have lunch around 1 pm at one or another of their favourite restaurants, shop for perhaps an hour after lunch, then come home. Sometimes, the shopping trips were more successful than at other times, but you have to have faith, Mrs Dietrich tells herself. Her
15   interior voice is calm, neutral, free of irony. Ever since her divorce her interior voice has been free of irony. You have to have faith.

     Tomorrow morning Nola returns to school in Maine; today will be spent at the mall. Mrs Dietrich has planned it
20   for days—there are numerous things Nola needs, mainly clothes, a pair of good shoes; Mrs Dietrich must buy a birthday present for one of her aunts; mother and daughter need the time together. At the mall, in such crowds of shoppers, moments of intimacy are possible as they are
25   rarely at home. (Seventeen-year-old Nola, home on spring break for a brief eight days, seems always to be *busy*, always out with her *friends*, the trip to the mall has been postponed

twice.) But Saturday, 10.30 am, they are in the car at last headed south on Route 12, a bleak March morning following a night of freezing rain; there's a metallic cast to the air and no sun anywhere in the sky but the light hurts Mrs Dietrich's eyes just the same. "Does it seem as if spring will ever come? It must be twenty degrees colder up in Maine," she says. Driving in heavy traffic always makes Mrs Dietrich nervous and she is overly sensitive to her daughter's silence, which seems deliberate, perverse, when they have so little time remaining together—not even a full day.

Nola asks politely if Mrs Dietrich would like her to drive and Mrs Dietrich says no, of course not, she's fine, it's only a few more miles and maybe traffic will lighten. Nola seems about to say something more, then thinks better of it. So much between them is precarious, chancy—but they've been kind to each other these past seven days. Nola's secrets remain her own and Mrs Dietrich isn't going to pry; she's beyond that. She loves Nola with a fierce unreasoned passion stronger than any she felt for the man who had been her husband for thirteen years, certainly far stronger than any she ever felt for her own mother. ...

Mrs Dietrich tries to engage her daughter in conversation of a harmless sort but Nola answers in monosyllables; Nola is rather tired from so many nights of partying with her friends, some of whom attend the local high school, some of whom are home on spring break from prep schools ... Late nights, but Mrs Dietrich doesn't consciously lie awake waiting for Nola to come home; they've been through all that before. Now Nola sits beside her mother looking wan, subdued, rather melancholy. Thinking her private thoughts. She is wearing a bulky quilted jacket Mrs Dietrich has never liked, the usual blue jeans, black calfskin boots zippered tightly to mid-calf. Her delicate profile, thick-lashed eyes. Mrs Dietrich must resist the temptation to ask, Why are you so quiet, Nola? What are you thinking? They've been through all that before.

Extract from "Shopping" by Joyce Carol Oates

1   The phrase "they've been through all that before" occurs twice in the last paragraph. What do you think this implies about the mother and daughter relationship? What else can you infer about their relationship?

2 The writer tells the story through the viewpoint of Mrs Dietrich. What effect does this have on you as a reader?

3 Mrs Dietrich is an example of a complex character. State in what ways you sympathize with her and in what ways you do not sympathize with her.

15.2 Character analysis

Definition—Character analysis

Character analysis refers to an analysis of the character's inner personality through looking at outward appearances or behavioural characteristics.

Purpose—Why do we need to analyse the characters?

We analyse the characters to

(a) understand the hidden motivations behind what they do and why they behave in a certain way

(b) understand their situation and background.

Method—How do we analyse a character?

When analysing a character, we should

(1) look at the author's comments about the character as well as outward attributes of the character (see the next section);

(2) say what these attributes imply about the character's personality or inner self;

(3) use adjectives to describe these qualities.

(1) What does the author say?

We can get a clearer idea of a character's personality by looking at the author's comments on the character. An author can comment on a character in several ways:

(a) A direct authorial comment on a character's personality

The author may comment directly on the character. In this case, the text is usually written in the third person and the narrator is positioned as one who is authoritative and omniscient (all-knowing).

For example, read this extract and state what the author is implying about the character's personality:

> In school, he was neither happy nor unhappy. He avoided those boys who teased him and tried to touch him. There was one, a brutal-looking fellow with a powerful, athletic body, who stalked him during the school recess to tease him,
> 5 but after he had gone to his teacher to complain, the fellow had left him alone. He did his work well, although he never shone, and he was always polite, so his teachers had no cause to be dissatisfied with him.
>
> *Extract from "Father and Son" by Catherine Lim*

(b) An authorial comment on a character's personality through a narrator or a speaker

In some first-person accounts, the author may comment on a character through his fictional narrator or speaker. For example, in the extract below, the author comments on the personality of Tim through his narrator:

> If there was any one thing that really won me over, it was his sense of humour. Beneath that quiet, polite, eager, agreeable exterior, Tim had a vein of wicked humour. He breathed cutting asides to me in the very presence of the person he
> 5 was making fun of: our teachers, my father, his father, our tennis coach, the giggly girls we'd meet.
>
> *Extract from "My Cousin Tim" by Simon Tay*

(c) An implied authorial comment on a character's personality through the character's name

Another authorial comment on a character's personality may be seen through the name given to that character. For example, in *Oliver Twist*, Charles Dickens provides a commentary on many of his characters by assigning names to them, for example,

Mr Bumble is a comic character who is full of contradictions, Mr Fang is a mean-spirited police magistrate and the Dodger is one of Oliver's acquaintances who introduces him to the life of crime and teaches him how to escape its consequences.

(2) What can be learnt of a character through his/her external attributes?

One of the purposes of creative writing is to entertain the reader. If the plot forms the basis upon which a story is built, then it is the characters that drive the plot forward. In order to move the reader, writers often create realistic yet fascinating characters following the "Show—don't tell" advice. This means that writers try not to openly judge their characters. Instead, by their use of various devices, the reader is able to infer the personalities of the characters on his own and, hence, becomes more involved in the story.

There are five means by which a character's personality may be inferred:
(a)   environment
(b)   appearance—physical appearance and dress
(c)   words and thoughts
(d)   actions and behaviour
(e)   relationship with others.

(a)   *Environment*

We can tell a lot about a character by looking at the **physical environment** or **setting**. For example, a character's home—the way it is designed externally and internally—provides hints about the character's social status and personality. To infer a character's personality from his environment, pick out descriptions concerning his home, his society or community, the physical landscape and then say what you can infer about the character.

Exercise 15B – Character (Environment)

From the description of the town, weather and behaviour of the townspeople, what is your impression of Maycomb?

> Maycomb was an old town, but it was a tired old town when I first knew it. In rainy weather the streets turned to red slop; grass grew on the sidewalks; the courthouse sagged in

the square. Somehow, it was hotter then: a black dog suffered on a summer's day; bony mules hitched to hoover carts flicked flies in the sweltering shade of the live oaks on the square. Men's stiff collars wilted by nine in the morning. Ladies bathed before noon, after their three o'clock naps, and by nightfall were like soft teacakes with frostings of sweat and sweet talcum.

People moved slowly then. They ambled across the square, shuffled in and out of the stores around it, took their time about everything. A day was twenty-four hours long but seemed longer. There was no hurry, for there was nowhere to go, nothing to buy and no money to buy it with, nothing to see outside the boundaries of Maycomb County.

Extract from To Kill a Mockingbird *by Harper Lee*

(b) *Appearance—physical appearance*

Writers often go to great lengths to describe a character's outward appearance, including his facial appearance, physical stature, and attire. For example, the opening sentence of the novel *Lord Jim* by Joseph Conrad reads:

> He was an inch, perhaps two, under six feet, powerfully built, and he advanced straight at you with a slight stoop of the shoulders, head forward, and a fixed from-under stare which made you think of a charging bull.

Why do you think Conrad begins his novel by describing the physical stature of Jim when he could have opened the story by describing Jim's background, his family or even his present circumstances? Perhaps this is not only to focus the reader's attention on the character of Jim but also to invite the reader to infer Jim's personality from his outward appearance. For example, we can infer from the comparison of Jim's physical appearance to that of a bull that he has a strong sense of inner rage within him. We can also say that Jim's style of "advancing straight" at others may reveal his intense need to be in control.

To infer personality from appearance, pick out descriptions of the character's dress, shoes, accessories, etc, and say what they imply about his personality.

Look at the physical description of the main character (his posture, facial expression, etc). What is your impression of him? What do you think his relationship with his son was in the last few years before his son passed away?

> The old man sat in the easy chair in his room all day; his posture was not that of repose but agitation, for he never leaned back but sat forward, gripping the sides of his chair as in readiness to spring up. The perturbation of spirits was
> 5 not only in the posture, it was in the very eyes glinting with anger, in the lines etched on the brow and cheeks and around the mouth and most of all, in the wild abundance of white hair which gave the aspect of outraged patriarchal authority.
> Visitors—but they rarely came now—approached the old
> 10 man with timid caution, his wife and daughters with resigned weariness and sometimes a little resentment. Of the son, no one dared to speak, for the old man was sure to snap in vexed impatience, "He's dead, he's dead and gone, and why speak of him to me! He's dead, I tell you!" and he would
> 15 point, triumphantly to the cutting from *The Straits Times* on the wall, now yellowing a little. "There! That's the announcement of his death—15 July 1973! His obituary. Are you satisfied now?"
>
> *Extract from "Father and Son" by Catherine Lim*

(c) *Words and thoughts*

The choice of words or language which a character uses in his speech often indicates the character's status. The character's tone, on the other hand, may indicate his personality, for example, whether he is humble or arrogant. Sometimes, however, what a character says may contradict his behaviour or personality. In this case, one indicator of the character's true self would be his thoughts.

A character may engage in **interior monologue**, which *occurs when the character talks aloud to himself/herself so that the reader is aware of his/her thoughts*. This is the most obvious way of learning about the character's true self. As you read,

(1) ask yourself what the character's thoughts or words reveal of him/her.

(2) Pay attention to any repeated words or ideas the character uses. For example in "The Tell-Tale Heart", the main character keeps telling the reader that he is not mad. This only serves to strengthen our suspicion that he is mad.

Exercise 15D – Character (Words and thoughts)

Examine the thoughts of the main character. What can you tell about her state of mind? What does the speaker mean in the last few lines and how do you think this story will continue?

> I am a little marionette. See my golden hair? See my little hands? Listen to my little feet scamper across the wooden stage. What do you see, when you see me? Bright blue sky in my clear eyes and black velvet ribbon in my hair. Touch me
> 5 if you dare, touch me if you dare. Sometimes I hang by my strings, sometimes I run as freely as I wish. But it wasn't always like this, I wasn't always like this. In this theatre of marionettes, I am the smallest but not the youngest. I am the most innocent but not the most naïve. And sometimes,
> 10 sometimes when I am not on the stage, when the lights are dark and there is no audience to charm, sometimes I remember things. Wonderful, terrible, beautiful things. I think I was once a little girl ...
>
> *Extract from "Theatre des Marionettes" by Maggie Tan*

(d) *Actions and behaviour*

We often infer a character's personality from his outward behaviour. For example, a person who constantly slouches may reveal a lackadaisical disposition. On the other hand, a person who quickly makes decisions or says things without adequate reflection may indicate an impulsive personality.

However, you should be very careful about judging a character too quickly. Try to think about what has motivated a character to act in a certain way and think about what this reveals of the character's needs. Pay attention to repeated behaviour or any strange habits the character has and then ask yourself what this implies about his/her inner character.

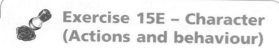

Exercise 15E – Character (Actions and behaviour)

Which particular words/phrases are emphasized in the following extract and what does the writer imply about the couple? What odd behaviour do you notice about this couple?

> Mr and Mrs Veneering were brand-new people in a brand-new house in a brand-new quarter of London. Everything about the Veneerings was spick and span new. All their furniture was new, all their servants were new, their
> 5 plate was new, their carriage was new, their harness was new, their horses were new, their pictures were new, they themselves were new, they were as newly married as was lawfully compatible with their having a brand-new baby, and if they had set up a great-grandfather, he would have
> 10 come home in matting from the Pantechnicon, without a scratch upon him, French polished to the crown of his head.
>   For, in the Veneering establishment, from the hall-chairs with the new coat of arms, to the grand pianoforte with the new action, and upstairs again to the new fire-escape, all
> 15 things were in a state of high varnish and polish. And what was observable in the furniture, was observable in the Veneerings—the surface smelt a little too much of the workshop and was a trifle sticky.

Extract from Our Mutual Friend *by Charles Dickens*

(e) *Relationship with others*

Finally, we can infer a character's personality through his relationship with others. For example, we may call a character a hypocrite when he behaves in the presence of others in a way which is contradictory to his true self. Another indicator of a character's personality is what other characters think of him. On the other hand, a whole community which thinks of a character in a particular manner may also reveal prejudice within that community. For example, the story of "Gimpel the fool" by Isaac Bashevis Singer begins:

> I am Gimpel the fool. I don't think myself a fool. On the contrary. But that's what folks call me. They gave me the name while I was still in school.

Although, to a certain extent, we may say that Gimpel is foolish to accept the title which others bestow on him, it is also true that the people in the town are mean-spirited bullies.

Exercise 15F – Character (Relationship with others)

Analyse Velan's relationship with his father in this extract. What can you infer about Velan's personality?

When he was eighteen, Velan left home. His father slapped his face one day for coming late with the midday meal, and he did that in the presence of others in the field. Velan put down the basket, glared at his father and left the
5   place. He just walked out of the village, and walked on and on till he came to the town. He starved for a couple of days, begged wherever he could and arrived in Malgudi, where after much knocking about, an old man took him on to assist him in laying out a garden. The garden existed only in the
10   mind of the gardener. What they could see now was acre upon acre of weed-covered land. Velan's main business consisted in destroying all the vegetation he saw. Day after day he sat in the sun and tore up by hand the unwanted plants. And all the jungle gradually disappeared and the
15   land stood as bare as a football field.

Extract from "The Axe" by R.K. Narayan

(3) Using adjectives to describe personality

When writing about character, avoid focusing on external, superficial appearances. For example, here is an opening sentence which reads, "Ms Chee often insisted on being driven around in a black limousine whenever she ventured abroad." A common mistake many students make is to summarize the superficial facts about the character rather than inferring the character's personality. For example, instead of stating that Ms Chee is a wealthy lady, you should aim to infer her personality from the facts in the text, for example, you could infer that she has an arrogant, snobbish personality. In other words, in answering questions on character, you should focus on **adjectives** which describe a character's personality instead of summarizing external, superficial facts about the character.

Instead of simply saying a character is "good" or "bad", you should try to use specific adjectives to describe the character. These are some words you could use:

positive	negative	boisterous	self-confident	introvert	extrovert
optimistic	pessimistic	dictatorial	domineering	reserved	arrogant
self-assured	modest	strong	melancholic	shy	snobbish
weak	stoic	altruistic	harmonious	distrusting	firm
influential	generous	uncivilized	discontented	nervous	bossy
insecure	confident	oppressive	accommodating	suspicious	coarse
egocentric	unstable	possessive	despondent	paranoid	vulgar

Can you think of more adjectives to describe personality?

 Group work: Vocabulary building

(1) Imagine possible scenarios such as taking a walk down Orchard Road, Arab Street, in Chinatown, a quiet HDB estate, and so on.

(2) Each group is to focus on one scenario and describe at least five common behavioural traits and style of dressing of the people in that community. The group must then brainstorm for possible words to describe these people and complete a table like the one below.

Summarizing a character's outward appearance or behaviour	Possible adjectives to describe personality
A person who appears untidy	Easy-going, nonchalant, lackadaisical
A person who is well dressed	Attention-seeking, creative, flamboyant, snobbish, arrogant, proud, meticulous

Links to real-world issues

In literature, you are often asked to empathize with characters. This means that even though a character may be depicted in an unfavourable manner, you must try to empathize with the character. You may criticize his actions but you must also be aware that he is a product of society and of his family upbringing. This comes from the basic belief that there is good in every one of us and even though people may falter at times, it is important to focus on the cause and not the act, the person and not the action. Think about someone you were unhappy with this week and try to put yourself in his or her shoes. What insights about yourself and about your unhappiness do you gain from this?

Exercise 15G – Character analysis

Read the following extract and answer the questions that follow.

The goalie. James suddenly recognized her. Devil-may-care woman with a crazy laugh when she made a spectacular save. Intense. Almost trembling with tension in a one to one situation. "She'd scare the hell out of me if I was in the dee
5 and had an open run with only her at the goal mouth waiting." With her pads and her wild hair, Ethel could look very fierce. "The ting about her," LeMercier once said, "is dat when you are dare coming arp to der gol', looking to see which leg her weight is on, you get scarte' ... because if the girl stops your
10 shot she'll laugh like a ghostly *pontianak*." LeMercier had a way of saying things.

But James did not know that she was also the State team goalkeeper. He had met her in the days when he was posted to Joo Chiat Station. He could not recognize her now
15 that she had grown up.

"Whoossat?" Mary asked.

"Ethel Richards, our goalie," Bertha replied.

Then James remembered. The Richardses who lived in that ramshackle bunch of wooden shacks by the sea at Siglap.
20 "Your people, Rodrigues," ASP Chandler had once said.

He hated them. Those good-for-nothing *geragoks* there. The scum of the earth. Always filthy-dirty. Always fighting, stealing. Always dead broke. Even when the sea was full of prawns. Letting the moneylender fellow bully them. That snivelling Williams. Always with some outlandish excuse or alibi. Bet he's got Indian blood in him.

This must be the eldest girl. He'd seen her in her grubby white 'jumpers', a sort of a one-piece suit like a baggy swimsuit or boilersuit but with short leg pieces, running from the coffee shop with condensed-milk tins of coffee hanging with strings from her finger, running like mad, spilling the coffee, jumping across the soft muddy patches to firm ground, with a confidence of knowing every puddle, laughing with her eyes sparkling.

When he first saw her, he cursed them inwardly for the way they were bringing up their children. Leaving them to get their meals when they wanted to eat from the pots which had been cooked early in the morning. Letting them sit around watching the card games till they fell asleep every night. Shouting at the them in the foulest language when they distracted them from their gambling.

Cards. Four digits. Huh. And blaring radios. They really couldn't afford them. Must be stolen, James used to think. He had tried to explain to them that it was far cheaper to make coffee at home than to buy it from the coffee shop. But they wouldn't listen. "But you doan known how many times the coffee we make at home is not finished." He had given up. He did not realize that buying coffee powder, sugar and milk needed more ready money than buying a few tins from the coffee shop in the morning. And when there was no money, there was no coffee.

He also gave up feeling sorry for their children after he encountered two of them on the mud track one day. That's it. It was her. The eldest Richards girl!

She was sitting astride the chest of a tiny Malay boy, her hands on his throat. He saw her face determined and savage. He heard the little boy's cries, "Aiyooh, Aiyooh ..." He had pulled the girl off grabbing her 'jumpers'. She turned round. He was in uniform. She took one look at him and bit his hand. He relaxed his hold with the shock; not so much the pain but the surprise at the way she reacted so quickly and bit him. She was gone before he could recover.

He pulled the skinny Malay boy up. "*Nama siapa? ... Tinggal di mana?*" The frightened child stared at him for a long time, then mumbled, "Mervin."

"Mervin? Mervin what?"

"Mervin Palmer."

James let him go as though he was contagious or covered with vermin. That girl! Her own people. My people. Serani.
70   Something boiled up in him. Some kind of rage mixed with disappointment. He was angry and confused.

From that day he avoided them if he could. He stopped trying to argue with and persuade them.

Adapted from The Shrimp People *by Rex Shelley*

1   Provide as many details as you can about the narrator James. What is your impression of his personality?

2   Discuss James's attitude to Ethel Richards. For this question, do not repeat what you wrote in your answer to question 1.

3   Which group of people does he describe as "scum of the earth" *(line 22)*? Is he justified in his opinions of them? Give reasons for your answer.

Exercise 15H – More practice in character analysis

Read the extract below and analyse Miss Emily's character.

When Miss Emily Grierson died, our whole town went to her funeral: the men through a sort of respectful affection for a fallen monument, the women mostly out of curiosity to see the inside of her house, which no one save an old
5   manservant—a combined gardener and cook—had seen in at least ten years.

It was a big, squarish frame house that had once been white, decorated with cupolas and spires and scrolled balconies in the heavily lightsome style of the seventies, set
10   on what had once been our most select street. But garages and cotton gins had encroached and obliterated even the august names of that neighbourhood; only Miss Emily's house was left, lifting its stubborn and coquettish decay above the cotton wagons and gasoline pumps—an eyesore
15   among eyesores.

Alive, Miss Emily had been a tradition, a duty, and a care; a sort of hereditary obligation upon the town, dating from the day in 1894 when Colonel Satoris, the mayor, invented a tale to allow her not to pay her taxes. When the

20   next generation, with its more modern ideas, became mayors and aldermen, this arrangement created some dissatisfaction. On the first of the year, they mailed her a tax notice. February came, and there was no reply. They wrote her a formal letter, asking her to call at the sheriff's office at her convenience. A

25   week later the mayor wrote her himself, offering to call or send his car for her, and received in reply a note on paper of an archaic type, in a thin, flowing calligraphy in faded ink, to the effect that she no longer went out at all. The tax notice was also enclosed, without comment.

30   They called a special meeting of the Board of Aldermen. A deputation waited upon her, knocked at the door through which no visitor had passed since she ceased giving china-painting lessons eight or ten years earlier. They were admitted by the old Negro into a dim hall from which a stairway

35   mounted into still more shadow. It smelled of dust and disuse—a close, dank smell. The Negro led them into the parlour. It was furnished in heavy, leather-covered furniture. When the Negro opened the blinds of one window, they could see that the leather was cracked; and when they sat

40   down, a faint dust rose sluggishly about their thighs, spinning with slow motes in the single sun-ray. On a tarnished gilt easel before the fireplace stood a crayon portrait of Miss Emily's father.

They rose when she entered—a small, fat woman in

45   black, with a thin gold chain descending to her waist and vanishing into her belt, leaning on an ebony cane with a tarnished gold head. Her skeleton was small and spare; perhaps that was why what would have been merely plumpness in another was obesity in her. She looked bloated,

50   like a body long submerged in motionless water, and of that pallid hue.

She did not ask them to sit. She just stood in the door and listened quietly until the spokesman came to a stumbling halt. Then they could hear the invisible watch ticking at the

55   end of the gold chain.

Her voice was dry and cold. "I have no taxes in Jefferson. Colonel Satoris explained it to me. Perhaps one of you can gain access to the city records and satisfy yourselves."

"But we have. We are the city authorities, Miss Emily.

60   Didn't you get a notice from the sheriff, signed by him?"

"I received the paper, yes," Miss Emily said. "Perhaps he considers himself the sheriff ... I have no taxes in Jefferson."

"But there is nothing on the books to show that. We must go by the—"

65   "See Colonel Satoris." (Colonel Satoris had been dead almost ten years.) "I have no taxes in Jefferson. Tobe!" The Negro appeared. "Show these gentlemen out."

Adapted from "A Rose for Emily" by William Faulkner

1   Analyse in detail the personality of Miss Emily by looking at the following five areas:

- her relationship with others—refer to the first and third paragraphs
- her environment (description of her home)—refer to the second and fourth paragraphs
- her physical appearance and dress—refer to the fifth paragraph
- her actions and behaviour—refer to the sixth paragraph
- her words and thoughts—refer to the seventh paragraph to the end of the text.

2   What is your impression of the people in the town? What does their relationship with Miss Emily reveal about them?

3   What are your feelings for Miss Emily at the end of the text? Provide evidence to support your answer.

Chapter **16**

THE TONE OF THE TEXT: COMIC, TRAGIC OR IRONIC

 Trigger activity

Read these two cartoons. Can you say why they make you laugh?

Chapter outline

16.1 Comedy

16.2 Tragedy

16.3 Irony

Cartoon A

Cartoon B

Look for other interesting cartoons or comic strips. Can you say what techniques the cartoonists use to create humour? Do you think prose writers employ similar techniques?

16.1 Comedy

Purpose—Why do writers employ humour?

Humour is used in stories for several reasons:

(a) to entertain or amuse the reader
(b) to poke fun at other people or society
(c) to laugh at ourselves (comedies are often a reflection of our own lives and behaviour).

Definition—What are the characteristics of comedy?

(a) Comedies usually have a resolution at the end, that is, the initial problem is solved.
(b) The main character wants something and attains it at the end.
(c) Comedy involves elements of humour (refer to the following table).

Method—How do we identify comic elements?

Comedy may be created through the following aspects:

(1) Comic situations	
(a) Exaggerated events	A incident which involves many exaggerated incidents, eg: someone trips over a paint bucket which spills on the cat, the cat gets angry and attacks the dog, which jumps on the sofa and overturns it, and so on.
(b) Unexpected events	Something we expect to happen does not happen but the opposite does, eg: character X is so stingy, saves all his money and locks it in a cupboard, but he loses the key.
(c) Slapstick	This involves a lot of physical action like chases, collisions, accidents, tripping, striking, falling, practical jokes, etc.

(2) Comic characters	
(a) Clumsy characters	Characters like clowns who often fall on each other or are prone to accidents
(b) Unusual appearance or voice	Characters who may dress in an exaggerated or unusual manner or characters who speak differently from the norm.
(c) Strange habits or exaggerated behaviour	Characters who have strange habits such as someone who loves to smell his feet. Usually comic characters have one personality trait which is slightly exaggerated; for example, a miser who is paranoid and constantly takes out his money bag, counts every cent and puts the money back again.
(3) Humour in language	
(a) Jokes	This involves humorous jokes that poke fun at people, certain social groups or organizations, certain leaders, and society in general.
(b) Puns or verbal wit	This involves clever wordplay such as punning, in which words with double meanings are used. For example, one common joke is the story of a panda which goes to a restaurant where it eats shoots and leaves.
(4) Ironic twist	
(a) Verbal irony	This involves the use of sarcasm where one character says one thing and means another.
(b) Situational irony	This involves a clever twist in events. What is expected to happen does not occur; instead the opposite does. For example, a driver yells at a man for knocking on his window only to find that it is a policeman.

Note: Irony will be covered in more detail in a later section of this chapter.

 Group work: Role-play

Work in a group of four or five.

(1) The objective of this activity, in the spirit of Charlie Chaplin, is to turn an ordinary, mundane event into a comic one. Here are some ordinary events that the group could choose from:

- a fly falls into someone's soup at a posh restaurant

- someone drops her earring in a crowded MRT coach
- a student's pen starts leaking ink midway during a test
- a student accidentally mixes the wrong chemicals during a laboratory session
- sending a message to someone only to realize later that it was delivered to the wrong person.

(2) Use the table above and try to incorporate at least three of the comic elements into your three-minute performance. During your performance, the rest of the class try to identify the comic elements in your play.

Exercise 16A – Humour

It had rained all morning and the management had decided to go out and have a long lunch. This is frequently their reaction to unpleasant weather. And so I was left in the house with the other dogs—dear old souls in many ways but
5 somewhat lacking in initiative. Reluctant to join in, if you know what I mean. I think they probably suffered from too much training during their formative years and never recovered. So, as I always do when cooped up and left to my own devices, I made a tour of the premises—checking the
10 kitchen for any edible traces of sloppy housekeeping, testing doors and electrical wiring, rearranging rugs, and generally making myself useful. And then, on a whim, I decided to have a look upstairs, where overnight visitors are locked up. For some reason, this has been designated a forbidden zone.
15 Heaven knows what they do up there, but it's been made clear to me that I'm not welcome.

So up the stairs I went and what did I find? The door had been left ajar and the delights of what they call the "guest suite" were available for inspection.
20 Well, once you've seen one bathroom, you've seen them all. Stark, uncomfortable places that reek of soap and cleanliness. But the bedroom was a different matter altogether —wall-to-wall carpet, cushions galore, a large bed. And rather a fine bed at that—not too high, with an ample supply of
25 pillows and an inviting expanse of what I later found out was an antique bedspread. It looked like the standard issue

white sheet to me, but antique linen isn't one of my interests. I incline more to the fur-rug school of interior decoration myself.

30 Nevertheless, the bed had a definite appeal—as it would to you—if you normally spent your nights in a basket on the floor—and so I hopped up. At first, I was a little disturbed by the degree of softness but once I adapted my movements I found I could explore in short and rather exhilarating

35 bounces, and I made my way up to the head of the bed where the pillows were kept. They were poorly organized, in my view, laid out in a neat row, which may suit the reclining human figure but is not a convenient arrangement for a dog. We like to be surrounded when we sleep. I think it may be a

40 subconscious desire to return to the womb, although I personally wouldn't want a second visit. As you may remember, I had to share with twelve others and I have no pleasant memories of the experience. Even so the instinct to surround oneself remains, possibly for protection, and I set

45 to work dragging the pillows to the middle of the bed until they formed a kind of circular nest. And there I settled, in great comfort, and dozed off.

Sometime later, I was wakened by the sound of a car. The management had obviously gorged enough and had

50 decided to return. I bounded downstairs to do my duty and lined up with the others as the management made their entrance. All was well until evening. Madame had gone up to put flowers in the guest room for visitors who were arriving the next day. She is fussy about these little touches and has

55 been known to agonize over such details as the choice of water to leave beside the bedside tables. She wants guests to be comfortable, you see, which I feel only encourages them to stay. Anyway, there was Madame upstairs in the suite when I heard distant cries of alarm. Put two and two together

60 and I assumed my adjustments to the bedding were causing some minor distress. Consequently, I was in the basket faster than a rat up a drainpipe and feigning the sleep of the innocent by the time she came down. There were three of us, I reasoned, and so there was a fair chance that one of the

65 others would be sentenced to bread and water while the true culprit escaped. Wrongful arrest and imprisonment is very popular these days, so I've heard, and I was hoping that this would be another chapter in the annals of injustice.

With eyes tightly shut and ears tuned in to the hurricane

70 warning, I listened to Madame as she waxed indignant about

footprints on the bedspread, ripped and rumpled pillows and one or two other small imperfections.

75 I heard her coming over to my basket, and I ventured a half-open eye. Madame's accusing figure stood before me, brandishing evidence, shaking the offending bedspread in front of me and carrying on as though I'd thrown up in her best hat (which I did once, but there was a good reason for it). I attempted a puzzled and indifferent look but what I'd failed to take into account was the size of my paws and the 80 traces of mud that remained in the bedsheets after the morning walk. Taking hold of one incriminating paw, she applied it to a large and well-defined footprint, and that was that. Dead to rights, guilty as charged, and serious repercussions on the way, I felt sure—unless I moved quickly.

Extract from A Dog's Life *by Peter Mayle*

1 What evidence tells you that the text is told from the point of view of a dog? How effective is this style of narration and why?

2 Explain how the writer creates humour in the text.

3 What is your impression of the narrator? Support your answer with reference to the text.

16.2 **Tragedy**

 Purpose—Why do we read serious texts?

Perhaps one of the more significant aspects of stories is that they can be thought-provoking. Through stories, we can learn something more of ourselves and of the world we live in. This is the primary function of serious stories—to reflect the real world so that their readers or audience may gain a greater understanding of their lives and the issues affecting the world.

Definition—Tragedy

Serious stories may range from the thought-provoking to the reflective, in which the writer poses a certain question or issue for consideration. Sometimes these stories may include some element of humour or irony. The more serious forms of stories are often **tragedies**.

Tragic stories are often characterized by the following:

(a) The story often ends in disaster, usually involving death.

(b) The main character is usually a noble figure with a flaw that may lead to fatal consequences.

(c) The main character often does not understand himself until the end. Here, he learns something of himself and the world (the reader or audience learns with him).

(d) The reader or audience feels sorry for the main character at the end.

 Method—How do we analyse a tragedy?

(1) Look at the subject matter of the text. Serious stories usually involve more realistic and heavy themes such as war, death, power or evil.

(2) Look at the setting in the text. Setting refers to time and place. The environment usually depicts the tone of the text as well as the psychology of the main character. Look at the issue of time in the text. Does the event happen in an hour, over a few months or years? What happens to the main character or the problem as time progresses? Identify the key changes.

(3) Identify the main problem in the text. Look at how the problem places the main character in a dilemma. What flaw in the main character is surfaced as he deals with the problem?

(4) Look at the ending. What is the outcome of the situation?

He showed me a picture of the Englishman who had founded the island on which I happened to be born. He was a tall man with a long nose. A proud man he looked. Haughty, I think, was the expression used to describe him. He didn't

5   look the sort of man who liked answering questions. My teacher told me that this haughty person was a man of vision, a man who saw what the island could become. I wasn't too sure. He seemed to be looking over our heads. Perhaps, he was looking into the future. Perhaps, he adopted

10 a lofty gaze to avoid looking into the eyes of the Malays he had cheated.

However, all this had happened a long time ago. When I came to be born on the island the British no longer approved of cheating, or gunboats or taking advantage of the weak.

15 Now, they talked of honour and the rights of men. They told us of truth which it was our duty to speak.

I thought it strange that men who had but recently enforced bargains with cannon and cunning should talk this way.

20 I asked my teacher and he said, "It does not matter why they say it. It matters that what they say is true. And you, my innocent, must always be prepared to fight for the rights of other men and to speak what you see as the truth."

I believed him. I had reason to. Honesty and fair play,

25 justice and honour must be good things for they had made the British masters of the land, rulers of the waves.

I came also to believe two things. First, that the British were invincible. Second, that they always played by the rules that I had come to hold so dear. I was wrong about both.

30 Far to the north of our island, in the mindless darkness of the South China Sea, several thuds were heard. They were Japanese bombs hitting the decks of the *Prince of Wales* and the *Repulse*, battleships which we had come to believe no power on earth could sink.

35 More thuds were heard. The air was filled with smoke and fire.

Unfamiliar aircraft crowded the skies and rained bombs on our island. Everything was on fire: houses, ships, people. The smell of burning invaded your nose and stayed there.

40 Soon, we saw them: the conquerors, the giants who had defeated the British. But they were not giants. They were little

men with bandy-legs and flat faces. Men who spoke in grunts
and smelled of the swamp from which they had just emerged.
These were men who didn't play by our rules. They raped
45 women, hit children, kicked the old out of their way. Justice
was whatever they said it was. The torture-chamber replaced
the courtroom, confessions, the truth.

Hungry and sick we forgot truth and justice and decency.
We cheated the unwary, robbed the weak. I was troubled.
50 Everything I held so dear seemed no longer to be true.

Extract from "The Personal History of an Island"
by Gopal Baratham

1 What is the narrator's attitude towards the British in the
above text?

2 Identify in the text, elements of tragedy affecting the
individual as well as the society. Provide examples to
support each point.

3 How does the writer make the experience of the Japanese
Occupation vivid and horrifying at the same time?

 Links to real-world issues

The narrator in the above passage states: "I came also to believe
two things. First, that the British were invincible. Second, that they
always played by the rules that I had come to hold so dear. I was
wrong about both." What lessons can we learn from the Japanese
Occupation of Singapore? Read and share examples of other stories
and historical accounts you know about what happened to Singapore
from 1942 to 1945. In today's context, who is responsible for the
defence of Singapore? What is the role of the ordinary Singapore
citizen in the war against terrorism and other threats?

16.3 Irony

A story can be written in a comic or tragic tone. In addition, a writer/
speaker may also adopt an ironic tone to convey an implied meaning.

 **Definition—Irony**

Irony refers to a **contradiction** between what is expected and what really happens. There are two main types of irony.

(1) Situational irony

Here, the irony occurs when what one expects to happen does not happen. Instead, the opposite occurs. For example, imagine you learn that a false rumour about yourself has been spreading in your school. You confide in your best friend about how you feel, only to find out later that it was your best friend who started that rumour!

(2) Verbal irony

This is commonly known as **sarcasm** and expresses a contradiction between what is said and what is actually meant. For example, a sarcastic tone is employed when you turn up half an hour late and your friend says, "You are so early today!"

 Purpose—Why do writers employ irony?

Usually this is because, as readers, we often enjoy a twist in the plot. For example, a story which ends in a way we expect is predictable and boring. Besides adding to the sense of unpredictability, irony engages our attention. In addition, irony can be used for a variety of purposes. Some are:

(a) To create humour

The writer may employ an ironic tone to poke fun at others. This gives the text a sense of humour and light-heartedness. This technique is commonly used in situation comedies on television. For example, we find it hilarious when a character puts on a show of bravado and enters a dark room only to jump in fright when a friend touches him on the shoulder.

(b) To criticize

Irony can also be used to criticize an issue or a community (for instance, a social group such as the upper class or the bourgeoisie or a political group such as the government of a country). For example, Jane Austen, a writer famous for her use of irony, often employs this technique to poke fun at certain characters and social groups as well as to criticize them. One of her main targets in *Pride and Prejudice* is the snobbish and hypocritical upper class.

(c) To add to the sense of tragedy

Finally, irony can be used to make a situation even more tragic. For example, imagine the scenario of a main character who has sold everything he has to finance the hospital bills of his dying mother. Because of his poor financial situation, his wife has left him. He walks home dejected, feeling that he is losing his mother and everything else that he loves. He wishes life could be kinder to him. Absorbed in his thoughts, he does not realize where he is going and as he crosses the road, he is hit by a truck and is fatally injured. The irony here is that as readers, we expect that something better would follow, especially since the character appears to be a good person and is already in a state of suffering. When the opposite occurs, the irony adds to an already tragic situation and hence, increases the reader's sympathy.

 Exercise 16C – Ironic tone

Read the extract below and identify elements of irony.

When the government became alarmed by the increasing tendency among graduate women to stay unmarried and thus deprive the country of the brainy children that would form the future pool of expertise for the country's economic
5   development, it started a matchmaking scheme whereby these women might meet the men who would lead them away from the errors of their ways.

On the morning after the Prime Minister himself, in a major policy speech, alerted the nation to the perils of this
10   trend, single graduate women woke up to find themselves suddenly on the national centre stage: everybody wanted to know why they hadn't gotten married, what they looked for in a marriage partner, were Singapore men deficient in any way, et cetera. Because these graduate women had been
15   invested with special importance as the providers of the much-needed brains to run the country in the future, they found themselves in the unique position of being cajoled and wooed by a government not normally given to these methods of getting things done, and naturally their views
20   were sought eagerly, and the men's not at all. The minister whose prestige was only slightly less than the Prime Minister's took upon himself the task of personally interviewing a sample of these graduate women to obtain firsthand

25 knowledge of why the educated Singapore woman no longer wanted to marry the educated Singapore man. What he found convinced him that it was all the fault of the Singapore male, so that, after the interviews were over, he turned his attention to the male graduates, berated them for their wrong attitudes and sternly advised them to change. For the men,

30 despite their education, were still stubbornly clinging to the old notion that, to marry happily, a man must marry an academic notch or two below him: a man with a university degree would do better to marry someone with A levels only, and a man with A levels had better, for his own peace of

35 mind, seek someone with O levels only, and so on. Only in this way could marital supremacy, so important to the Asian male, be ensured. The result was that the very large crop of female graduates produced by the university each year, a crop that was moreover becoming bigger each year with a

40 rise in female ambition, was left largely unsought, and therefore, in the words of a concerned government official, "deprived of the primary function of womanhood".

From "The English Language Teacher's Secret"
by Catherine Lim

1 In this extract, the writer makes a number of assumptions about Singapore society (its government and its citizens). What assumptions are these? Support your answer with reference to the text.

2 Look at the last sentence in the extract. Can you say what is ironic about it and why?

3 What do you think the writer's intention in writing this story is? Does she approve or disapprove of the minister's view about the fault lying with the Singapore male? Give evidence to support your answer.

4 What is your opinion on this issue about why graduate women stay unmarried? Could there be reasons other than those offered in this story?

Chapter 17
ANALYSING LANGUAGE IN PROSE

Trigger activity

Chapter outline

17.1 Literary techniques in prose

Study this example of a street graffiti.

(Source: http://www.bigfoto.com)

1   What do you think this picture depicts?

2   Where do you think the graffiti artists painted the picture? What seems to have been their intention for doing so?

Like paintings, literary texts are works of art. Instead of images and colour, however, the writer uses words. Language is what transforms an ordinary story into a literary work of art; that is, a story which is rich in meaning, and which contains a treasure of emotions and a wealth of insights.

Definition—What does analysing language involve?

Analysing language in prose **refers to a close analysis of word choice and other language devices** such as imagery, sound and rhythm.

Purpose—Why analyse language in prose?

One question that is often asked in examinations is the "how" question, for example: "How does the writer convey a sense of excitement in the text?" We can answer such questions by referring to characterization, development of tension and style of narration in the text. But in order to answer the question fully, we should also talk about the writer's use of language. Close analysis of language is applicable both to the analysis of poetry and to the analysis of prose. In prose, meaning, mood and the writer's attitude are often conveyed in the choice of words and other language devices used.

Method—How do we analyse language in prose?

(1) Pick out **literary techniques** (the use of literary devices such as symbolism, figurative language, word order, rhythm and sound) and state how these techniques contribute to the meaning or the mood of the text. (Refer to Section II for more information on each of these devices.)

(2) Pick out **repetition of words or ideas** and look at what is emphasized in the text or what patterns emerge from the repetition.

(3) Look at whether there is a **trend**, that is, a change or changes in the value of repeated words as the text progresses. Identify what is developed and how it contributes to your understanding of the mood or character.

17.1 Literary techniques in prose

Familiarize yourself with these terms: **symbolism, figurative language, word order, rhythm** and **sound**. (Refer to Section II and the glossary at the back of this book for their definitions and uses.)

Exercise 17A – Language analysis

Analyse the following text, paying attention to literary devices (diction, imagery and sound effects).

Now he noticed that the sky had grown much darker. The rain was heavier every second, pressing down as if the earth had to be flooded before nightfall. The oaks ahead blurred and the ground drummed. He began to run. And as
5   he ran he heard a deeper sound running with him. He whirled around. The horse was in the middle of the clearing. It might have been running to get out of the terrific rain except that it was coming straight for him, scattering clay and stones, with an immense supple and powerful motion. He let out a tearing
10 roar and threw the stone in his right hand. The result was instantaneous. Whether at the roar or the stone, the horse reared as if against a wall and shied to the left. As it dropped back on its forefeet he flung his second stone, at ten yards' range, and saw a bright mud blotch suddenly appear on the
15 glistening black flank. The horse surged down the wood, splashing the earth like water, tossing its long tail as it plunged out of sight among the hawthorns.
        He looked around for stones. The encounter had set the blood beating in his head and had given him a savage
20 energy. He could have killed the horse at that moment. He came out at the woodside, in open battle now, still searching for the right stones. There were plenty here, piled and scattered where they had been ploughed out of the field. He selected two, then straightened and saw the horse twenty
25 yards off in the middle of the steep field, watching him calmly.

Extract from The Rain Horse *by Ted Hughes*

How does the writer make the sense of tension vivid in this text?

1   Analyse the imagery in the extract and state the specific techniques used, the purpose of each and how effective it is (your response). The first one has been done for you.

Evidence	Technique	Contribution to meaning	Effect
"The oaks ahead <u>blurred</u> and the ground <u>drummed</u>."	Personi-fication	The writer uses personification, a device by which non-human things are given human attributes. Through the examples, the oaks "blurred" and the ground "drummed", we are given the impression that nature, represented by the vegetation (oaks) and earth (ground), is working against the man on foot. The two images reinforce the idea that natural things are antagonistic towards him in the situation.	The effect created is that the natural environment is violently opposed to the man—like an enemy. Together with the strange, wild behaviour of the horse, it gives the impression that everything is against him and adds to the sense of extreme danger—one of man versus hostile nature.

2   Analyse sound devices in the extract and state the specific techniques used, the purpose of each and how effective it is (your response). The first one has been done for you.

Evidence	Technique	Contribution to meaning	Effect
"The oaks ahea<u>d</u> blurre<u>d</u> and the groun<u>d</u> drumme<u>d</u>."	Use of consonance	The writer uses consonance in repeating the "d" consonant at the end of certain words. This creates a strong, heavy sound which complements the strength and power of the rain.	The sound seems to echo in the mind of the reader like a drumbeat signifying the intensity and terror of the rain, thus increasing the sense of foreboding.

3   Study the writer's choice of words in the text. How do these words contribute to the meaning (message, mood and attitude) of the text?

Choice of words	Denotative meaning	Connotative meaning
"The encounter had set blood beating in his head and had given him a <u>savage energy</u>."	The word "savage" describes the behaviour as violent and destructive.	The word also suggests an almost primitive, barbaric quality about the main character. The word serves to show the intensity of his rage and contributes to the tension in the text.

Exercise 17B – More practice in language analysis

The story is about Mr Tan, a radical and dynamic teacher who teaches a class of scholars.

As the weeks passed, this general opinion of Tan was strengthened: he was interesting as long as he didn't talk politics. His worst enemies had to admit that he conducted a lively and informative class; and what most nearly won
5 Laurence's admiration was that he had a surprising grasp of science for an Arts man, could toss back almost any technical ball they threw at him. Occasionally he gathered the Science and Arts Sixths together for lectures on subjects which he demonstrated to be of mutual interest; he called the Science
10 class Philistines and the Arts class ignoramuses, and conducted monologues on his own brand of doctrine which he called Humanism.

He took them through an elementary survey of the Theory of Relativity; then they went on to theories of cosmic entropy,
15 and passed on to the origin of the universe. Ling was massacred for his earnest affirmation of faith, and put on his best Father-forgive-them-for-they-know-not-what-they-do-look; Chow, displaying what he thought was hard-headed scientific positivism, was steam-rollered and called as much
20 a Fundamentalist as Ling. Inevitably, someone asked Tan what he really believed.

"Well, then, my credo: I believe in the dignity of the human spirit, and the enduring value of its achievements. I believe that it cannot be entirely suppressed by any amount

25 of oppression; there will always be some men who manage to retain their integrity, and always be some who aspire to higher goals than those at hand. I think the ultimate sin is to attempt to stifle such aspirations and a man's most precious possession is his freedom—from pressures economic or

30 political—to pursue his own particular star." Tan grinned. "Which is why I'm spending my life in trying to lift the blinkers off you poor myopic materialists, to get you to recognize some of the richness and glory of human achievement. And a pox on the fetters of your syllabus and

35 your examinations, and on the prestige of science over letters in this society!"

"Well, you know Singapore has to think of its political needs, sir," Chow said. "Science is important for progress in this modern world."

40 "And we have enough lawyers and economists," Laurence added: "and what's the use to the nation of so many graduates in History and English?"

Tan cocked an eye at him. "You seem to think of the educational process as a machine which turns out specialized

45 tools, each designed and sharpened to serve a particular function in the state. I grant you that specialists in the Arts have limited functions, except, like viruses, to propagate their own kind. But you might try asking, what is the value to the community of a leavening knowledge of the humanities

50 throughout the population? Every citizen of the democratic state, who hopes to play an intelligent part in the affairs of the nation, should have some knowledge of history, literature and law."

"I don't see how it helps us to know a set of dates by

55 heart," said Chow, "or to be able to recite the plays of Shakespeare, or to know all about contract law."

Tan buried his face in his hands. "God have mercy, is that the conception you bunch of adding-machines have of the Arts? Drawn, I suppose, from the 'history lessons' or

60 'poetry classes' of your infancy? Heaven help you! Come on, notebooks!" He reached for the chalk. "Assignments for next week, usual work groups." He began to write on the board, "'Literature: one man's fiction, all men's truth.' 'History: only a fool makes the same mistakes twice.' 'Jurisprudence:

65 study of the anatomy of society.'"

Extract from "The Scholarship" by Stella Kon

1   Mr Tan calls his Science class "Philistines"—what do you think he means by this? Pick out other examples of interesting words used in this text and analyse their connotative meanings.

2   By paying close attention to language and other devices, discuss how the writer conveys the differences between Mr Tan and his students.

3   What repeated image of the students does Mr Tan convey? How does his attitude and tone towards them develop in the course of the text?

4   Look at the last line of the text. Imagine you are one of the students in Mr Tan's class. Paraphrase and simplify each statement he has written on the board. What is your opinion of Mr Tan's views?

 Links to real-world issues

Do you think there is a place in our education system for the study of the arts (literature, music, fine arts and the humanities such as history)? Think about why the study of literature is important. What do you think are some of the objectives of literature education in schools? Can literature be relevant and practical in the real world? What are some fundamental skills we can gain from the study of literature? Discuss.

Chapter 18
KEYS TO GAINING A DEEPER INSIGHT INTO THE TEXT (PART I)

Aside from a close reading of the text, students need to think about the underlying message the text may be conveying and the purpose/s for which it was written. This section focuses on teaching the more advanced skills of appreciation to enable students to formulate a critical and insightful response to literature.

Chapter outline

18.1 An understanding of the term "insight"

18.2 Analysing the way the text is structured

 Trigger activity

Look at these images. What do you see?

Picture A

Picture B

These pictures are typical examples of the gestalt theory which was popularized in the early twentieth century. They illustrate the simple principle that sometimes a picture or any text can mean more than what it shows at first glance.

For example, in Picture A, if we focus on the white space, we see two people facing each other. If we focus on the black background, we see a vase.

What about Picture B? Whether we see a young woman or an old woman depends on whether we focus on the contrast between the upper black space against the white point nose (in which case, we see a young girl) or the contrast between the lower black space and the white point below the black line (in which case, we see an old woman).

18.1 An understanding of the term "insight"

What does the term "insight" mean? Many people mistake this to mean original thought. However, while having an original view of a text is wonderful, it would hardly seem a reasonable requirement for a student who only has 50 minutes to analyse a text and write a response to it.

 Definition—Insight

According to the *Oxford Dictionary,* having an **insight** into something means **being able to see and understand the truth about people and situations.**

The point is that all stories have been written for a reason and most contain a message about the world we live in or about human nature. As critical readers, we need to discern what this philosophical statement or message is.

 Purpose—Where do philosophical insight and response fit in our analysis of the unseen text?

Recall the diagrammatic presentation of approaching the Unseen in Chapter 1, page 4.

Stage 1: Understanding overall meaning

Question to ask: What is the text about?

- Obtain a basic understanding of the text's meaning.
- Identify the genre of the text and the subject matter.
- Identify the overall mood of the text.

> **Stage 2: Close reading**
>
> *Question to ask: What devices does the writer use to convey meaning to the reader?*
>
> - Poetic devices—diction, word order, figurative language, rhythm, sound.
> - Prose techniques—plot structure, narration, characterization, tension, repetition and development.

> **Stage 3: Philosophical insight and response**
>
> *Questions to ask: What issues about the world and human nature does the text highlight? What is my response to them?*

The rationale behind this is that, as critics, we need to be able to look at the text from different perspectives. We first need to have a broad overview of what it is about. Next, we need to pay close attention to devices and techniques by which the writer conveys his meaning to the reader. Finally, we need to discern and respond to the underlying meaning of the text and what it says about the world and about human nature.

 Method—How do we identify the text's underlying message?

One way of obtaining an insight into the text's underlying message is to look at two aspects:

(a) the way in which an idea is developed through the way the text is structured

(b) the way the text develops and how this conveys the writer's intended message.

Each of these aspects will be covered in detail in this and the following chapter.

18.2 Analysing the way the text is structured

All texts are structured in a specific way to convey an intended message. By examining the central oppositional structure of the text, we can identify these ideas.

To identify the central oppositional structure in the text, do the following:

(1) Identify the key subject matter and its contrasting subject matter (look at the title and the first stanza or paragraph of the text).

(2) Pick out words and phrases describing both the subject and its contrasting subject. Look especially for repeated ideas that contribute to the overall impression of the subject and show how this is defined against the contrasting subject.

(3) Say what philosophical truth about the world or human nature is expressed through the oppositions.

Application example

For example, read this poem:

The Eagle

He clasps the crag with crooked hands;
Close to the sun in lonely lands,
Ringed with the azure world, he stands.

The wrinkled sea beneath him crawls;
5   He watches from his mountain walls,
And like a thunderbolt he falls.

Alfred Tennyson

In this poem, the eagle is defined against its natural landscape:

Main opposition: Eagle	vs	Natural world
Depictions of the eagle	**Depictions of natural landscape**	
In control—the phrases "He clasps" and "He stands" depict the eagle's position of stability and control over his world.	Chaotic, empty—"lonely lands" and "wrinkled sea" depict the vast emptiness and lack of control in the natural landscape.	
Sense of power and authority—the eagle "watches from his mountain walls", giving him an omnipotent, almost omnipresent quality.	Peaceful, serene—"azure"—the colour blue implies harmony and peace.	
Great strength and might—the simile comparing his speed with a "thunderbolt" indicates the intensity of his strength as he falls presumably on his prey.	Weak—the sea is described as "beneath" the eagle and "crawls" underneath his presence. This depicts the inferiority of nature compared with the majesty and power of the eagle.	

In summary, we can say that the poem celebrates the eagle's power and presence through an oppositional structure in which the eagle is set against his own natural world. In this case, we see that the eagle's strength, versatility and control are clearly defined when set against a natural landscape that is formless, empty and whose weakness allows the eagle to have dominance over it.

 **Purpose—What is the purpose of identifying the central oppositional structure of the text?**

Identifying the central oppositional structure of the text helps us identify its underlying meaning and thematic focus. Since the world is often structured in terms of opposites (eg, light versus dark, day versus night, good versus evil), literary themes which reflect the world are also structured in terms of opposites.

Examples of common oppositional themes

Category of values	Common oppositional terms		
Transcendental values	good reality truth love life	*versus*	evil appearance hypocrisy hate death
Social values	justice peace harmony	*versus*	injustice war disharmony
Moral values	sacrifice generosity	*versus*	self-centredness greed
Leadership values	power courage leader	*versus*	weakness cowardice follower

Application example

In Tennyson's poem "The Eagle", we could say that the eagle's might set against an empty background depicts the universal idea that those in power will naturally have dominance over their own environment.

Group work: Discussion

Look at the above categories of oppositional structures and answer the following questions.

Work in a group of four or five.

1 Brainstorm other examples of themes that can be expressed in an oppositional structure.

2 For each oppositional structure described in the table above as well as those that you have come up with, phrase the oppositional structure into a statement that is a philosophical truth about human nature or society in general. For example, the oppositional structure "appearance versus reality" exemplifies the notion that truth is often tainted with hypocrisy and deception because people mask their intentions or motives.

Group work: Inference (Real-world case study)

The example below is adapted from an actual email scam sent to millions of people all over the world. Surprisingly, email scams like this make a profit of a few hundred million dollars a year. What do you think makes people fall for these scams? One answer to this question is naiveté. Some of us may take things too literally and hence approach a text with complete trust. On the other hand, literature teaches us to think critically and to question the underlying meaning of the text.

> Dear Sir,
>
> I am Jeremy Eliot, only child of the late Mr and Mrs Eliot. My father was a very wealthy coca merchant based in Abidjan before he was poisoned by his business associates on an
> 5 outing. Permit me to inform you of my desire to go into a business relationship with you. I got your name and contact from a random list on the Internet. I prayed over it and selected your name over other names due to its esteemable nature.

10 I wish to confide in you about a simple and sincere business. Before the death of my father on 24th November 2005, he secretly called me to his bedside and told me that he had a sum of US$16 million left in an account in a local bank here in Abidjan. He explained to me that it was because of this

15 wealth that he was murdered by his business associates and that I should look for a foreign partner in a country of my choice where I could transfer the money. I seek your permission to provide details of your bank account where this money may be transferred. Moreover, sir, I am willing to

20 offer you 15% of the total sum as compensation for your effort.

Thank you.

Jeremy Eliot

Work in a group of four or five and analyse the text by doing the following:

1 What is the genre of the text? What is its mood or tone?

2 The basic oppositional structure of the text is built on ambiguity on the part of the writer and specificity on the part of the reader. For example, the writer provides very vague details about his request. We do not know the following: the name of his father, what happened to his mother, what the name and nature of his father's business was, what his bank account is, what his address is, and how and when the money will be transferred to the reader. On the other hand, the request asked of the reader is very specific and straightforward—to provide details of the reader's bank account. Pick out two examples to support this point.

3 What other evidence in the text tells you that it does not come from a credible source?

 Links to real-world issues

Give examples of other email scams you have heard of. Why is it important to cultivate a critical mind before we act? What strategies can we adopt to prevent ourselves falling prey to such deceit?

Exercise 18A – Structural oppositions

Text A

Anthem for Doomed Youth

What passing-bells for these who die as cattle?
   Only the monstrous anger of the guns.
   Only the stuttering riffles' rapid rattle
Can patter out their hasty orisons.
5   No mockeries now for them; no prayers nor bells,
   Nor any voice of mourning save the choirs —
The shrill, demented choirs of wailing shells;
   And bugles calling for them from sad shires.

What candles may be held to speed them all?
10   Not in the hands of boys, but in their eyes
Shall shine the holy glimmers of good-byes.
   The pallor of girls' brows shall be their pall;
Their flowers the tenderness of patient minds,
And each slow dusk a drawing down of blinds.

Wilfred Owen

Text B

   … I've never been at home with my mind. It thinks too much. Like now. I'm seeing the little boy and the woman in black. My mind is not. I hate Descartes. I think therefore I am not. I do not want to be predicated. I want to remain the
5 subject. I want to lie down on this mattress and relax. After all, I took off from work. I don't know why. But I am lying down on this old mattress. The birds have become quieter for some reason. Maybe they are getting fed up of the white around them. I don't like white very much. When I was eight
10 I wore a pair of white pants to school. I remember the teacher —she was a pretty girl—held my pants and laughed. All the other boys laughed too. Since then I have not liked white pants. My wife likes them. White. It comes between me and my wife. Now it is coming between me and the ceiling fan. As
15 I see white, my mind is still engrossed on those two buffoons.

I call them buffoons because they sang songs which made good melody but which nobody understood. We still await the second coming. We still cannot hold our heads up high. Our minds are still not without fear. I don't know what I am thinking or what I am seeing. It is getting rather confused. But I know I'm lying on an old mattress in my living room in my own house. ...

20

Extract from "Monologue" by Kirpal Singh

1 Refer to Text A and Text B above. What are the texts about? What is the central conflict in each text? At which point in the text is this made clear to you and why?

2 Refer to the following table and provide examples of values expressed as opposites. As a start, one example is given.

Oppositional structure (theme) 1:	
Life versus Death	
Descriptions (implied in the poem):	**Descriptions:**
• Possibility of enjoying a full varied life • Bliss • The possibility of enjoying life with others	• Futility—end of all opportunities: "each slow dusk a drawing down of blinds" • Loss of bliss—"Nor any voice of mourning save the choirs" • Loss of relationships with others—"The pallor of girls' brows shall be their pall"
Universal truth War is futile and dying in war results in many missed opportunities of enjoying life to the full.	

Now, in each of the two texts above, identify two other oppositional structures in the same manner as shown in the table above and explain what philosophical truths about the world or human nature these texts convey.

Chapter 19
KEYS TO GAINING A DEEPER INSIGHT INTO THE TEXT (PART II)

Trigger activity

Read this short excerpt and discuss your responses in your usual group:

Wife:	I'm so tired—I don't know how I'm going to finish this report and cook dinner as well.
Husband:	Why don't you finish what you have to do and then cook the dinner?
Wife:	It's a lot of work. By the time I finish, it may be late.
Husband:	It's okay, I'm not hungry yet. Take your time.
Wife:	*(irritated)* I might not have any more energy left after that!
Husband:	Oh, then maybe you could get the dinner ready first and then you have the rest of the night to work on your report.
Wife:	Forget it! I'm going back to the office! *(She goes out, banging the door.)*
Husband:	Honey, what's wrong? I thought you said you were tired!

- What do you think went wrong in this conversation?
- What was the wife's intention?

Chapter outline

19.1 Inferring the writer's intention

19.2 Identifying repetition

19.3 Tracking development

Purpose—Why do we need to think about intention?

Misunderstanding occurs in relationships primarily because human beings communicate differently. One way to prevent misunderstanding is to think about what the other party is trying to say. In the above example, the wife repeatedly mentioned she was tired. In so doing, she was actually hinting to her husband to offer to cook for her. However, her husband misinterpreted her hints and assumed she was asking for his advice on how to handle her work and the cooking.

When we begin to consider the reason why a person says or asks something, we are on the way to a better understanding of the other party. Similarly, to understand a text, we must consider why the text was written in the first place. When we do this, we are thinking about the writer's intention.

19.1 Inferring the writer's intention

We can gain a deeper insight into the text when we consider the writer's **intention**.

Definition—Intention

This **refers to the writer's purpose or purposes** for writing the text. However, most often, the writer's intention is obscured by language or form. Also, the narrator in the text may deliberately try to mislead the reader.

Method—How do we analyse intention?

According to literary theorist Wolfgang Iser, one way to find out the meaning of a text is to know what question the writer had in mind before he wrote the text and then to find out how the text answers the question he had. Thus, to understand the underlying meaning of the text and the intention of the writer, we need to imagine the question the text is answering.

There are two ways of identifying the meaning of a text and the writer's intention:

(a)   Look at what point or idea is repeatedly emphasized in the text.

(b) Look at whether there is development or change in the feelings associated with the idea as the text progresses.

Each of these aspects will be covered in detail in the following subsections.

19.2 Identifying repetition

Repetition is often used to emphasize a point or an idea. For example, read this extract about what a gang of boys are planning to do to an old man's house.

> "I found out things," T said. He continued to stare at his feet, not meeting anybody's **eyes**, as though he were absorbed in some dream he was unwilling—or ashamed—to share.
> "What things?"
> 5 "Old Misery's going to be away all tomorrow and Bank Holiday."
> Blackie said with relief, "You mean we could break in?"
> "And steal things?" somebody asked.
> Blackie said, "Nobody's going to steal things. Breaking
> 10 in—that's good enough, isn't it? We don't want any court stuff."
> "I don't want to steal anything," T said. "I've got a better idea."
> "What is it?"
> 15 T raised his **eyes**, as grey and disturbed as the drab August day. "We'll pull it down," T said. "We'll <u>destroy</u> it."
>
> *Extract from "The <u>Destructors</u>" by Graham Greene*

In the extract above, there is the repetition of certain words such as "destroy" and "Destructors" (the words are underlined). Writers repeat words not because they have a limited vocabulary. They do so deliberately to emphasize a point. In this case, the writer is attempting to convey the impression of violence and angst in these boys, particularly the main character, T.

In addition to repeating certain words, writers may iterate ideas. For example, the phrases "He continued to stare at his feet, not meeting anybody's eyes" and "T raised his eyes, as grey and disturbed as the drab August day" both emphasize T's eyes (the words are in bold print). It is often said that the eyes are the windows of the soul (personality). In this case, the writer may be referring to T as an inwardly troubled youth.

Bala, his wife, Margaret, and their son, Babu, have returned by sea, only to be greeted by Mariama and informed that his mother is dead.

"I am Mariama," she wailed. "Your mother is dead."

Pinned under this mountain of flesh Bala feared that he would soon join his recently deceased parent.

"I am the oldest member of her village and therefore

5   took upon myself the heavy burden of greeting you with this sorrowful news."

Turning his head fractionally (Mariama's embrace only permitted fractional movements), Bala could see Margaret retreating hastily up the gangway pursued by Uncle

10   Sambasivam.

Margaret had been uncertain as to the kind of welcome they would receive. She had expected a touching family reunion at the quayside, but had not quite envisaged the degree of bodily contact this would entail. She was horrified

15   by what she saw happening to Bala. When Uncle Sambasivam broke away from the crowd and started up the gangway, eyes bloodshot, exuding fumes of alcohol almost undiluted with air, hoarsely screaming, "*Premai, premai.* Dearest, dearest," she feared some kind of sexual assault

20   was imminent and fled.

Babu, sensing his mother's panic, joined her in flight, attempting meanwhile to hide in the folds of her sari. From the increasing alcoholic content of the air, she realized that Uncle Sambasivam was gaining on her. Suddenly she felt

25   something warm and vaguely human moving about her thighs. For a moment she feared that Uncle Sambasivam had by some transcendental manoeuver managed to project a portion of himself under her clothes. Diving into the sea between ship and the quay seemed a tempting avenue of

30   escape, but even before she could consider this possibility further, Uncle Sambasivam caught up with her and, as soon as Babu had extricated himself from the folds of her sari, included both of them in a highly alcoholic but unmistakably avuncular embrace.

35   Meanwhile, Bala, stilled pinned under Mariama, noticed that one of the suitcases which had slipped from his grasp had burst open, strewing Margaret's underwear and Babu's

40 toys on the dockside. Women and children, assuming these were intended as gifts, were already helping themselves to them. He noticed this only momentarily for now Mariama was weeping copiously into his face. Her tears, which were as profuse as her person, found their way individually into his eyes, a feat which required unerring accuracy and impeccable timing. They succeeded in almost totally blinding
45 him and he thought that they too were black till he realized that this was an effect produced by the liberal use of mascara on her lower lashes. Bewildered, breathless, and now virtually blinded, Bala was acutely aware of a fact as inescapable as the embrace he was in.
50   He was home.

Extract from "Welcome" by Gopal Baratham

1 What words best describe the reception Bala and his family received? Consider whether the title of the short story from which this excerpt is taken is helpful for your answer.

2 What idea is repeated about the characters of Mariama and Uncle Sambasivam? Point to evidence in the text to suggest how Bala and his family responded to the greeting they received.

3 The story ends with the sentence, "He was home." Did Bala feel at home?

19.3 Tracking development

Being aware of repeated words or ideas is not enough. Your next step should be to analyse whether there has been a change in the intensity of feeling associated with the repeated words. Remember that every story progresses with time. The key is to know what it is that changes and when the change actually begins. Changes can take place through character development. They can also occur through a change in the mood or tone in the text. For example, the sense of fear and mystery may become heightened as the text progresses. Sometimes, the tone or mood of the text may also change entirely. For example, a text which begins in a light-hearted, humorous mood may end up becoming ironic and even cynical. In addition to identifying the type of change, you also need to identify the point at which this change occurs. One way of tracking development is to pay careful attention to the language used in describing either the character or the mood.

Application example

In the previous extract from "The Destructors", we noted that a group of boys were planning to destroy the house of an old man, Mr Thomas. Now, they have locked him in his outdoor toilet. Read what happens to the end of the extract and try to identify how the writer develops our sympathy for the old man as he witnesses the collapse of his house.

Mr Thomas pleaded desperately. "A joke's a joke, boy. Let me out and I won't say a thing. I've got rheumatics. I have to sleep comfortable."

"You wouldn't be comfortable, not in your house, you wouldn't. Not now."

"What do you mean, boy?" but the footsteps receded. **There was only the silence of night**: no sound of sawing. Mr Thomas tried one more yell, but he was daunted and rebuked by the silence—a long way off **an owl hooted** and made away again on its muffled flight through the soundless world.

At seven next morning the driver came to fetch his lorry. He climbed into the seat and tried to start the engine. **He was vaguely aware of a voice shouting**, but it didn't concern him. At last the engine responded and he backed the lorry until it touched the great wooden shore that supported Mr Thomas's house. That way he could drive right out and down the street without reversing. The lorry moved forward, was momentarily checked as though something were pulling it from behind, and then went on to the **sound of a long rumbling crash**. The driver was astonished to see bricks bouncing ahead of him, while stones hit the roof of his cab. He put on his brakes. When he climbed out the whole landscape had suddenly altered. There was no house beside the car park, only a hill of rubble. He went round and examined the back of his lorry for damage, and found a rope tied there that was still twisted at the other end round part of a wooden strut.

The driver again became aware of somebody shouting. It came from the wooden erection which was the nearest thing to a house in that desolation of broken bricks. The driver climbed the smashed wall and unlocked the door. Mr Thomas came out of the loo. He was wearing a grey blanket to which flakes of pastry adhered. **He gave a sobbing cry.** "My house," he said. "Where's my house?"

"Search me," the driver said. His eye lit on the remains of a bath and what had once been a dresser and he began to laugh. There wasn't anything left anywhere.

> "How dare you laugh," Mr Thomas said. "It was my house. My house."
>
> *Extract from "The Destructors" by Graham Greene*

One way in which the writer develops our sympathy for the old man, Mr Thomas, is through the description of sounds (note the phrases in bold).

- At the beginning of this extract, there is an unnerving silence in the surroundings as expressed by the phrase, "There was only the silence of night". This ominous sense in the mood is emphasized through the fact that "an owl hooted". We feel a sense of sympathy for Mr Thomas who has to spend the night alone and has to endure the uncertainty of the entire situation.
- The writer then develops tension in the scene by bringing in sounds—at first, pitched low. When the driver arrives early in the morning, he becomes "vaguely aware of a voice shouting". This muffled sound increases our anxiety for Mr Thomas.
- The silence is then interrupted by the sudden "sound of a long rumbling crash". This loud sound is coupled with the shouting which the driver now seems to hear clearly, "The driver again became aware of somebody shouting." Here, tension is at its height and the reader feels a greater sense of anxiety for Mr Thomas.
- Finally, our sympathy reaches a high point when the sound of Mr Thomas's shouting now becomes "a sobbing cry". We feel his agony and pain as he witnesses the destruction of his home.

In conclusion, the writer, Graham Greene, effectively uses sound to complement the mood of the text. In so doing, he also influences and develops the reader's sympathy for the victim in the story.

 Point to note

Insight = ability to see patterns and trends in the text

Your ability to recognize repeated words/ideas and to trace the changes in the ideas will help you gain insight into a text and become more sensitive to the text as it progresses. One useful method of keeping track of repetition and trends is to circle or underline repeated words/ideas and then link them together at a later stage. After that, check the circled or underlined words to see whether there has been a change in the value of the words used.

Read this poem and then conduct a short debate in class about the nature of war.

The Soldier

If I should die, think only this of me;
   That there's some corner of a foreign field
That is for ever England. There shall be
   In that rich earth a richer dust concealed;
5 A dust whom England bore, shaped, made aware,
   Gave, once, her flowers to love, her ways to roam,
A body of England's, breathing English air,
   Washed by the rivers, blest by suns of home.

And think, this heart, all evil shed away,
10   A pulse in the eternal mind, no less
     Gives somewhere back the thoughts by England given;
Her sights and sounds; dreams happy as her day;
And laughter, learnt of friends; and gentleness,
   In hearts at peace, under an English heaven.

Rupert Brooke

Work in a group of four or five.

(1) Select one debate motion and one position from this table; select another group to debate this against.

Debate motion	Proposition's view	Opposition's view
1	The writer's intention is to highlight the glory and honour of soldiers who fight for their country and die in foreign lands.	The writer's intention is to highlight the plight of soldiers who fight for their country and die in foreign lands.
2	The writer's intention is to express patriotism.	The writer's intention is to express the futility of war.
3	The speaker speaks of death and expresses his fear and the sadness of death.	The speaker speaks of death and expresses a fearlessness towards death.

Debate motion	Proposition's view	Opposition's view
4	We admire the speaker for his courage and spirit.	We do not admire the speaker and tend to view him as naïve and overly-sentimental.

(2) Each group must defend its position with examples from the text as well as be ready to rebut its opponent's points.

Links to real-world issues

Occasionally we read about young men in Singapore having to do national service. Why do you think national service is compulsory in Singapore and why is this important? In the above poem, the speaker expresses his love for his country, England. Do you find this same spirit of patriotism in Singapore? Why?

Exercise 19B – Tracking development

Text A

For a child born dead

What ceremony can we fit
You into now? If you had come
Out of a warm and noisy room
To this, there'd be an opposite
5   For us to know you by. We could
Imagine you in lively mood

And then look at the other side,
The mood drawn out of you, the breath
Defeated by the power of death.
10   But we have never seen you stride
Ambitiously the world we know.
You could not come and yet you go.

But there is nothing now to mar
Your clear refusal of our world.
15 Not in our memories can we mould
You or distort your character.
Then all our consolation is
That grief can be as pure as this.

Elizabeth Jennings

1 To which genre does this text belong? Be prepared to defend your answer.

2 Is there an oppositional pattern in the text (see the application examples in this and the previous chapter for an idea of this)? Support your answer with reference to the text.

3 Are there repeated words and ideas in this text and what pattern emerges as a result? Why do you think the poet wrote this text? At which point in the text is her intention the clearest?

4 What are your feelings as you read the text? Do you laugh or feel sad as you read it? Do your feelings change as you read the text? Say why.

Text B

A terrible scream—a prolonged yell of horror and anguish burst out of the silence of the moor. That frightful cry turned the blood to ice in my veins.

"Oh my God!" I gasped. "What is it? What does it mean?"

5 Holmes sprang to his feet, and I saw his dark, athletic outline at the door of the hut, his shoulders stooping, his head thrust forward, his face peering into the darkness.

"Hush!" he whispered. "Hush!"

The cry had been loud on account of its vehemence, but
10 it had pealed out from somewhere far off on the shadowy plain. Now it burst upon our ears, nearer, louder, and more urgent than before.

"Where is it?" Holmes whispered; and I knew from the thrill of his voice that he, the man of iron, was shaken to the
15 soul. "Where is it, Watson?"

"There I think." I pointed into the darkness.

"No, there!"

Again the agonized cry swept through the silent night, louder and much near than ever. And a new sound mingled
20 with it, a deep, muttered rumble, musical and yet menacing,

rising and falling like the low, constant murmur of the sea.

"The hound!" cried Holmes. "Come, Watson, come! Great heavens, if we are too late!"

25 He had started running swiftly over the moor, and I had followed at his heels. But now from somewhere among the broken ground immediately in front of us there came one last despairing yell and then a dull, heavy thud. We halted and listened. Not another sound broke the heavy silence of the windless night.

30 Blindly we ran through the gloom, blundering against boulders, forcing our way through gorse bushes, panting up hills and rushing down slopes, heading always in the direction whence those dreadful sounds had come. At every rise Holmes looked eagerly round him, but the shadows

35 were thick upon the moor and nothing moved upon its dreary face.

"Can you see anything?

"Nothing."

"But hark, what is that?"

40 A low moan had fallen upon our ears. There it was again upon our left! On that side a ridge of rocks ended in a sheer cliff which overlooked a stone-strewn slope. On its jagged face was spread-eagled some dark, irregular object. As we ran towards it, the vague outline hardened into a

45 definite shape. It was a prostrate man face downward upon the ground, the head doubled under him at a horrible angle, the shoulders rounded and the body hunched together as if in the act of throwing a somersault. So grotesque was the attitude that I could not for the instant realize that that moan

50 had been the passing of his soul. Not a whisper, not a rustle, rose now from the dark figure over which we stooped. Holmes laid his hand upon him and held it up with an exclamation of horror. The gleam of the match which he struck shone upon his clotted fingers and upon the ghastly pool which

55 widened slowly from the crushed skull of the victim.

Extract from The Hound of the Baskervilles
by Sir Arthur Conan Doyle

1 The passage begins with a terrible scream. How does this set the tone for the rest of the text? Identify other words related to sound in the passage. How do they contribute to the mood of the text?

2 In what ways are Holmes's and Watson's feelings intensified in the course of the text? Show evidence of this through changes in the language used to describe their feelings.

Chapter 20
HOW TO ORGANIZE AND WRITE THE ESSAY

In order to do well in the Unseen, analysing the text
in detail is not enough. Students must also be able to
express their ideas coherently and persuasively. This
section focuses on practical strategies in writing the
Literature essay.

Chapter outline

20.1 Skills in the analysis of text

20.2 Skills in the organization of an essay

20.3 Sample essays and commentary

The aim of practical criticism

Before you start writing an essay, it is important to keep in mind
the two main aims of practical criticism. In general, the Unseen
section of the examination paper tests the following two skills:

(a) the ability to critique and analyse the text while displaying
     keen sensitivity to the techniques used;

(b) the ability to communicate your argument coherently to
     the examiner through clear writing and effective
     organization.

Why is it important to organize the essay?

In general, it is both your ability to analyse the text and your
ability to organize and write your essay well which will determine
the grade you will get. The following table refers to the Unseen
assessment rubrics prepared by the University of Cambridge
Local Examinations Syndicate for the GCE 'N' and 'O' level
Literature in English examinations. Familiarize yourself with the
skills you will need in order to do well.

Band descriptors for the Unseen

Level	Grade for Normal	Grade for Express	Description of analytical skills	Description of writing skills
Level 1: Comprehension	E to C	F to D	• Superficial understanding of the text demonstrated largely through paraphrase. • Some misreading of the text. • Candidate does not respond fully to the demands of the question.	• Inappropriate substantiation. • Manages to communicate with some difficulty. • Expression may be hampered by lack of clarity.
Level 2: Interpretation	B	C	• Shows sound basic understanding of the text and how to respond to it. • The question is addressed. • There is some evidence of analysis and evaluation though these may be brief, mechanical or naïve.	• Shows some engagement, and substantiates with appropriate references to the text. • The candidate communicates clearly and puts forward a coherent argument.
Level 3: Analysis	A	B	• Competent grasp of subject matter. Evidence of analysis and evaluation which is likely to reflect conscientiousness rather than sophistication. • Answer is related to the question but may not address some of the key issues. • Evidence of close reading though this may not be sustained throughout the answer.	• The candidate makes a personal response to the text, often providing relevant substantiation. • Answer pursues a thorough, though rather unsophisticated argument. • Work is generally coherent and clear, though it may lack polish and subtlety of expression.

Level	Grade for Normal	Grade for Express	Description of analytical skills	Description of writing skills
Level 4: Insight	A+	A	• Intelligent grasp of subject matter. Answer demonstrates a freshness of insight. Good analysis and evaluation of content and presentation, and where appropriate, evidence of ability to critically appreciate the text. • Well focused on the question and addresses most of its key issues.	• Active and close engagement with the text. Sensitive and informed personal response. • Ideas developed effectively and well supported by textual evidence. • Answer reflects a highly coherent argument and clarity of thought and expression.

Copyright "Unseen Band Descriptors", Singapore Examinations and Assessment Board, 2006

According to the table above, a good Literature student must show two qualities:

- a close engagement with the text and
- an ability to communicate a coherent argument.

Each of these aspects will be treated in detail in the following sections.

20.1 Skills in the analysis of text

Displaying a close engagement with the text in the essay

In general, there are four levels of analytical skills you should attempt to display in your writing:

- a clear awareness of the text's meaning,
- a logical interpretation of the text,
- a detailed analysis and evaluation of the text, and
- finally, an insightful response to the text.

 Method—How can we demonstrate each of these levels in the essay?

(1) Comprehension

Try to spend no more than five minutes reading through and analysing the text before you start writing. After reading the text through once, immediately **jot down your impression of the text's meaning**:

- what it is about,
- its genre/theme,
- its mood, and
- its themes and issues.

The reason for doing this is that most of the questions in the Unseen will relate to your understanding of at least one of these components: the meaning of the text, the mood of the text and the issues highlighted by the text. If you are unsure of what the text is about after your first or second reading, attempt the second unseen text offered in the examination paper instead. This is because getting the right meaning is crucial to achieving at least a pass grade in the paper. In fact, one of the main reasons students do not do well in the Unseen is that they fail to spend adequate time understanding what the text is about. For example, it would be difficult to score in an unseen essay if you wrote about the sense of despair and sorrow in a text when the story is actually meant to be comical and ironic.

(2) Interpretation

Having understood the general meaning of the text, you should then try to **interpret the text**. Interpretation basically implies that you need to go beyond a superficial reading and begin to *question specific words, ideas or values* posed by the text. One useful strategy to adopt is the "Why X and not Y?" formula.

As you read the text, highlight any interesting words in it and then ask yourself why the writer chose that word instead of another. For example, in the poem by Robert Hayden called "Those Winter Sundays", you might want to ask yourself why the writer chose to set his poem in winter rather than summer. Could this be to convey a certain mood? Could he be implying something about his family since Sunday represents rest day or family day? When you think about why a writer uses a specific word instead of another, you become more aware and sensitive to the skills involved in crafting a poem or piece of prose.

(3) Analysis

Many students are able to demonstrate a clear understanding of the text and to go on to explain its implied meaning (interpretation). However, what is often neglected is a **detailed analysis of the text**. This consists of two components: analysis of the techniques used by the writer to achieve an effect and the ability to track patterns and development of character or mood in the text.

(a) Identifying techniques
As you read the text, try to **pick out various techniques and devices** used by the writer. Keep in mind, however, that you should

not just mention that a technique exists. More importantly, you must **state what the purpose of the technique is and how it affects the reader**.

For example, in the poem "In Memoriam VII" by Alfred Tennyson reproduced on the next page, one way of explaining a technique is as follows: "Alliteration is used in 'On the bald street breaks the blank day'. Here, the heavy 'b' consonant sound is repeated, thus contributing to the bleak mood of the poem (contribution/purpose)."

(b) **Tracking development**

As you analyse poetry or prose, you should also try to **pick out trends or changes in language, tone or mood**. Ask yourself whether the words have become stronger, more intense and why.

An example of a trend statement based on the poem "In Memoriam VII" is as follows: "For example, in the first stanza, the poet looks back at the past in the phrase 'my heart was used to beat'. This shows that he longs for the happy times he had with his lover. The word 'used' also indicates a tinge of regret on his part. In the third stanza, his tone becomes heavier. The rainy weather creates a bleak mood and even the tone seems more mournful, as indicated by the phrase 'ghastly through the drizzling rain'."

Note that the writer points out how the language indicates a change in the mood of the poem and tone of the speaker.

(4) **Insight and response**

An excellent essay is able to go a step further by **offering an insight into the text**. This refers to the ability to step out of the text to give a philosophical interpretation of what the text may be saying about human nature and the world (refer to Chapter 18). The ability to express an insight requires keen sensitivity to the text and a sharp eye for detail. For example, in the sample paragraph on page 226, the writer is able to make an insightful comment on the depth of pain felt when one reflects on the past. In order to attain insight, you need to train your eyes and mind to read between the lines. One way to start is by doing more practice exercises and by cultivating critical reading skills each time you pick up a book!

Point to note

Response must be supported by textual evidence.

One danger in giving a response is to make it too personal. Do not preach or make subjective comments when giving a response. For example, on reading a poem about war, do not write about your personal opinions on the issue of war. Instead, refer closely to the text and respond to the language, imagery and ideas the writer conveys through the poem. A good way to think about providing a response is to see yourself as representing a community of readers. Your response should be objective, empathetic and, more importantly, supported by textual evidence.

Application example

For example, let us examine a sample paragraph answer to a poem. Each of the four areas highlighted will be explained in greater detail following this sample.

In Memoriam VII

Dark house, by which once more I stand
    Here in the long unlovely street,
    Doors, where my heart was used to beat
So quickly, waiting for a hand,

5   A hand that can be clasped no more —
    Behold me, for I cannot sleep,
    And like a guilty thing I creep
At earliest morning to the door.

He is not here; but far away
10   The noise of life begins again,
    And ghastly through the drizzling rain
On the bald street breaks the blank day.

                    Alfred Tennyson

Question: What is the mood of the poem?

Sample paragraph answer:

(1) *Begins with a focused introduction which demonstrates a clear understanding of the text's **general meaning***

(2) *Displays sensitivity to language through **interpretation***

(3) *Evidence of **analysis**: explains techniques used and identifies trends*

(4) *Concludes with a personal **insight** and response*

The mood of the poem is bleak and sad. It starts off in a nostalgic mood and moves to a depressing one. For example, in the first stanza, the poet looks back at the past in the phrase "my heart was used to beat". This shows that he longs for the happy times he had with his lover. The word "used" also indicates a tinge of regret on his part. In the third stanza, his tone becomes heavier. The rainy weather creates a bleak mood and even the tone seems more mournful, as indicated by the phrase "ghastly through the drizzling rain". The heavy mood at the end is conveyed through the alliteration in the final line: "On the bald street breaks the blank day", which repeats the heavy "b" consonant sound, thus contributing to the bleak mood of the poem. The shift in mood indicates the degree of pain within the speaker. The increasing and intensifying sense of nostalgia helps the reader develop sympathy for the speaker of the poem. As the speaker reflects on his past, feelings of pain and regret surface and overwhelm him.

20.2 Skills in the organization of an essay

Besides displaying a close engagement with the text in your essay, you need to communicate a clear and coherent argument. In general, a good Literature essay should be organized into three distinct sections.

(1) The introduction

Always **start your essay with a statement which immediately answers the question and which states your standpoint**. Then, note down the points you will be making in the body of the essay. For example, in answer to the question "Examine how the sense of tension is created in the text", a typical introductory paragraph might read:

> The sense of tension is gradually built up as the text progresses. Even though the tone is light-hearted in the beginning, a disturbing sense of coming disruption gradually intensifies. This is created through the use of various techniques in the text such as lighting, mood, choice of words and setting.

Notice that in this paragraph, the first sentence expresses the main point that the student is going to make in the essay—that the "tension is gradually built up". In the second sentence, the student states her overall view of the text structure and then goes on to summarize the evidence in support of her view in her third sentence. Thus, **an organized introduction** consists of three components:

- a clear assertion which forms the basis of your essay;
- an overall view of the point or issue; and
- a summary of the key points which will serve as evidence in support of your view.

(2) The body

The body of your essay consists of the main points you mentioned in the introduction. You should organize it into about five to eight paragraphs, with each paragraph making a clear point supporting the initial assertion. A useful acronym to remember when writing the body and the conclusion is the **PEEP** principle: *point, evidence, elaboration* and *personal response*.

(a) Point

Begin the first sentence of a paragraph with a point that answers the question. One method of ensuring that your answers are to the point is to underline the key word of the question and then make it a habit to repeat that key word in your point. For example, if a question asks: "What is your impression of character X?", your first sentence should read, "My impression of character X is ..." You should always make it a habit to keep that key word in mind as you write your essay and to repeat it or another word with a similar meaning throughout your essay. For example, the first sentence of another paragraph could begin with "My view of character X is ..." In this way, your essay will be organized and focused yet will not sound monotonous and repetitive.

(b) Evidence

Every major point you make should be supported by evidence from the text. There are two forms of evidence you can use:

(i) One form is a **direct quote** from the text. For example, you could say: "I think character X has a courageous, admirable personality as indicated by the sentence, 'Mr X stared at the thief, refusing to budge.'"

(ii) The other form of evidence is a **paraphrase** of the text. For example, a variation of the previous example would read, "I think character X is both courageous and admirable as during the incident he firmly stood his ground in spite of the threats he received from the thief."

Keep in mind that the more evidence you can provide to support your point, the stronger your point will be. For example, a sentence that reads, "The atmosphere in the text appears gloomy and cold as suggested by the phrases 'ancient ruins', 'stone walls', 'barren island', 'dark clouds'" will sound stronger than a sentence with only one example, such as, "The atmosphere in the text appears gloomy and cold as seen in the fact that the story is set on a 'barren island'." Therefore, in your planning stage, try to always link words or expressions that convey a similar meaning, mood or attitude so that when you write your essay you will be able to easily provide more than one example to support your point.

(c) **Elaboration**

Besides making a point and providing evidence to support it, you will need to elaborate on your point. This means that you need to **explain how your evidence links to and proves the point you have made**. An example of such a statement would read:

> *My impression of character Y is that he is an insecure person. For example, he constantly looks around him and clutches a stick as if expecting someone to pounce on him at any moment. His constant uncertainty shows the degree of tension and anxiety within him.*

Notice that in the last sentence, the word "shows" links the evidence with the point. Note also that the elaboration sounds logical and convincing. If the writer had said, "My impression of character Y is that he is an insecure person. For example, he constantly stares at the floor. This shows the degree of tension within him", the last sentence would not sound convincing for two reasons. Firstly, there is no logical connection. What has staring at the floor to do with insecurity? And secondly, the writer has failed to give a clear, detailed explanation.

Thus, when you elaborate, you should always aim to provide logical and clear reasons for your points. In fact, the more detailed your elaboration is, the more convincing your point will be. You could begin your elaboration of the evidence with such common phrases as "This shows", "This reveals", "This conveys the idea that", etc, and then go on to state what the evidence shows.

(d) **Personal response**

A response basically means that you should express how you feel towards the character or event. For example, do you sympathize with, admire, feel angry about the character or event? If you do, explain why you feel this way. This implies that you need to use words such as "admire", "dislike", "empathize with", "identify with", "disgusted". An example of a response statement would read:

I think character X has a courageous, admirable personality as indicated by the sentence, "Mr X stared at the thief, refusing to budge." This illustrates how firm he could be even in the midst of danger, causing us to <u>admire</u> his inner strength.

Note that it is not always necessary to write a response at the end of each paragraph. However, you should at least give a response as part of the conclusion to your essay. Secondly, your response should be one that is well supported by textual evidence. Write as though you are representing the views of the general reader.

(3) The conclusion

So far, what you have seen is how to make a detailed analysis of the text. Now, look at how to conclude your essay. You could do the following:

- Reiterate the major claim or argument of your essay. This is especially helpful since most Literature essays are argumentative in nature and stronger essays are those which are convincing.
- Summarize the key points you have made in your essay.
- Provide a philosophical insight and summative response to the issues raised in the text (refer to Chapter 18 for details on how to do this).

A note about quoting from the text

It is very important that you substantiate your points with evidence (particularly quotations) from the text. However, you should keep in mind these two suggestions when quoting:

(1) Quotes used should add value to the point made and not merely repeat the point.

For example, compare the following statements. Which is better?

Example A	Example B
When Romeo sees Juliet for the first time, he falls in love with her. For example, he says: "Did my heart love till now? Forswear it sight / For I ne'er saw true beauty till this night." When Romeo sees Juliet, he realizes that she is probably the most beautiful girl he has seen and thus becomes deeply attracted to her.	When Romeo sees Juliet for the first time, the evidence that his love is an infatuation is clear. For example, the phrase "true beauty" in the lines: "Did my heart love till now? Forswear it sight / For I ne'er saw true beauty till this night" appears to be an exaggeration as it is hard to believe how anyone can understand true beauty so quickly. Furthermore, this infatuation is based on his "sight"—he loves her for her external beauty rather than appreciating her for her personality or character.

A key difference between example A and example B is that the quote in example A simply repeats the point made in the first sentence whereas the same quote in example B substantiates the point made in the first sentence. Also, the sentence following the quote in example A is simply a paraphrase of the quotation. On the other hand, the sentence following the quote in example B explains and analyses specific words in the quote to provide a deeper insight into the character in the text.

(2) As far as possible, quotes should be included within the sentence or point made. Do not simply start a sentence with a quote.

For example, compare the following statements. Which is better?

Example A	Example B
"So shows a snowy dove trooping with crows"—this is a metaphorical statement which compares Juliet to a dove and implies she is both innocent and beautiful at the same time. Thus, Shakespeare shows us the qualities which attract Romeo to Juliet when he sees her for the first time.	Shakespeare shows us the extent of Romeo's awe when he sees Juliet for the first time through the use of the metaphor which compares Juliet to a "snowy dove trooping with crows". The dove connotes both innocence and beauty at the same time and it is these qualities which capture Romeo's attention.

In example A, the student begins with a quote. As readers, we are thus unclear about the point she is making until the end of the paragraph. Also, the quote exists as a statement on its own; this appears awkward and unsophisticated and gives the impression that the student is making notes rather than developing an argument. On the other hand, the student in example B begins with a point that is then substantiated with the quote. The quote is incorporated very neatly into the sentence, making it seem fluid and coherent.

20.3 Sample essays and commentary

Having looked at the skills needed for analysing a text and writing the essay, let us now examine three sample student essays. The text for the samples is taken from "The Man Who Lived Underground" by Richard Wright and can be found in Section VI (page 274).

 **Group work**

Work in a group of four.

(1) Read the text—an extract from "The Man Who Lived Underground"—and then attempt to answer the following two questions. Do NOT read the sample essays yet.

 Q1: How is tension introduced and developed in the text?

 Q2: What is your impression of the main character?

(2) Next, read the three sample student essays. The students are from a Secondary Four Express class. Using the unseen rubrics provided at the beginning of this chapter, give each essay a grade.

(3) Then read the marker's commentary at the end of this chapter and discuss whether you agree or disagree with the opinions expressed. Share your views with the other groups in class.

(4) At the end of this exercise, compare the sample essays with your group's essay. Which student essay is closest to yours in terms of style? With reference to the band descriptors, what grade should you get? Finally, identify five ways by which you can improve your essay.

Student essay 1—by Paul

Q1 The mood in the text is very tense. The story begins with the main character trying to hide. "I've got to hide," he tells himself. He later proceeds to the middle of the street. He constantly thinks that the policemen are after him. I feel that he is very strange. He keeps getting worried for no reason and keeps wanting to hide. His behaviour is very weird. Next he finds a manhole and jumps into it thinking that this will help him escape from the police.

 The situation is very tense because the manhole is black. "Water rustled in the black depths." He later jumps into the hole but we are not sure where the hole leads to. He hangs inside there waiting for the police to pass by but each time he keeps feeling that he is going to get caught anytime. He hangs inside the hole for a long time with his fingertips. Then he slowly tries to let his body sink so that he can feel the floor. However the current appears very strong and it is as if it can sweep him away anytime. Luckily, he manages to grab hold of a hole in the wall and steady himself. However, the tension is not over yet. The most tense moment in the passage occurs in the fourth paragraph. "They had found him! Looming above his head in the rain, a white face hovered over the hole." The main character thinks that the police have caught him only to find out later that he was mistaken. It is also quite weird that even when the police go away he can remain in the hole thinking. Most people would have taken the opportunity to get away. This shows that the man does not have any common sense. He is most probably a crazy person who has escaped from an asylum.

Q2 My impression of the main character is that he is very strange. He behaves in a very unusual manner. For example, he keeps repeating himself. He keeps telling himself "I've got to hide". Why does he keep feeling he has to hide—most probably it is because he has done something wrong. I think he may have committed a crime such as robbing a bank and now he feels very guilty and feels that he needs to run away. He seems to be very afraid of the police. Every time he hears a siren he jumps in fright thinking they are going to catch him. This again tells us that he is very guilty.

I also think that he can't think very straight. He is not very intelligent. He could have hidden anywhere in the street but he chooses a hole. He could have gone into a shop or gone into one of the houses but instead he chooses to go into a hole. How anyone can remain in a smelly black hole with water for such a long time puzzles me. Most probably the man may have been drinking—that is why he can't think so clearly.

The whole story is about a man who is trying to run away from the police but the man goes through such torment just because he wants to hide from them. When he hears the car, he describes it like the hum of the plane. This again shows that he cannot think clearly, for how is it possible for a car to sound like a plane? I felt very scared for the man when I read the passage. When the man was in the hole, he was in a very dangerous position. For example, it says that he hung for a long time to the rim and then later he dropped into the water. The current was very strong and this made his head hit the wall. He even wondered whether he was going to die. Luckily with some effort, he managed to steady himself and stand in the water. This story shows me that when we do something wrong, it is sometimes better to own up than run and hide.

Grade: _____

Reasons:

Student essay 2—by Devi

Q1 The writer introduces the tension in the beginning with the words "I've got to hide". This already arouses a sense of curiosity in the reader. We are not sure what the speaker is trying to hide from. The speaker is also not given a name, which creates a sense of mystery about him. As the story goes on, we are made aware that the speaker is trying to hide from the police. He debates within himself about whether he should hide or surrender. This suggests he is guilty. He has committed a crime. He is therefore a fugitive and this establishes the conflict between the criminal and the authorities.

In the second paragraph, the writer then develops the tension through the use of sound devices. The repetition of the word "siren" adds to a sense of fear in the text because the siren is red, which implies danger. The repeated idea of the man waiting also adds to the sense of suspense because we are not sure whether he will soon get caught.

In the third paragraph, the sense of tension is great when the siren appears to sound very near the man. This forces him to go into the hole. The writer uses animal imagery to show how desperate he is. For example, the phrases "Fist over fist, he let his body sink" and "Frenziedly his fingers clawed" convey the image of a monkey or a wolf. This shows how the act of running away has dehumanized him and how desperate he has become.

In the fourth paragraph, the situation is most tense because despite his escape into the hole, it appears as if the policemen have found him. The use of words like "looming" and "hovered" seem to convey the idea that the authorities have power over him and that his life is in their hands. This causes the reader to feel a great sense of fear for the speaker.

In the final paragraph, the sense of tension is slightly relieved when the policemen eventually leave. However, we continue to feel disturbed for the speaker, who appears to remain in the dank hole and, in fact, seems to feel comfortable remaining there. Ironically however, it is the real world that begins to seem strange to the fugitive. For example, he describes a passing car to be like a plane speeding through a cloud; he also states that "everything seemed strange and unreal under here". This suggests that as the fugitive becomes increasingly used to the idea of running away, the reality of the real world also seems to slip away. This sense of conflict between the world of the fugitive and the real world sustains the mood of tension in the text.

Q2 My impression of the main character is that he is an overly cautious character. In the first paragraph, he constantly repeats to himself that he has to hide. His cautiousness may be observed in the words used to describe his movements such as "crouching in a dark corner", "He crept", "He gritted his teeth". Another evidence of his cautious behaviour can be seen in that he is very observant. While deciding where to hide, he notices vapour coming from a manhole cover and this gives him the idea that he should hide there. The fact that he jumps into the manhole without thinking about the dangers this may pose him later shows that though he is overly cautious, he lacks the ability to think ahead and strategize. It appears as if he lives and reacts to things at the moment.

The second and third paragraphs convey the impression that he has an over-active imagination. For example, when he looks at the manhole, it says that he is "half expecting the cover to leap up again". This suggests that he has a tendency to exaggerate things. Also, he constantly thinks that the police have found him and in fact, he is found to be mistaken several times. In the third paragraph, he starts in terror when the siren sounds near him and thinks the police have found him. This causes him to quickly jump into the hole without thinking. Even when he is in the hole, the descriptions are exaggerated. For example, the water in the hole is described as "watery darkness" and "an ocean of warm, leaping water". The currents are described as so powerful that at one point in the text, he imagines that he will be killed by it. In his panic, his head is battered against the wall and he frenziedly clings to the edges. Only when he manages to calm down and steady himself does he realize that actually the water is only flowing beneath his knees!

Again in the last two paragraphs, the writer repeats the idea that the main character is overly imaginative and even paranoid. For example, he screams to himself that the police have found him when, in fact, they are merely trying to close the manhole cover. In fact, nowhere in the text is there evidence to suggest that the police are actively on the lookout for him. Even when the police have left, he remains in the hole and in semi-darkness for a long time because being underground gives him a greater sense of security than being in the real world with its ever-present danger. The writer uses the current to parallel the sense of fear within the main character. For example, the current described as moving with "fearful velocity" earlier is now described as "streaking" to suggest the greater sense of peace the main character feels when he is away from the real world.

Grade: _____

Reasons:

Student essay 3—by May Lin

Q1 In the beginning of the text, the sense of uncertainty and tension is introduced through the setting of the text. Firstly, the story takes place on a dark night, as expressed by the phrase "dark corner of the vestibule". The repetition of the idea of darkness, for example, the phrases "could see nothing" and "fogged plate glass", adds to the oppressive and gloomy mood of the scene. Secondly, there is also a sense of oppression in the mood. For example, the words "grey", "clogged" and "black" all evoke feelings of being in a hostile environment. This is further accentuated by the fact that it is raining, as indicated by the phrase "swished through the rain". Rain creates a very bleak and gloomy environment and it also foreshadows more dangers to come.

This sense of tension is gradually built up through several techniques, namely, the introduction of the conflict, the development of paranoia in the character, and the use of sound devices.

The conflict is introduced in the first paragraph where the character debates within himself whether he should hide or surrender. The presence of the police intensifies the degree of tension in the scene. This sense of disturbance is added to by the sense of unpredictability about the whole environment. For example, just as he is contemplating his plans, a police car swishes by. We are told later that "a sudden movement" catches his attention.

Later on, the nearness of the siren shocks him. The emphasis on suddenness adds to the sense of uncertainty throughout the text. Also, we note that the main character is in a very dangerous and precarious situation. For example, phrases like "his head was battered" and "his fingers clawed" all show his nervousness and this increasingly intensifies in the situation. The fact that the main character is alone against a hostile, larger organization (the police) creates a greater sense of anxiety in the text.

Next, the development of the paranoia of the main character contributes to the increasing tension in the passage. In the beginning, the man behaves in a collected fashion; for example, in the second paragraph, he plans to hide from the police: "He hatched a tentative plan". Later on, however, he begins to lose his collected frame of mind. For example, in the next paragraph, he "started with terror", emphasizing his already unbalanced frame of mind. Soon his fear overpowers his ability to reason. For example, the mental exclamations "Oh God! They had found him!" reveal his capacity to over-react in moments of great stress.

In addition, the use of sound devices increases the tension of the scene. For example, the passage begins with a quiet setting where the main character crouches in a dark and quiet corner of the vestibule. When he first hears the police car, the onomatopoeic "swish" creates a soft, quick sound illustrating the oncoming presence of the police. Later on, this "swish" sound intensifies to a "hoot" nearer to him. The "hoot" parallels that of an owl which foreshadows imminent doom since the owl is commonly symbolic of death. This sense of disturbance is then added to in the following paragraph where the "hoot" becomes a "scream", as seen in the phrase "He heard a prolonged scream of the brakes". The increasing loudness of the sounds demonstrates the nearness of his captivity and heightens the sense of anxiety felt by the main character and the reader.

Q2 My impression of the main character is that he is an extremely unstable and insecure person.

Firstly, his instability is demonstrated by his paranoia. His fears are unfounded—for example, he gets nervous and agitated easily and through this, the author subtly hints to us that he may be mentally and psychologically unstable. Throughout the passage, we see how the main character reacts to fear. He is so unbalanced in his mind that he sees the policemen as bad people and bullies who will endanger his life. For example, the constant repetition of "I've got to hide" and similar phrases all show how focused he is on running away. Further evidence of this imbalance is seen in the fact that he does not consider the risks or consequences of his actions. For example, he risks his life by hiding in a manhole and at times, the danger is expressed, as in the phrase "He swayed in the dank space". Perhaps his desire to stay in the manhole is symbolic of how trapped in his warped thinking he is.

Secondly, the main character's insecurity is constantly emphasized in the text through the character's monologue, in which we get a glimpse of his state of mind, as well as through the use of rhetorical questions. For instance, the main character constantly talks to himself, saying or thinking, for example, "I've got to hide". This strongly hints to us that something is wrong because normal people do not talk in such an agitated and frustrated manner. Also, he constantly asks himself rhetorical questions such as "but where?" This shows his uncertainty and doubt about himself and his environment. Through his constant self-consciousness, the insecurity of the main character is emphasized.

Thirdly, my impression of the main character is that he is an extremely nervous person. Part of this nervousness can be attributed to his sense of being trapped and outnumbered by hostile forces in his world (such as the police) as well as his own longing to escape. The sense of frustration is brought out at the ending when the cover falls back into place and he heaves a great sigh of relief. However, prior to that, the sense of anxiety and frustration is illustrated through the use of sound effects in the text. For example, "the prolonged scream of the brakes" is likely to be the scream of inner torment as he waits in fear of being caught by the police. Later on, when the police move away, he breathes again but with an "aching chest", implying the intensity and pressure of tension within him.

Finally, in spite of his many flaws, the main character is also a person of courage and fortitude. For example, even though it is stated at the beginning that he is "tired of running and dodging", he never surrenders. Instead, his immense desire to escape and be free can be proved by the fact that not only has he been running away for a long period of time, he is also willing to do anything in order to escape. In fact, the main character becomes more and more like an animal in his desire to escape. For example, words and phrases like "crouching", "crept", "his fingers clawed" all reveal his almost barbaric nature. Yet, this desire to escape reveals his free-spirited nature and his strong will to remain independent, which is worthy of our admiration.

Grade: _____

Reasons:

Marker's comments

Note: These grades and comments are suggestions provided by the authors of this book. They are open to discussion and alternative views.

Comments on student essay 1

Grade: Express = D   Normal = C

Reasons:

- The student shows a basic understanding of the text but the answer is characterized largely by paraphrase. For example, in the second paragraph of his answer to Q1, the student tells step by step the process by which the main character manages to survive in the hole.

- As a result of trying to paraphrase the text, the student does not fully answer the question. Although he manages to give some examples of tension, he does not show how the writer develops and intensifies the sense of tension.

- The student tends to focus on the content of the text rather than the style of the writer. For example, in the second paragraph of his answer to Q1, he states: "The situation is very tense because the manhole is black." A better answer would be one where the student specifically states the technique used by the writer to create tension. For example, a good topic statement could be: "The writer makes the situation tense through the use of setting."

- In the answer to the second question, the student has not attempted to analyse the personality of the main character. The answer is superficial and is characterized by attention to external details. The student could have looked at the external details such as outward behaviour and inferred what this would suggest about the main character's personality.

- Throughout the essay, there is inappropriate substantiation. Although the student manages to communicate his ideas, there is a lack of clarity in this. The use of words like "weird" and "strange" makes the commentary vague and ambiguous. More specific adjectives such as "paranoid", "nervous" and "insecure" would have been more appropriate.

- Finally, the student has a tendency to preach and jump to conclusions without attempting to understand the character fully. For example, the sentences "Most people would have taken the opportunity to get away. This shows that the man does not have any common sense" are examples of sweeping statements that should be avoided.

Comments on student essay 2

Grade: Express = B/B- Normal = A/A-

Reasons:
- The student has a competent grasp of the text and addresses most of the requirements of the question.

- There is evidence of analysis although this tends to be rather unsophisticated. One reason for its lack of sophistication is that her analysis of the text tends to proceed from one paragraph to the next. There is little attempt to link points and evidence from various parts of the text.

- In some parts of the essay, the student shows good insightful analysis. For example, in the third paragraph of her answer to Q1, she is able to identify the animal imagery used. It would have been better if she had elaborated on the effectiveness of such an imagery.

- The student pays attention to the writer's style as in his choice of words, imagery and various techniques such as repetition that are used. It would have been better if, instead of simply identifying the techniques used, the student had also evaluated these techniques. For example, she could have written about why these devices are effective.

- The student's answer is coherent, organized and clear although it may lack subtlety of expression. Examples of statements which could have been better phrased are: "This suggests he is guilty. He has committed a crime. He is therefore a fugitive and this establishes the conflict between the criminal and the authorities." The student could have rephrased these so that the ideas are clearly linked to the key word of the question, "tension". For example, the following statement would have a clearer link to the question: "This suggests that he feels guilty because of the crime he has committed. The sense of tension is established through the central conflict in the text between the criminal and the authorities."

- Finally, although the essay is generally structured into paragraphs, the use of connectives would have made the essay more coherent.

Comments on student essay 3

Grade: Express = A   Normal = A+

Reasons:

- In terms of analysis, the writer shows a close and sensitive response to the text. There is a keen awareness of the various literary devices present in the text. The writer also demonstrates her ability to describe the contribution of certain techniques to the overall mood and sense of the text.

- The writer's sensitivity to language is demonstrated by her ability to pick out repeated ideas, to connect these ideas and show their development in the text.

- The essay as a whole is clearly organized, with the use of connectors linking each paragraph to another.

- The points made are adequately supported by textual evidence and an explanation.

- Lastly, the student uses a wide range of vocabulary which lends clarity to her arguments.

The essay could, however, be improved by taking the following suggestions into account:

(a) Avoiding generalizations and sweeping statements, such as "normal people do not talk in such an agitated and frustrated manner";

(b) Explaining some of the techniques such as rhetorical questions and the use of monologue in more detail, emphasizing the writer's intentions in using these devices;

(c) More analysis on the reader's response to the effects of specific techniques used by the writer, for example, what effect the sound devices have on the reader as he reads the text; and

(d) Ending with a conclusion that sums up the main points of the essay.

On the whole, however, the well-organized, convincing and insightful arguments meet the criteria of the grade.

A more detailed analysis of this "A" grade essay with marker's comments on the side is provided below.

Marker's commentary on student essay 3

Q1: How is tension introduced and developed in the text?

> *Student demonstrates an understanding of the question—she shows how tension is **introduced**. In her second paragraph, she shows how tension is **developed**.*

In the beginning of the text, the sense of uncertainty and tension is introduced through the setting of the text. Firstly, the story takes place on a dark night, as expressed by the phrase "dark corner of the vestibule". The repetition of the idea of darkness, for example, the phrases "could see nothing" and "fogged plate glass", adds to the oppressive and gloomy mood of the scene. Secondly, there is also a sense of oppression in the mood. For example, the words "grey", "clogged" and "black" all evoke feelings of being in a hostile environment. This is further accentuated by the fact that it is raining, as indicated by the phrase "swished through the rain". Rain creates a very bleak and gloomy environment and it also foreshadows more dangers to come.

> *Student makes use of introductory paragraphs before developing her points.*

This sense of tension is gradually built up through several techniques, namely, the introduction of the conflict, the development of paranoia in the character, and the use of sound devices

The conflict is introduced in the first paragraph where the character debates within himself whether he should hide or surrender. The presence of the police intensifies the degree of tension in the scene. This sense of disturbance is added to by the sense of unpredictability about the whole environment. For example, just as he is contemplating his plans, a police car swishes by. We are told later that "a sudden movement" catches his attention.

> *Student shows sensitivity to word choice.*

Later on, the nearness of the siren shocks him. The emphasis on suddenness adds to the sense of uncertainty throughout the text. Also, we note that the main character is in a very dangerous and precarious situation. For example, phrases like "his head was battered" and "his fingers clawed" all show his nervousness and

240

this increasingly intensifies in the situation. The fact that the main character is alone against a hostile, larger organization (the police) creates a greater sense of anxiety in the text.

Next, the development of the paranoia of the main character contributes to the increasing tension in the passage. In the beginning, the man behaves in a collected fashion; for example, in the second paragraph, he plans to hide from the police: "He hatched a tentative plan". Later on, however, he begins to lose his collected frame of mind. For example, in the next paragraph, he "started with terror", emphasizing his already unbalanced frame of mind. Soon his fear overpowers his ability to reason. For example, the mental exclamations "Oh God! They had found him!" reveal his capacity to over-react in moments of great stress.

In addition, the use of sound devices increases the tension of the scene. For example, the passage begins with a quiet setting where the main character crouches in a dark and quiet corner of the vestibule. When he first hears the police car, the onomatopoeic "swish" creates a soft, quick sound illustrating the oncoming presence of the police. Later on, this "swish" sound intensifies to a "hoot" nearer to him. The "hoot" parallels that of an owl which foreshadows imminent doom since the owl is commonly symbolic of death. This sense of disturbance is then added to in the following paragraph where the "hoot" becomes a "scream", as seen in the phrase "He heard a prolonged scream of the brakes". The increasing loudness of the sounds demonstrates the nearness of his captivity and heightens the sense of anxiety felt by the main character and the reader.

Q2: What is your impression of the main character?

My impression of the main character is that he is an extremely unstable and insecure person.

Firstly, his instability is demonstrated by his paranoia. His fears are unfounded—for example, he gets nervous and agitated easily and through this, the author subtly hints to us that he may be mentally and psychologically unstable. Throughout the passage, we see how the main character reacts to fear. He is so unbalanced in his mind that he sees the policemen as bad people and bullies who will endanger his life. For example, the constant repetition of "I've got to hide" and similar phrases all show how focused he is on running away. Further evidence of this imbalance is seen in the fact that he does not consider the risks or consequences of his actions. For example, he risks his life by hiding in a manhole and at times, the danger is expressed, as in the phrase "He swayed in the dank space". Perhaps his desire to stay in the manhole is symbolic of how trapped in his warped thinking he is.

Student is able to connect evidence from various parts of the text and draw the links between them.

Student is able to track development in language.

Student uses connectors to organize ideas and paragraphs.

Student makes insightful comment by relating mythology of the owl to the text.

Student shows ability to connect and show links between words.

Student demonstrates focus by answering the question immediately.

Student uses adjectives to describe personality rather than external characteristics, which shows that she understands the requirements of the question.

Secondly, the main character's insecurity is constantly emphasized in the text through the character's monologue, in which we get a glimpse of his state of mind, as well as through the use of rhetorical questions. For instance, the main character constantly talks to himself, saying or thinking, for example, "I've got to hide". This strongly hints to us that something is wrong because normal people do not talk in such an agitated and frustrated manner. Also, he constantly asks himself rhetorical questions such as "but where?" This shows his uncertainty and doubt about himself and his environment. Through his constant self-consciousness, the insecurity of the main character is emphasized.

Thirdly, my impression of the main character is that he is an extremely nervous person. Part of this nervousness can be attributed to his sense of being trapped and outnumbered by hostile forces in his world (such as the police) as well as his own longing to escape. The sense of frustration is brought out at the ending when the cover falls back into place and he heaves a great sigh of relief. However, prior to that, the sense of anxiety and frustration is illustrated through the use of sound effects in the text. For example, "the prolonged scream of the brakes" is likely to be the scream of inner torment as he waits in fear of being caught by the police. Later on, when the police move away, he breathes again but with an "aching chest", implying the intensity and pressure of tension within him.

Finally, in spite of his many flaws, the main character is also a person of courage and fortitude. For example, even though it is stated at the beginning that he is "tired of running and dodging", he never surrenders. Instead, his immense desire to escape and be free can be proved by the fact that not only has he been running away for a long period of time, he is also willing to do anything in order to escape. In fact, the main character becomes more and more like an animal in his desire to escape. For example, words and phrases like "crouching", "crept", "his fingers clawed" all reveal his almost barbaric nature. Yet, this desire to escape reveals his free-spirited nature and his strong will to remain independent, which is worthy of admiration.

PRACTICE EXERCISES ON POETRY AND PROSE

INTRODUCTION

Included in this section are twenty poems and twenty prose passages which are a combination of Singaporean texts and texts from other countries dealing with a variety of themes. The poems and prose passages are separated into two parts. Each part is further divided into three segments:

POETRY

(1) Guided close reading: Poetry exercises 1 to 5

(2) Four-level question scaffold: Poetry exercises 6 to 10

(3) GCE 'N' and 'O' level past examination unseen questions: Poetry exercises 11 to 20

PROSE

(1) Guided close reading: Prose exercises 1 to 5

(2) Four-level question scaffold: Prose exercises 6 to 10

(3) GCE 'N' and 'O' level past examination unseen questions: Prose exercises 11 to 20

A note on the three segments

(1) Guided close reading

The poems and prose texts in their respective segments each have annotations and questions in boxes at the side(s). The objective behind this is to guide students towards a habit of close reading and of learning to question word choice and various techniques used by the writer. In addition, following each poem or prose passage there are also general and broad questions for discussion. Students may use their answers to the guided questions to answer the broad questions posed.

(2) Four-level question scaffold

The exercises in this segment contain questions arranged according to four levels of analysis based on the Unseen assessment rubrics. Refer to Chapter 20, pages 220 to 226, for more details about these four levels of analysis.

Level 1: Comprehension—this refers to questions related to a basic understanding of the text: what it is about, its genre/theme, its mood, and the issues the text highlights to the reader.

Level 2: Interpretation—this refers to questions which test students' ability to interpret specific words, imagery and ideas posed in the text.

Level 3: Analysis—this refers to questions requiring a detailed analysis of the text. Students are required to analyse techniques used by the writer to achieve effects as well as track patterns and development of character or mood in the text.

Level 4: Insight and response—this refers to questions which encourage students to step out of the text to give a philosophical interpretation to what the text may be saying about human nature and the world (refer to Chapter 18).

(3) GCE 'N' and 'O' level past examination unseen questions

This segment contains GCE 'N' and 'O' level unseen texts and questions on them from the years 2001 to 2005.

Poetry Exercise 1
Guided Close Reading

Who is Sean and what is his relationship with the speaker? Looking at the title, what do you think this poem is about?

How does the writer use the seasons to connote a change in their relationship?

Comment on this interesting choice of word, "pathos"—use a dictionary and find out what it means. Then infer what the speaker is implying about his feelings for Sean.

Explain what the writer is saying in the last two lines of this stanza. What words would you use to describe the tone of the speaker here?

Walking Away
(for Sean)

It is eighteen years ago, almost to the day—
A sunny day with the leaves just turning,
The touch-lines new-ruled—since I watched
    you play
Your first game of football, then, like a satellite
5 Wrenched from its orbit, go drifting away

Behind a scatter of boys. I can see
You walking away from me towards the school
With the pathos of a half-fledged thing set free
Into a wilderness, the gait of one
10 Who finds no path where the path should be.

That hesitant figure, ebbying away
Like a winged seed loosened from its parent
    stem,
Has something I never quite grasp to convey
About nature's give-and-take—the small, the
    scorching
15 Ordeals which fire one's irresolute clay.

I had worse partings, but none that so
Gnaws at my mind still. Perhaps it is roughly
Saying what God alone could perfectly show—
How selfhood begins with a walking away,
20 And love is proved in the letting go.

C. Day Lewis

The poem begins with "It is eighteen years ago". This indicates that the poem is a recollection of a past event. How would you describe the mood of the poem?

Comment on the use of simile in these lines. What is the speaker implying?

The writer uses another interesting phrase "ebbing away". What idea is often associated with this phrase and what does the speaker imply by this? Comment on any other interesting word or words in this stanza.

Further questions for discussion:

1   What do you think this poem is about?

2   What is your impression of the relationship between the speaker and Sean? Support your answer with reference to the text.

3   The poet uses several images to talk about the boy's walking away from his father. What are they and how do these images contribute to the mood of the poem?

Having read the poem once through, state the number of ways this title can be interpreted.

What is the effect of the rhyming words "still" and "until"?

What does the phrase "Contoured by choice" mean? What image comes to your mind? What could the writer be implying?

There are several phrases with unusual word order or grammatical structure. For example, the writer begins a sentence with "And". What other example of unusual word structure can you find? Explain its purpose.

Women without Men

Already ringed by daughters
And no son, they keep
Trying and trying still
And trying until
5   Tired out, afraid of mothering
More women,
They stop.

Contoured by choice,
They manage people over
10   The children they can't imagine
Bearing or diapering. Or the men
They won't concede lives to.
Work pushes old
Age off.

15   Unused to the new,
Some, not knowing
What to do, are afraid,
Though it may be a blessing
That women outlive men,
20   And singleness is theirs
Again.

Leong Liew Geok

What is the meaning of "ringed"? Why do you think the writer has used this word?

Comment on the use of run-on lines in the first stanza. How effective is this?

Who are these "people" they manage? What is their relationship with their husbands? What impression does this give you of the women?

Explain why the poem ends with one word "Again". What is the point the writer is trying to convey? Give reasons.

Further questions for discussion:

1   What is the subject matter of the poem and what is the speaker's feeling or attitude towards the subject matter? Show evidence to support your points.

2   Explain the phrases "ringed by daughters" *(line 1)* and "Contoured by choice" *(line 8)*. How do these phrases add to the significance of the subject matter? What other interesting words can you find in the poem? Explain the implied meanings of these words.

3   How do you feel about the women in the poem? Why?

Poetry Exercise 3
Guided Close Reading

Why do you think the writer begins each stanza with "I am …"?

What is the difference between the colour of the carriage and the colour of smoke? Why does the writer repeat the word "colour"? What other examples of repetition are there? Explain them.

How would you describe the rhyme scheme in the first and second stanzas? What is the effect of this?

Who do you think "they" refers to? What does the speaker mean when he says "lest one day / I dare to grow"?

The Man in the Bowler Hat

I am the unnoticed, the unnoticeable man:
The man who sat on your right in the morning
    train:
The man you looked through like a
    windowpane:
The man who was the colour of the carriage,
    the colour of the mounting
5 Morning pipe smoke.

I am the man too busy with a living to live,
Too hurried and worried to see and smell and
    touch:
The man who is patient too long and obeys
    too much
And wishes too softly and seldom.

10 I am the man they call the nation's backbone,
Who am boneless—playable catgut, pliable
    clay:
The Man they label Little lest one day
I dare to grow.

I am the rails on which the moment passes,
15 The megaphone for many words and voices:
I am the graph diagram,
Composite face.

I am the led, the easily-fed,
The tool, the not-quite-fool,
20 The would-be-safe-and-sound,
The uncomplaining bound,
The dust fine-ground,
Stone-for-a-statue waveworn pebble-round.

A.S.J. Tessimond

What is the difference between "unnoticed" and "unnoticeable"?

The writer employs wordplay with the words "living" and "live". What is he saying in these lines?

Analyse the play of words with "playable" and "pliable". What is the difference? What is the writer suggesting?

Explain the metaphors "rails", "megaphone", "graph diagram". What do they imply? What connects all these images?

The writer employs the technique of "listing" in giving a continuous series of description. What is the purpose of this?

Further questions for discussion:

1   In the first stanza, identify and describe in your own words, two distinguishing actions of the man in the bowler hat and say if the actions are significant.

2 Do you think he has the qualities of a (a) leader or (b) follower? Show evidence to support your points.

3 A bowler hat was worn in England by businessmen in the past. What do you think the writer is saying about life in modern society? Give reasons for your answer.

Poetry Exercise 4
Guided Close Reading

Describe the situation in the poem in terms of who is writing to whom. What is the effect of framing this poem in the form of a letter?

Based on this stanza, can you say what the nature of the conflict between the speaker and his landlord was?

The writer employs juxtaposition by contrasting the speaker's behaviour with that of the other tenants. What is the purpose of this?

Did the landlord treat all his tenants equally? Give some reasons why he did not extend the speaker's lease.

To My landlord

This final notice, *fait accompli**—it
only shows how much attention you gave
my last appeal, the moral grounds.

I wasn't asking for a lease in perpetuity,
5 like your own titles, all freehold,
in fee simple. Just a few more years.

Never behind with my rent, I've kept
your house (mine too?) in good condition.
got along well with my neighbours.

10 Even vacating, I will have left your
premises no worse than when I came,
discharged every single obligation.

Consider some of your other tenants—who
bring your name into disrepute, still
15 enjoying your house a longer lease.

You didn't think to rap them earlier—
the troublemakers of the earth? Easier
to bless the meek—and then dismiss?

Explain why the speaker uses the term "fait accompli" here. What does he mean?

Find out the meaning of the terms "lease in perpetuity", "titles", "freehold" and "in fee simple".

Why do you think the speaker describes the house as "mine too"?

Why do you think the stanzas in this poem are each structured in three lines? How does this complement the tone of the poem?

Who are these "troublemakers" the speaker is referring to? What contradictions in the landlord's behaviour does the speaker criticize?

---

* Fait accompli: a thing that has been done and cannot be altered [French origin]

Do you think "sufficient notice" was given? Identify two other examples of verbal irony and say what the speaker is implying. What is the effect of employing verbal irony in the poem?

20 I find it hard to understand.
more so your sense of humour—
What man proposes, God disposes.

This note will not make a difference—
that's certain! I know you are
all-powerful etc. so, good day, SIR!

25 Oh! I thank you all the same
for the sufficient notice—enough
to say goodbye to the neighbours.

Ee Tiang Hong

Describe the tone of the speaker at the beginning of the poem. Does the tone change towards the end? Why?

Further questions for discussion:

1   What is the tone of the speaker (that is, his attitude to the person he addresses) and what does it tell you about his feelings?

2   What is your impression of the speaker in the poem? Support your answer with reference to the poem.

3   Ee Tiang Hong (1933–90) was a Malaysian poet who emigrated to Australia in 1975. One of his reasons for leaving was that he felt he was discriminated against racially. Why do you think the poet chose to discuss his relationship with his country of birth in these terms?

4   How does the poet convey sarcasm and develop the sense of frustration as the poem progresses? What do you think his message is?

How would you describe the rhyme scheme in this poem? How does this rhyme scheme contribute to the overall meaning and mood of the poem?

What is the simile used in these first lines? Comment also on the use of alliteration.

Explain the switch between the objective overview description in the first stanza and the first-person description in the second stanza. What is the purpose of this switch?

What is the purpose of repeating the colour "green"? Identify words or phrases which connote colour. What is the effect of this?

The writer uses two conditional "if" statements here—why do you think the writer uses them?

The writer employs hyperbole or exaggeration in the phrase "All went lame; all blind"—what is the effect of this? Pick out other examples of hyperbole in the poem.

Comment on the use of run-on lines in the second stanza.

Why does the third stanza only consist of two lines unlike the others? The writer also lists three consecutive verbs "guttering, choking, drowning"— what is the effect of this?

Why do you think the writer has chosen to use an old Latin proverb in the last lines of this poem to bring his message across?

Dulce et Decorum Est

Bent double, like old beggars under sacks,
Knock-kneed, coughing like hags, we cursed
    through sludge,
Till on the haunting flares we turned out backs
And towards our distant rest began to trudge.
5 Men marched asleep. Many had lost their boots
But limped on, blood-shod. All went lame; all
    blind;
Drunk with fatigue; deaf even to the hoots
Of gas shells dropping softly behind.

Gas! GAS! Quick, boys!—An ecstasy of fumbling,
10 Fitting the clumsy helmets just in time;
But someone still was yelling out and stumbling
And flound'ring like a man in fire or lime ...
Dim, through the misty panes and thick green
    light,
As under a green sea, I saw him drowning.

15 In all my dreams, before my helpless sight,
He plunges at me, guttering, choking, drowning.

If in some smothering dreams you too could pace
Behind the wagon that we flung him in,
And watch the white eyes writhing in his face,
20 His hanging face, like a devil's sick of sin;
If you could hear, at every jolt, the blood
Come gargling from the froth-corrupted lungs,
Obscene as cancer, bitter as the cud
Of vile, incurable sores on innocent tongues, —
25 My friend, you would not tell with such high zest
To children ardent for some desperate glory,
The old Lie: *Dulce et decorum est
Pro patria mori.**

Wilfred Owen

* From a Latin quote meaning "it is sweet and fitting to die for one's country."

Further questions for discussion:

1   "Bent double, like old beggars under sacks ..." What are the literal and implied meanings of this line?

2   By analysing the first stanza of the poem, describe your impression of the soldiers. Give reasons for your answer.

3   Analyse the sound devices and rhythmic structure of the poem. State how they contribute to the mood and increasing tension in the poem.

4   Comment on the use of light imagery in the poem. What is the effect of this?

5   How does the writer develop the sense of irony in the poem? How effective is this? Support your answer with reference to the text.

6   As you reach the end of the poem, what do you think the poet's message is? Do you agree with his views? Why?

Poetry Exercise 6
Four-level Question Scaffold

Boys in Jungle Green

These are our common boys in jungle green
Upon whom we trust a role at home.
For will and muscle to grow on bone,
Young men will have to be brave men.

5   The parade ground is harsh bitumen
And harder still the corporal's lash.
Hours drag like a sacrifice ...
Tomorrow is the same refrain.

Jungle, river, valley and hill
10   The elemental lash of rain and sun.
Despite blisters, cramps, faintings even,
The mud on your face is soil, your soil.

Here you will dig a trench today
So your neighbour will know
15 You're doing it for a tomorrow
You shall greet a five each day.

Rooting green and steady
Among the people sent
That they may know, when we all plant
20 Tomorrow grows on our tree.

So these our boys in jungle green
Shall secure our home.
Will and muscle shall grow on bone
And young men be brave men.

Robert Yeo

Level 1: Comprehension

1 a What do you understand by the reference to "jungle green" in line 1? Explain in one sentence what this poem is about.

b When the poet writes, in line 12, "The mud on your face is soil, your soil", who is he addressing?

Level 2: Interpretation

2 Explain what is meant by "Tomorrow grows on our tree", in line 20. What image connects the words "rooting" and "plant"? Why does the writer use these images?

Level 3: Analysis

3 a Pick out words or phrases whose sounds complement the meaning of the poem. Identify the sound devices and say how effectively they contribute to its meaning.

b The ideas in lines 2 and 3 are repeated in lines 23 and 24, but with a difference. How effective is the repetition?

Level 4: Insight and response

4 Does the writer intend his poem to be a patriotic one? How does the style of writing convey his attitude towards the issue of national service? Support your answer with reference to the text.

Do not go gentle into that good night

Do not go gentle into that good night,
Old age should burn and rave at close of day;
Rage, rage against the dying of the light.

Though wise men at their end know dark is right,
5 Because their words had forked no lightning they
Do not go gentle into that good night.

Good men, the last wave by, crying how bright
Their frail deeds might have danced in a green bay,
Rage, rage against the dying of the light.

10 Wild men who caught and sang the sun in flight,
And learn, too late, they grieved it on its way,
Do not go gentle into that good night.

Grave men, near death, who see with blinding sight
Blind eyes could blaze like meteors and be gay,
15 Rage, rage against the dying of the light.

And you, my father, there on the sad height,
Curse, bless me now with your fierce tears, I pray.
Do not go gentle into that good night.
Rage, rage against the dying of the light.

Dylan Thomas

Level 1: Comprehension

1 **a** In your own words, state what the poem is about.

   b Who is the speaker addressing in this poem? What is
       the speaker telling this person?

Level 2: Interpretation

2 **a** What do "night" and "light" represent in the poem?
       What clues do you use?

b The writer describes different types of men in the poem—wise men, good men, wild men and grave men. What does he say about the men of each type and their attitude towards death?

3 **a** Pick out images (similes or metaphors) in the poem and explain their contribution to the poem's meaning.

b The writer employs the use of antithesis in the poem—this refers to words or ideas in a phrase which are directly opposed to each other. One example of this is: "Blind eyes could blaze like meteors". Pick out other examples of antithesis and comment on the effectiveness of their use.

c The poem is structured in the form of a villanelle. The is a French verse form characterized by the following:

- nineteen lines organized into five three-line stanzas and ending with a four-line stanza.
- A regular rhyme scheme of this structure: **aba aba aba aba aba abaa**.
- The first line of the first stanza is repeated as the last line of the second and the fourth stanza while the third line of first stanza is repeated in the third and the fifth stanza. These two lines are then repeated as a couplet in the last two lines of the final stanza.*

Why do you think the poet has written this poem in the form of a villanelle? Support your answer with reference to the text.

Level 4: Insight and response

4 **a** Would you describe this poem as inspiring? Why?

b How does the writer convey the sense of persuasion in this poem? Support your answer with textual evidence.

---

* Source: Murfin, R. and Ray, S. The Bedford Glossary of Critical and Literary Terms. New York: Bedford Books, 1998.

Night Shift

another night, youre making your round
every half hour, now its 0105, & most
patients are asleep, some snoring loudly
(youd prefer that, actually), Fatimahs gone

5   home already, & for now youre the only
nurse left in charge of this ward / some
time, 0145 or so, someone howls suddenly,
eerie, limbs flail, body contorts, you call

10   for assistance, & soon several colleagues,
doctor, come rushing in, but within minutes,
mr s (a friendly oldman with whom youd
just chatted hours earlier) is pronounced

dead / white sheet over body, toe tagged
with number, body wheeled out to morgue
15   discretely located behind at deserted corner
of hospital, some patients, awake, watch

silently, as one woman starts to sob, mum
bling to herself, so you rub yr eyes, fill out
the details, all necessary paperwork settled,
20   wait for first sliver of light, another day

Yeow Kai Chai

Level 1: Comprehension

1 **a** Identify the person in the poem who is being addressed, providing relevant details like gender, profession and so on.

   b What does the title "Night Shift" mean? In one sentence, state what this poem is about.

Level 2: Interpretation

2 **a** Which group of people is referred to in lines 4 and 5, indicated by "Fatimahs gone / home"?

b Attempt to describe accurately the emotional state of mind of the person on the night shift as the poem progresses.

Level 3: Analysis

3 a Pick out two examples of unusual punctuation in this text. Why do you think the writer uses them and what is the effect of this?

b Pick out two examples of run-on lines in the poem and comment on their effectiveness.

c Many words and phrases in the poem appear ungrammatical because of, for example, the use of abbreviations, the use of the lower case at the beginning of sentences, etc. Suggest reasons why the poem is structured in this manner.

Level 4: Insight and response

4 Does the poem accurately describe the work of a nurse on night shift? What are your various feelings as you read the poem?

> ### Poetry Exercise 9
> *Four-level Question Scaffold*

Digging

Between my finger and my thumb
The squat pen rests; snug as a gun.

Under my window, a clean rasping sound
When the spade sinks into gravelly ground:
5   My father, digging. I look down

Till his straining rump among the flowerbeds
Bends low, comes up twenty years away
Stooping in rhythm through potato drills
Where he was digging.

10 The coarse boot nestled on the lug, the shaft
Against the inside knee was levered firmly.

He rooted out tall tops, buried the bright edge deep
To scatter new potatoes that we picked
Loving their cool hardness in our hands.

15 By God, the old man could handle a spade.
Just like his old man.

My grandfather cut more turf in a day
Than any other man on Toner's bog.
Once I carried him milk in a bottle
20 Corked sloppily with paper. He straightened up
To drink it, then fell to right away
Nicking and slicing neatly, heaving sods
Over his shoulder, going down and down
For the good turf. Digging.

25 The cold smell of potato mould, the squelch and slap
Of soggy peat, the curt cuts of an edge
Through living roots awaken in my head.
But I've no spade to follow men like them.

Between my finger and my thumb
30 The squat pen rests.
I'll dig with it.

Seamus Heaney

Level 1: Comprehension

1 Briefly describe what the speaker is doing, with reference to the first three stanzas of the poem.

Level 2: Interpretation

2 **a** The speaker describes his father at work in the second and third stanzas. What is your impression of the father?

  b Is the speaker's attitude towards his grandfather similar to or different from his attitude towards his father? Support your answer with reference to the poem.

Level 3: Analysis

3 **a** Find four examples of the use of the word "digging" in the poem and discuss the effect of this repetition.

b In the last stanza, the speaker says he will dig with his pen. What does he mean by this? Explain why the first and the last stanza begin and end with the speaker and his pen. Why is the poem structured in this manner and what is the effect of this?

Level 4: Insight and response

4 What can you say about the difference between the occupation of the speaker and that of his father and grandfather? What is the point the poet may be making in the poem? Give reasons for your answer.

> ### Poetry Exercise 10
> ### *Four-level Question Scaffold*

AIDS Diary

I want to eat.
Eating is important.
Eating alone is just
As important.

5   The sky is full of messages.
Or else it would not change
Its colours that way.

This book I'm working on.
I don't have a title for it yet.
10   It will come to me in a dream.
The first chapter:
I am convinced I will not
Remember that dream.

I take naps all the time.
15   They used to give me headaches.
I take certain naps where
I break out into sweat
And the fan is just
One arm's length away
20   But I lie still and smell
The burning of my skin.

Oh my God the people
Are still walking
Carrying things in their hands
25   Looking left and right
And crossing the roads!

These pills I'm taking.
It used to be difficult
To get me to take pills.
30   I had a mother
Who would point out
An imaginary lizard
On the ceiling.
The last people
35   To hold my body
Will do so
With rubber gloves.

Cartoons used to be funnier
When I was a kid.

40   I used to pray.
I used to read a lot.
I used to have a comment
For each person I knew.
I used to.
45   I used.

I think happiness
Is to say that you are happy
And to trust yourself
That you have said
50   The right word.

Alfian Bin Sa'at

Level 1: Comprehension

1   Give a brief description of the speaker's condition and how he is spending his time.

Level 2: Interpretation

2   Pick out one example each of (a) physical and (b) mental suffering and describe how they affect the person concerned.

3   a   Point to repetition as a feature in the speaker's diary entry and say whether you think the use of repetition is effective.

b   What features in this poem indicate that it is a diary entry? Why do you think the poet chose to write the poem in the style of a diary? How effective is this style in causing the reader to sympathize with the speaker?

Level 4: Insight and response

4   What are your feelings towards the speaker? As the poem progresses, do your feelings change? State the point in the poem at which your feeling is the strongest and give reasons for your answer.

Poetry Exercise 11
GCE 'N' Level 2017/1 Literature in English (October 2001)

Read the poem below and answer the questions that follow it.

Mushrooms

Overnight, very
Whitely, discreetly,
Very quietly

Our toes, our noses
5   Take hold on the loam,
Acquire the air.

Nobody sees us,
Stops us, betrays us;
The small grains make room.

10   Soft fists insist on
Heaving the needles,
The leafy bedding,

Even the paving.
Our hammers, our rams,
15   Earless and eyeless,

Perfectly voiceless,
Widen the crannies,
Shoulder through holes. We

Diet on water,
20   On crumbs of shadow,
Bland-mannered, asking

Little or nothing.
So many of us!
So many of us!

25   We are shelves, we are
Tables, we are meek,
We are edible,

Nudgers and shovers
In spite of ourselves
30   Our kind multiplies:

We shall by morning
Inherit the earth.
Our foot's in the door.

Sylvia Plath

1   With careful reference to the poem, show how Sylvia Plath makes the mushrooms seem almost human. How does she also help us to see them as mushrooms?

2   What in the poem suggests that the mushrooms might be dangerous and threatening?

3   After they have read this poem, do you think people might feel differently about mushrooms from the way they felt before?

In this poem, the writer remembers an experience she had as a schoolgirl. Read the poem carefully and answer the questions which follow it.

Quieter than snow

I went to school a day too soon
And couldn't understand
Why silence hung in the yard like sheets
Nothing to flap or spin, no creaks
5   Or shocks of voices, only air.

And the car-park empty of teachers' cars
Only the first September leaves
Dropping like paper. No racks of bikes
No kicking legs, no fights,
10   No voices, laughter, anything.

Yet the door was open. My feet
Sucked down the corridor. My reflection
Walked with me past the hall.
My classroom smelt of nothing. And the silence
15   Rolled like thunder in my ears.

At every desk a still child stared at me
Teachers walked through walls and back again
Cupboard doors swung open, and out crept
More silent children, and still more.

20   They tiptoed round me
Touched me with ice-cold hands
And opened up their mouths with laughter
That was

Quieter than snow.

Berlie Doherty

1   How does the poet help you to understand how quiet and deserted her school seemed when she went there a day too soon?

2 Describe how you think she felt when she entered the school building.

3 What feelings do **you** have when you read the last nine lines of the poem?

Poetry Exercise 13
GCE 'N' Level 2017/1 Literature in English (October 2003)

Read the poem below carefully, and then answer the questions that follow it.

(This poem tells us of what is going through the mind of a child playing "hide and seek". This is a game where one child is given a few minutes to find a hiding place and then some friends search for her/him. If the friends are successful, they win; if they are not successful, the child wins.)

Call out. Call loud: "I'm ready! Come and find me!"
The sacks in the toolshed smell like the seaside.
They'll never find you in this salty dark,
But be careful that your feet aren't sticking out.
5   Wiser not to risk another shout.
The floor is cold. They'll probably be searching
The bushes near the swing. Whatever happens
You mustn't sneeze when they come prowling in.
And here they are, whispering at the door;
10   You've never heard them sound so hushed before.
Don't breathe. Don't move. Stay dumb. Hide in your
      blindness.
They're moving closer, someone stumbles, mutters;
Their words and laughter scuffle, and they're gone.
But don't come out just yet; they'll try the lane
15   And then the greenhouse and back here again.
They must be thinking that you're very clever,
Getting more puzzled as they search all over.
It seems a long time since they went away.
Your legs are stiff, the cold bites through your coat;
20   The dark damp smell of sand moves in your throat.
It's time to let them know that you're the winner.
Push off the sacks. Uncurl and stretch. That's better!

Out of the shed and call to them: "I've won!
Here I am! Come and own up I've caught you!"
25 The darkening garden watches. Nothing stirs.
The bushes hold their breath; the sun is gone.
Yes, here you are. But where are they who sought you?

Vernon Scannell

1 Describe the child's hiding place and what he thinks about it.

2 With close reference to the child's thoughts, show how his feelings gradually change in the course of the poem.

3 What feelings do **you** have when you read the last five lines of the poem? Say how the poet makes you feel that way.

Poetry Exercise 14
GCE 'N' Level 2017/1 Literature in English (October 2004)

Read this poem carefully, and then answer the questions that follow it.

My Grandmother

She kept an antique shop—or it kept her.
Among Apostle spoons and Bristol glass,*
The faded silks, the heavy furniture,
She watched her own reflection in the brass
5 Salvers and silver bowls, as if to prove
Polish was all, there was no need of love.

And I remember how I once refused
To go out with her, since I was afraid.
It was perhaps a wish not to be used
10 Like antique objects. Though she never said
That she was hurt, I still could feel the guilt
Of that refusal, guessing how she felt.

---

* Apostle spoons and Bristol glass: old, valuable types of spoons and glass, often
sold in antique shops.

264

Later, too frail to keep a shop, she put
All her best things in one long narrow room.
15   The place smelt old, of things too long kept shut,
The smell of absences where shadows come
That can't be polished. There was nothing then
To give her own reflection back again.

And when she died I felt no grief at all,
20   Only the guilt of what I once refused.
I walked into her room among the tall
Sideboards and cupboards—things she never used
But needed; and no finger-marks were there,
Only the new dust falling through the air.

Elizabeth Jennings

1   Describe the grandmother's character and her way of life.

2   What do you think the poet felt about her grandmother, from the way she writes about her in this poem?

3   What are **your** feelings about the relationship between the poet and her grandmother? Refer closely to the poem to support your opinion.

Poetry Exercise 15
GCE 'N' Level 2017/1 Literature in English (October 2005)

Read this poem carefully, and then answer the questions that follow it.

First Day at School

A millionbillionwillion miles from home
Waiting for the bell to go. (To go where?)
Why are they all so big, other children?
So noisy? So much at home they

5　　　must have been born in uniform
　　　Lived all their lives in playgrounds
　　　Spend the years inventing games
　　　that don't let me in. Games
　　　that are rough, that swallow you up.

10　　And the railings.
　　　All around, the railings.
　　　Are they to keep out wolves and monsters?
　　　Things that carry off and eat children?
　　　Things you don't take sweets from?
15　　Perhaps they're to stop us getting out
　　　Running away from the lessins. Lessin.
　　　What does a lessin look like?
　　　Sounds small and slimy.
　　　They keep them in glassrooms.
20　　Whole rooms made out of glass. Imagine.

　　　I wish I could remember my name
　　　Mummy said it would come in useful.
　　　Like wellies.* When there's puddles.
　　　Yellowwellies. I wish she was here.
25　　I think my name is sewn on somewhere
　　　Perhaps the teacher will read it for me.
　　　Tea-cher. The one who makes the tea.

Roger McGough

1　In this poem, a small child is experiencing her or his first day at school. How do the words help us to understand how young and inexperienced the child is?

2　In your own words, describe what makes the child anxious on this first day at school.

3　What feelings do **you** have for the child when you read about what he or she thinks and imagines? Remember to refer closely to the poem to explain your feelings.

* wellies: waterproof, rubber boots.

Read this poem carefully and then answer the questions that follow it.

War Photographer

In his darkroom he is finally alone
with spools of suffering set out in ordered rows.
The only light is red and softly glows,
as though this were a church and he
5   a priest preparing to intone a Mass.
Belfast. Beirut. Phnom Penh.* All flesh is grass.

He has a job to do. Solutions slop in trays
beneath his hands which did not tremble then
though seem to now. Rural England. Home again
10   to ordinary pain which simple weather can dispel,
to fields which don't explode beneath the feet
of running children in a nightmare heat.

Something is happening. A stranger's features
faintly start to twist before his eyes,
15   a half-formed ghost. He remembers the cries
of this man's wife, how he sought approval
without words to do what someone must
and how the blood stained into foreign dust.

A hundred agonies in black-and-white
20   from which his editor will pick out five or six
for Sunday's supplement. The reader's eyeballs prick
with tears between the bath and pre-lunch beers.
From the aeroplane he stares impassively at where
he earns his living and they do not care.

Carol Ann Duffy

1   Explain what the photographer is thinking as he develops photographs in his darkroom.

---

* Belfast, Beirut, Phnom Penh are all places which have suffered great destruction as a result of bombing.

2 What are your feelings about the photographer and his work as you read the poem? Show how the words of the poem have created these feelings in you.

Remember to refer closely to the poem in support of your answers to both questions.

This poem depicts a scene in a zoo. Read it carefully and then answer the questions that follow it.

The Jaguar

The apes yawn and adore their fleas in the sun.
The parrots shriek as if they were on fire, or strut
Like cheap tarts to attract the stroller with the nut.
Fatigued with indolence, tiger and lion

5 Lie still as the sun. The boa-constrictor's coil
Is a fossil. Cage after cage seems empty, or
Stinks of sleepers from the breathing straw.
It might be painted on a nursery wall.

But who runs like the rest past these arrives
10 At a cage where the crowd stands, stares, mesmerized,
As a child at a dream, at a jaguar hurrying enraged
Through prison darkness after the drills of his eyes

On a short fierce fuse. Not in boredom —
The eye satisfied to be blind in fire,
15 By the bang of blood in the brain deaf the ear —
He spins from the bars, but there's no cage to him

More than to the visionary* his cell:
His stride is wilderness of freedom:
The world rolls under the long thrust of his heel.
20 Over the cage floor the horizons come.

Ted Hughes

* A visionary is someone who lives in his imagination, cut off from the practical world.

268

1 What does the poet convey about the characters of the apes, the parrots, the tiger and the lion in the first two verses of the poem?

2 In what ways does the poet show that the jaguar is different from the other animals and how does he make these differences clear?

3 What are your feelings for the jaguar by the end of the poem? You should remember to examine closely the words and images that the poet uses.

Poetry Exercise 18
GCE 'O' Level 2015 Literature in English (November 2003)

This poem is about a man who suffers from astigmatism, a condition which means he has extremely weak eyesight. Read it carefully and then answer the questions that follow it:

The Astigmatic

At seven the sun that lit my world blew out
Leaving me only mist. Through which I probed
My way to school, guessed wildly at the sums
Whose marks on the board I couldn't even see.

5   They wanted to send me away to a special school.
I refused, and coped as best I could with half
The light lost in the mist, screwing my tears
Into my work, my gritted teeth, my writing —

Which crawled along and writhed. Think thoughts at will,
10   None of it comes across. Even now friends ask
"How do you read that scrawl?" the fact is, I don't;
Nobody could. I guess. But how would you

Like my world where parallels actually join,
Perspectives vary at sight? Once in a pub
15   I walked towards a sign marked gents over
A grating and crashed through the floor —

Well, it looked all right to me. Those steep stairs
People told me of later flattened to lines
In my half-world. The rest imagination
20   Supplied: when you've half a line you extend it.

The lenses drag their framework down my nose,
I still can't look strangers in the face,
Wilting behind a wall of glass at them.
It makes me look shifty at interviews.

25   I wake up with a headache, chew all day
Aspirins, go to bed dispirited,
Still with a dull pain somewhere in my skull,
And sleep. Then, in my dreams, the sun comes out.

Philip Hobsbaum

NB: Remember to refer closely to the words and images of the poem in answering these questions.

1   Explain briefly how the poet makes us feel sympathy for the child in lines 1–9.

2   In what ways do you think that the poet's poor eyesight has affected his later life and attitudes? How does it make you feel towards him?

3   What do you understand by the last sentence of the poem, and what impact does it have on you?

My Box

My box is made of golden oak,
my lover's gift to me.
He fitted hinges and a lock
of brass and a bright key.
5   He made it out of winter nights,
sanded and oiled and planed,
engraved inside the heavy lid
in brass, a golden tree.

In my box are twelve black books
10 where I have written down
how we have sanded, oiled and planed,
planted a garden, built a wall,
seen jays and goldcrests, rare red kites[1],
found the wild heartsease[2], drilled a well,
15 harvested apples and words and days
and planted a golden tree.

On an open shelf I keep my box.
Its key is in the lock.
I leave it there for you to read,
20 or them, when we are dead,
how everything is slowly made,
how slowly things made me,
a tree, a lover, words, a box,
books and a golden tree.

Gillian Clarke

1   For what reasons is the box important to the poet?

2   How do the words and images that the poet uses convey
the strength of her feelings to you? Remember to support
your ideas by close reference to the poem.

---

[1] *jays, goldcrests, red kites: types of bird.*
[2] *heartsease: a flower.*

271

Read this poem carefully, and then answer the questions that follow it.

The Choosing

We were first equal Mary and I
with same coloured ribbons in mouse-coloured hair
and with equal shyness,
we curtseyed to the lady councillor[1]
5   for copies of Collins' Children's Classics[2].
First equal, equally proud.

Best friends too Mary and I
a common bond of being cleverest (equal)
in our small school's small class.
10   I remember
the competition for top desk
or to read aloud the lesson
at school service.
And my terrible fear
15   of her superiority at sums.

I remember the housing scheme
where we both stayed.
The same houses, different homes,
where the choices got made.

20   I don't know exactly why they moved,
but anyway they went.
Something about a three-apartment[3]
and a cheaper rent.
But from the top deck of the high-school bus

---

[1] councillor: local government officer.
[2] Collins' Children's Classics: English literature books given as school prizes.
[3] three-apartment: accommodation with three bedrooms.

25   I'd glimpse among the others on the corner
              Mary's father, mufflered[4], contrasting strangely
              With the elegant greyhounds[5] by his side.

              He didn't believe in high-school education,
              especially for girls
30   or in forking out for uniforms.

              Ten years later on a Saturday —
              I am coming from the library —
              sitting near me on the bus,
              Mary
35   with a husband who is tall,
              curly haired, has eyes
              for no one else but Mary.

              Her arms are round the full-shaped vase
              that is her body.
40   Oh, you can see where the attraction lies
              in Mary's life —
              not that I envy her, really.

              And I am coming from the library
              with my arms full of books.
45   I think of those prizes that were ours for the taking
              and wonder when the choices got made
              we don't remember making.

By Liz Lochhead

1   By what means does the poet convey the similarity between the two girls in lines 1–19 of the poem?

2   What do you find striking about the ways in which the poet conveys the developments and changes in the girls' lives as they have grown older?

Remember to refer closely to the words and images of the poem.

---

[4] mufflered: *wrapped in a scarf.*
[5] greyhounds: *racing dogs.*

In this passage, a fugitive is on the run from the police and finds a place to hide in the underground tunnels of the city.

> The writer uses words like "crouching" and "crept" to depict the movements of the man. What image is associated with these words?

I've got to hide, he told himself. His chest heaved as he waited, crouching in a dark corner of the vestibule.* He was tired of running and dodging. Either he had to find a place to hide or he had to surrender. A police car swished by through the rain, its siren rising sharply. They're looking for me all over ... He crept to the door and squinted through the fogged plate glass. He stiffened as the siren rose and died in the distance. Yes, he had to hide, but where? He gritted his teeth. Then a sudden movement in the street caught his attention. A throng of tiny columns of water snaked into the air from the perforations of a manhole cover. The columns rose abruptly, as though the perforations had become clogged; a grey spout of sewer water jutted up from the underground and lifted the circular metal cover, juggled it for a moment, then let it fall with a clang.

> The writer juxtaposes the man's thoughts with an objective description of his movements. What is the effect of this?

> Analyse the writer's use of colour in the first two paragraphs. How do they complement the mood of the scene?

He hatched a tentative plan: he would wait until the siren sounded far off, then he would go out. He smoked and waited, tense. At last, the siren gave him his signal; it wailed, dying, going away from him. He stepped to the sidewalk, then paused and looked curiously at the open manhole, half expecting the cover to leap up again. He went to the centre of the street and stopped and peered into the hole, but could see nothing. Water rustled in the black depths.

> Trace the growing intensity of the sound of the siren in the first three paragraphs. How does this contribute to the sense of tension in the text?

He started with terror; the siren sounded so near that he had the idea that he had been dreaming and had awakened to find the car upon him. He dropped instinctively to his knees and his hands grasped the rim of the manhole. The siren seemed to hoot directly above him and with a wild gasp of exertion he snatched the cover far enough off to admit his body. He swung his legs over the opening and lowered himself into the watery darkness. He hung for an eternal moment to the rim by his fingertips, then he felt rough metal prongs and at once, he knew that sewer workmen had used these ridges to lower themselves into the manholes. Fist over fist, he let his body sink until he

> What animals are associated with the words "hoot" and "howl"? Why do you think the writer uses these words? How do they contribute to your impression of the main character?

Line numbers: 5, 10, 15, 20, 25, 30, 35

---

* vestibule: lobby or entrance to a hall.

could feel no more prongs. He swayed in the dank space;
the siren seemed to howl at the very rim of the manhole.
He dropped and was washed violently into an ocean of
40 warm, leaping water. His head was battered against a wall
and he wondered if this were death. Frenziedly his fingers
clawed and sank into a crevice. He steadied himself and
measured the strength of the current with his own muscular
tension. He stood slowly in water that dashed past his
45 knees in fearful velocity.

He heard a prolonged scream of brakes and the siren
broke off. Oh God! They had found him! Looming above
his head in the rain, a white face hovered over the hole.
"How did this thing get off?" he heard a policeman ask. He
50 saw the steel cover move slowly until the hole looked like
a quarter moon turned black. "Give me a hand here,"
someone called. The cover clanged into place, muffling the
sighs and sounds of the upper world. Knee-deep in the
pulsing current, he breathed with aching chest, filling his
55 lungs with the hot stench of yeasty rot.

From the perforations of the manhole cover, delicate
lances of hazy violet sifted down and wove a mottled pattern
upon the surface of the streaking current. His lips parted as
a car swept past along the wet pavement overhead, its
60 heavy rumble soon dying out, like the hum of a plane
speeding through a dense cloud. He had never thought
that cars could sound like that; everything seemed strange
and unreal under here. He stood in darkness for a long
time, knee-deep in rustling water, musing.

Extract from "The Man Who Lived Underground"
by Richard Wright

What animals are associated with the following phrases: "swung his legs ... hung for an eternal moment" and "Frenziedly his fingers clawed"? How do they contribute to your impression of the main character?

The writer uses personification to describe the "leaping water". He later describes it as a "pulsing current". How do they contribute to the setting?

What is the simile used to describe the sound of the passing car? What is the purpose of this?

Why do you think the main character stood in the darkness even after the police had left?

Further questions for discussion:

1 What is your impression of the main character?

2 By paying close attention to repeated words and images,
show how the writer conveys and develops the sense of fear
within the main character. How effective is he in doing this?
Give evidence to support your answer.

3 How would you describe the mood in the text? Support
your answer with reference to the text.

4 What techniques does the writer use to create tension and
suspense as he builds the story up to its climax?

In this passage, the narrator reflects on her relationships with men and thinks of ways to gain control over them.

Why do you think the story begins with one word "Men"? What does this suggest about the attitude of the narrator towards men?

Comment on the narrator's use of simile when she compares men to a tap?

Why does the writer begin the second and third paragraphs with the word "Sometimes"? How does this add to the overall mood?

What kind of job does the narrator have? Show evidence from other parts of the text.

Comment on the use of disjointed, ungrammatical sentences. How does this add to a conversational tone?

Men. Men are difficult. So hard to understand. They seem to operate on a very simple basis, like a tap. They're either turned on or turned off. But unlike a tap you can't control their switching from one state to another. You can't reach out your hand and say "on" or "off". Instead you have to put up with whatever state they're in—unwelcome attentions or hurtful silence.

Sometimes I feel I've spent my whole life trying to work out how to handle them. From the moment my mother started pressuring me to keep my legs together—"Otherwise not nice." And especially from the time when I had to learn how to manage during my period. And learning how to apply make-up. "Not too much, not too little"—as if I were a pot on a stove that needed salt. And learning how to walk in high heels.

Sometimes I think it's too much. A permanent fashion parade. Forever swaying down an endless spotlit catwalk. Male faces eagerly upturned in the shadows. My job hardly helps. I have to smile until my jaws ache. I come home after a shift feeling like a punchbag, only it's not punches that have been thrown at me but the silly jokes of businessmen and tourists. "Any discounts on the room? A nice girl like you should give discount."

Once when I'd just left school, when I'd messed up with a tall handsome boy (they're always handsome in your memory—you forget their sweat, their failure to take regular baths or to clean under their fingernails) I thought I'd turn my back on men. Strike out. Live for myself. He'd just started National Service. I was rather sweet on him. Such a cute smile. Like a child's. The night before he enlisted we spent an eternity in one another's arms. Whispering our love and devotion. But once he was in the army things changed. He was so silent on weekends. Or if he talked it would be about the army. What he'd done that week. What he'd do next week. I used to listen, but it meant nothing to me. And he'd be so tired, so irritable. He'd snap at me for no reason. And when I got upset he'd make me feel guilty for being upset, for spoiling his few hours of freedom.

5

10

15

20

25

30

35

He'd look at his watch and count down the hours. He'd
40 mention some sergeant who he said had marked him but
when I hugged him and said I was sorry he shrugged me
off; I could not understand, he said. He was right; I could
not understand.

45 So I stopped seeing him. There's a limit to how many
problems I can take on board before I begin to sink. My
parents could see how he was upsetting me. They were
relieved when we broke up. But he, he kept accusing. I was
faithless. I had lied to him. I had betrayed him. I put down
the phone when I heard his voice.

50 And I stopped seeing men. I bought no new clothes. I
stopped using eyeshadow. I bought myself comfortable
shoes and said to hell with the whole race of men.

But of course no man is an island. Least of all a
woman. Jobs were hard to come by. They always are. And
55 all the interviewers are men. You can feel their eyes crawling
all over you as you sit timidly, eyes downcast, hands folded
in your lap, on the edge of the chair.

As the rejection slips mounted my parents grew more
restless. Times are hard, they said. Everyone must pull
60 their weight. My mother said, you have to look good. So I
daubed on mascara and bought a new outfit. I outfaced
my interviewers. I presented them with a new face that I'd
applied in front of a mirror that morning. I hid myself
away inside a charming lady, whose every gesture sought
65 to flatter the spectator. My lips trembled. My hand brushed
invitingly across my body. My voice became gentler. I
matched him comment for comment, yet making clear that
ultimately he was in control.

Extract from The Third Eye *by Philip Jeyaretnam*

> Explain what caused the relationship between the narrator and her lover to fall apart.

> Why does the writer describe in detail the actions of the narrator after her breakup? How is this effective in contributing to your impression of her?

> What is meant by the sentences "No man is an island. Least of all a woman"?

> Who was really in control at the interview? What can you say about the narrator's character from this?

Further questions for discussion:

1 What is the narrator's view of men in general and, in particular, her boyfriend?

2 Identify the internal and external conflicts in the text.

3 Discuss how the tone and style of narration are appropriate in this extract.

4 How does the writer develop our sympathy for the protagonist? Support your answer with reference to the text.

5 The writer of this extract is a male person. Do you feel that his depiction of the female persona is stereotypical? Give reasons for your answer.

Prose Exercise 3
Guided Close Reading

A reporter meets a vampire in a bar by chance and now proceeds to interview him on his life story.

> Describe how lighting and setting in the first paragraph contribute to the mood.

"I see ..." said the vampire thoughtfully, and slowly he walked across the room towards the window. For a long time he stood there against the dim light from Divisadero Street and the passing beams of traffic. The boy could see
5 the furnishings of the room more clearly now, the round oak table, the chairs. A washbasin hung on one wall with a mirror. He set his briefcase on the table and waited.

> Look carefully at the language spoken by the vampire. What can you infer of his character?

"But how much tape do you have with you?" asked the vampire, turning now so the boy could see his profile.
10 "Enough for the story of a life?"

"Sure, if it's a good life. Sometimes I interview as many as three or four people a night if I'm lucky. But it has to be a good story. That's only fair, isn't it?"

> Look at the manner in which the boy speaks to the vampire. How would you describe his reaction to the vampire here?

"Admirably fair," the vampire answered. "I would like
15 to tell you the story of my life, then. I would like to do that very much."

"Great," said the boy. And quickly he removed the small tape recorder from his briefcase, making a check of the cassette and the batteries. "I'm really anxious to hear
20 why you believe this, why you ..."

"No," said the vampire abruptly. "We can't begin that way. Is your equipment ready?"

"Yes," said the boy.

"Then sit down. I'm going to turn on the overhead
25 light."

> What is it about the vampire's mannerism that disturbs the boy?

"But I thought vampires didn't like light," said the boy. "If you think the dark adds to the atmosphere ..." But then he stopped. The vampire was watching him with his back to the window. The boy could make out nothing of his face

30 now, and something about the still figure there distracted him. He started to say something again but he said nothing. And then he sighed with relief when the vampire moved towards the table and reached for the overhead cord.

35 At once the room was flooded with a harsh yellow light. And the boy, staring up at the vampire, could not repress a gasp. His fingers danced backwards on the table to grasp the edge. "Dear God!" he whispered, and then he gazed, speechless, at the vampire.

40 The vampire was utterly white and smooth, as if he were sculpted from bleached bone, and his face was as seemingly inanimate as a statue, except for two brilliant green eyes that looked down at the boy intently like flames in a skull. But then the vampire smiled almost wistfully, and the smooth white substance of his face moved with the

45 infinitely flexible but minimal lines of a cartoon. "Do you see?" he asked softly.

The boy shuddered, lifting his hand as if to shield himself from a powerful light. His eyes moved slowly over the finely tailored black coat he'd only glimpsed in the bar,

50 the long folds of the cape, the black silk tie knotted at the throat, and the gleam of the white collar that was as white as the vampire's flesh. He stared at the vampire's full black hair, the waves that were combed back over the tips of the ears, the curls that barely touched the edge of the white

55 collar.

"Now, do you still want the interview?" the vampire asked.

The boy's mouth was open before the sound came out. He was nodding. Then he said, "Yes."

60 The vampire sat down slowly opposite him and, leaning forward, said gently, confidentially, "Don't be afraid. Just start the tape."

And then he reached out over the length of the table. The boy recoiled, sweat running down the sides of his face.

65 The vampire clamped a hand on the boy's shoulder and said, "Believe me, I won't hurt you. I want this opportunity. It's more important to me than you can realize now. I want you to begin." And he withdrew his hand and sat collected, waiting.

70 It took a moment for the boy to wipe his forehead and his lips with a handkerchief, to stammer that the microphone was in the machine, to press the button, to say that the machine was on.

"You weren't always a vampire, were you?" he began.

Why do you think the writer first describes the boy's reaction to the vampire when the light is turned on before describing what the vampire looks like?

The writer employs three similes to describe the vampire. Explore how these similes contribute to your impression of the vampire.

The writer juxtaposes the colour black with white. What is the effect of this?

The writer carefully describes the behaviour of the vampire and the reaction of the boy. Why does she do this? How effective is this in sustaining the reader's interest?

How is the vampire's behaviour a contrast to his external appearance?

75   "No," answered the vampire. "I was a twenty-five-year-
old man when I became a vampire and the year was
1791."

Extract from Interview with the Vampire *by Anne Rice*

Further questions for discussion:

1   Vampires are traditionally known to be evil and cruel in
nature. Does the vampire in this extract appear to be
different? Can you say how? Provide examples to support
your point.

2   What evidence can you find to show that the boy becomes
increasingly uneasy during the interview?

3   The boy appears to be in control of the interview at the
beginning of the text. Show how the vampire takes control
of the interview as it progresses.

Prose Exercise 4
Guided Close Reading

During his vacation in Vietnam with his friends, the main
character, Nick, encounters various incidents which cause him
to reflect on his own life.

Describe the day's activities of the tourists in lines 1 to 6? Does their excursion seem exciting or monotonous?

They woke early next morning and bundled up in
their jackets, put out to sea, just the three of them in a big
boat, heading towards an island with a big cave.
They walked through the limestone passages, stood in
5   enormous caverns, cruised the waters waving at people
who lived on boats smaller than the one they were riding
in.

What does the writer mean when he says that Nick "was with the local people again"? What differentiates Nick from the other tourists?

A small fast boat drew up alongside and a small girl
held up a piece of coral to Nick. He saw that it had cut her
10   finger and that she was bleeding. Suddenly, he was with
the local people again, for a brief moment, away from his
friends on the deck and with this little girl with the cut on
her finger. His heart ached for her and he wondered to

what end would be all his understanding about the
environment and the advice from books telling him not to
buy things like coral from the locals because it would only
encourage them to harvest more, killing the reefs. But it
was food for a little girl with a cut finger and he did not
know what to do or say to her. ...

It was almost ten when they left Ha Long Bay, snug
and comfortable in the sanctuary of the Toyota, secure in
the thought that it was the reliable Mr Ngoc at the wheel
and not any one of them. The miles rushed by and this
time, they were too tired to talk and fell in and out of sleep.
Nick thought about the little girl with the coral and felt a
weariness inside that was not pity, just a tiredness from
being able to do so little—or nothing, in her case—to help in
any way. He remembered how his father had always gone
to the roadside hawkers when his sister and he always
voted for the coffee house, his father saying that the old
women needed the money more than they did. He thought
it was because his father had sold cakes by the road too
when he was a small boy, but a similar experience was not
necessary for empathy. Nick had learned to close his eyes,
his ears and his heart to other people's sufferings, telling
himself that if he could not help, he should not feel too
badly about it.

He still knew that to be true and to be important if one
wanted to function normally. He was a case in point. He
had grown up ruthlessly efficient, organized and prepared
for most things. But something had been suppressed, kept
dormant and he knew that it was pity. Not a condescending
pity, but a pity that sought to do something so that another's
pain could be eased. ... Maybe this was what he had come
to Vietnam to rediscover, unknown to himself. Maybe it
was not his friends that he had come all the way to be
reunited with. Maybe it was not the hostel good times he
had come to relive. Maybe all it was, really, was that sense
of pity that let him connect with other people. He had lost
it or denied its existence for so long, and it was his inability
to connect that had cost him the closeness with his
councillors, the closeness with his family, the closeness
with his hall friends that had suddenly seemed so
vulnerable. And maybe that was why he had been lonely
after all—a free-floating organism disconnected from the
empathy that made one human. And it had taken a journey
alone to find this sense of pity again.

15
20
25
30
35
40
45
50
55

Describe the
epiphany that
Nick has when
he encounters
the girl with the
piece of coral.

Why do you
think this story
is written in the
third person
even though it
centres on the
thoughts and
reflection of the
main character,
Nick? How does
the writer
manage to make
the story
personal?

According to
Nick, what is one
problem that is
a result of
modernization
and a quest for
the material?

The writer
employs listing
to depict the
thoughts going
through Nick's
mind. How
effective is this
in conveying what
Nick is feeling
at this point?

60

65

70

75

He felt the car slowing down, Mr Ngoc stopping to wait for a ferry across the river. The moment he stopped, children appeared with fruits and quails' eggs, sugarcane and other tidbits. Mr Ngoc tried to keep them away, but Nick said it's alright. We all need lunch anyway. ...

— Nick saw her standing a little further back, letting the children run ahead of her. She was an older girl, a head taller than the rest of the little ones—a conical hat shading her face and a flat, round basket before her. She smiled at him and he smiled back. He stepped away from the car, from Mr Ngoc, from his two friends—to buy a bag of tangerines.

She put the basket down and sat on a rock to count them out. He knelt before her to wait and handed her the note when she held up the bag to him, her thin, brown arm straining with the weight of the bag on her extended arm. She smiled sweetly, obviously pleased that he had bought something from her and said *cam on ong* shyly. *Khong co chi*, he said. Then he took a fruit from his bag, peeled it, broke it and offered half to her. She was surprised but smiled again and accepted the fruit. He smiled, she smiled, and he knew that in that moment, it was all that mattered.

Extract from Tangerine *by Colin Cheong*

How is Nick's reaction to this girl different from his reaction to the girl in the first paragraph? What has caused this change?

"He stepped away from the car, from Mr Ngoc, from his two friends"— what is the literal and implied meaning of this sentence?

Further questions for discussion:

1   What do you think the tangerine symbolizes?

2   Discuss the writer's use of point of view and style of narration. How do they enhance your understanding of the narrator's character?

3   What kinds of conflict are evident in this extract? Do you think any of those conflicts are resolved by the end of this passage?

This short story relates Mrs Mallard's reaction to news of her husband's death.

Knowing that Mrs Mallard was afflicted with a heart trouble, great care was taken to break to her as gently as possible the news of her husband's death.

5   It was her sister Josephine who told her, in broken sentences; veiled hints that revealed in half concealing. Her husband's friend Richards was there, too, near her. It was he who had been in the newspaper office when intelligence of the railroad disaster was received, with Brently Mallard's name leading the list of "killed". He had
10   only taken the time to assure himself of its truth by a second telegram, and had hastened to forestall any less careful, less tender friend in bearing the sad message.

She did not hear the story as many women have heard the same, with a paralysed inability to accept its
15   significance. She wept at once, with sudden, wild abandonment, in her sister's arms. When the storm of grief had spent itself she went away to her room alone. She would have no one follow her.

There stood, facing the open window, a comfortable,
20   roomy armchair. Into this she sank, pressed down by a physical exhaustion that haunted her body and seemed to reach into her soul.

She could see in the open square before her house the tops of trees that were all aquiver with the new spring life.
25   The delicious breath of rain was in the air. In the street below a pedlar was crying his wares. The notes of a distant song which someone was singing reached her faintly, and countless sparrows were twittering in the eaves. ...

She sat with her head thrown back upon the cushion
30   of the chair, quite motionless, except when a sob came up into her throat and shook her, as a child who has cried itself to sleep continues to sob in its dreams. ...

There was something coming to her and she was waiting for it, fearfully. What was it? She did not know; it
35   was too subtle and elusive to name. But she felt it, creeping

---

Give two reasons why Mrs Mallard's sister and her husband's friend are so careful about informing her of her husband's death. What do they predict her reaction would be?

The writer repeats the idea of spontaneity in the words "sudden" and "wild abandonment". What could she be implying about Mrs Mallard's personality?

Why do you think the writer pays great attention to describing what Mrs Mallard sees? What is she implying? Why does she repeat the word "open" in the fourth and fifth paragraphs?

The writer cleverly uses an ironic twist in the fourth and fifth paragraphs. Can you identify the twist and say why it is effective in engaging the reader?

out of the sky, reaching towards her through the sounds, the scents, the colour that filled the air.

Now her bosom rose and fell tumultuously. She was beginning to recognize this thing that was approaching to possess her, and she was striving to beat it back with her will—as powerless as her two white slender hands would have been. ...

She did not stop to ask if it were or were not a monstrous joy that held her. A clear and exalted perception enabled her to dismiss the suggestion as trivial.

She knew that she would weep again when she saw the kind, tender hands folded in death; the face that had never looked save with love upon her, fixed and grey and dead. But she saw beyond that bitter moment a long procession of years to come that would belong to her absolutely. And she opened and spread her arms out to them in welcome.

There would be no one to live for during those coming years; she would live for herself. There would be no powerful will bending hers in that blind persistence with which men and women believe they have a right to impose a private will upon a fellow-creature. A kind intention or a cruel intention made the act seem no less a crime as she looked upon it in that brief moment of illumination.

And yet she had loved him—sometimes. Often she had not. What did it matter! What could love, the unsolved mystery, count for in face of this possession of self-assertion which she suddenly recognized as the strongest impulse of her being! ...

She arose at length and opened the door to her sister's importunities. There was a feverish triumph in her eyes, and she carried herself unwittingly like a goddess of Victory. She clasped her sister's waist, and together they descended the stairs. Richards stood waiting for them at the bottom.

Someone was opening the front door with a latchkey. It was Brently Mallard who entered, a little travel-stained, composedly carrying his grip-sack and umbrella. He had been far from the scene of accident, and did not even know there had been one. He stood amazed at Josephine's piercing cry; at Richards's quick motion to screen him from the view of his wife.

But Richards was too late.

When the doctors came they said she had died of heart disease—of joy that kills.

Adapted from "The Story of an Hour" by Kate Chopin

How is Mrs Mallard feeling in this paragraph?

From lines 46 to 57, infer Mrs Mallard's relationship with her husband. Why is she relieved that he is dead?

Would this story have been better if it had been written in the first person, from Mrs Mallard's point of view? Why?

What is the contradiction in these lines: "And yet she had loved him—sometimes. Often she had not"? Do you think Mrs Mallard loved her husband at all?

How does the writer introduce the appearance of Brently Mallard? Why is this effective?

Why do you think Richards tries to shield Mrs Mallard from seeing her husband?

What do you think the real cause of Mrs Mallard's death is?

40

45

50

55

60

65

70

75

Further questions for discussion:

1   How would you describe the setting and atmosphere of this scene? How does the setting complement the inner feelings of Mrs Mallard?

2   In what way has Mrs Mallard been repressed in her marriage? What other impression do you have of Mrs Mallard and what are your feelings for her at the end of the text?

3   Why is the conclusion of this story ironic? How does the writer develop the story towards its ironic conclusion?

Prose Exercise 6
Four-level Question Scaffold

Lee arrives at the airport to pick up his daughter, who has spent the last eight years growing up in California. His daughter will now be living with him in Singapore.

At first, he couldn't pick his daughter out from the crowd at the airport when he went to meet her, and he panicked, imagining all sorts of things. All he had was a rather smudged photograph to go by, showing a girl with long Janis Joplin

5   hair framing her face, her smile wide and lopsided. He saw her finally, by the soft-drinks machine, inserting coins; no drink emerged and she kicked the machine, once, twice, three times. He should have recognized the flowing hair, but her clothes—a black man's jacket and tight red jeans—had

10 led him to suppose it was someone older. She looked up, her forehead furrowing in doubt, when he came up.

"Are you my dad?" she asked in a pronounced American accent.

"Li Wen?"

15 "Yeah. But everyone calls me Lee."

Clumsily he hugged her and she accepted it with a sort of grudging nonchalance. She kept looking at him with a certain measured surprise—they hadn't met in eight years, he remembered, not since his ex-wife, having won custody of

20 their eight-year-old child, had taken the first plane out to California and never come back. He'd heard that she'd got a job at a refugee centre, helping displaced Asians settle in their new country. Three weeks ago, she had drowned accidentally in a friend's swimming pool in LA, hence Li
25 Wen's return. To be with her kith and kin, as his mother had sonorously put it. He had had great difficulty in persuading his mother to stay away that night; he'd needed, he said, to be alone when he met Li Wen. "Is that a new-fangled Western concept or what?" his mother had demanded. She had never
30 understood that one sometimes needed a modicum of privacy, a moment to take stock; everything had to be done As Family.

He picked up Li Wen's luggage, all three small pieces of it—"Oh, just my favorite shirts and a couple of records"—
35 while she swung her own tennis racket carelessly and walked ahead of him. Her step was jaunty, light-footed; it was almost like cat-walking. She was as tall as he and he was five foot nine. She was sixteen.

"Hey," Lee said, when he caught up with her, "it's kind
40 of hot here, isn't it?"

"Don't you remember anything about your country?"

He dumped the luggage in the back of the car.

"My country?" Lee said, as if not sure what he meant. "Oh. Yeah. Some. Not much. Not the humidity."
45 "You won't need that jacket here."

She looked down at it, flicking an infinitesimal speck of dust off the lapel, and an odd reflective look came over her face; he was to recognize it well; it was the look which signified she was back in LA in her mind.
50 "I guess not," she said.

In the car, she made straight for the radio, her hair swashing over the gears. Backing out, he didn't pay attention to her restless flicking of channels, her sarcastic exclamations of "Oh my God" and "Can this be real?"
55 "Man, is that all the radio there is? M.O.R. and Bach?" She sounded flabbergasted.

"We don't believe in being swamped by the media here," he said in amusement.

"Hey—stop," she commanded. Her tone was imperative.
60 "Why?" They were near the exit of the car park.

"I gotta get my Walkman out from the back. I can't listen to this junk. Kenny Rogers—" She rolled her eyes.

"Do you have to listen to anything right now?"

Lee said intensely, "I need the music, man."

65　　　　He was about to say, No, annoyed, then relented. So he
stopped the car and she was out and back in a flash; now
she sat contentedly, legs tucked under her, swivelling her
head round in curiosity at things which caught her attention
along the road. She played the music loud and he could
70　　hear it above the noise of the traffic; in a way, it was a relief
not to have to talk.

Extract from "Lee" in Fascist Rock: Stories of Rebellion
by Claire Tham

Level 1: Comprehension

1　Why is the father unable to recognize his daughter when he
first sees her?

Level 2: Interpretation

2　What is your impression of Li Wen? How well do you think
she will be able to adjust to her new environment? Give
evidence to support your points.

Level 3: Analysis

3　**a**　How does the writer depict the tension between father
and daughter in this extract? Support your answer with
reference to the text.

　　b　How does the writer effectively convey the changing
attitude of the father towards his daughter as the text
progresses? Support your answer with reference to the
text.

Level 4: Insight and response

4　In what way does the writer highlight the conflict between
East and West? What are your feelings towards the father
and daughter in the story?

Michael Obi, the newly appointed headmaster of a school in an African village, has ambitious hopes of modernizing the village. However, he comes into conflict with some of the local villagers.

Michael Obi's hopes were fulfilled much earlier than he had expected. He was appointed headmaster of Ndume Central School in January 1949. It had always been an unprogressive school, so the Mission authorities decided to

5 send a young and energetic man to run it. Obi accepted this responsibility with enthusiasm. He had many wonderful ideas and this was an opportunity to put them into practice. He had had sound secondary school education, which designated him a "pivotal teacher" in the official records and

10 set him apart from the other headmasters in the mission field. He was outspoken in his condemnation of the narrow views of these older and often less-educated ones.

"We shall make a good job of it, shan't we?" he asked his young wife when they first heard the joyful news of his

15 promotion.

"We shall do our best," she replied. "We shall have such beautiful gardens and everything will be just *modern* and delightful ..." In their two years of married life she had become completely infected by his passion for "modern methods"

20 and his denigration of "these old and superannuated people in the teaching field who would be better employed as traders in the Onitsha market". She began to see herself already as the admired wife of the young headmaster, the queen of the school.

25 The wives of the other teachers would envy her position. She would set the fashion in everything ... Then, suddenly, it occurred to her that there might not be other wives. Wavering between hope and fear, she asked her husband, looking anxiously at him.

30 "All our colleagues are young and unmarried," he said with enthusiasm which for once she did not share. "Which is a good thing," he continued.

"Why?"

"Why? They will give all their time and energy to the

35 school."

Nancy was downcast. For a few minutes she became sceptical about the new school; but it was only for a few minutes. Her little personal misfortune could not blind her to her husband's happy prospects. She looked at him as he sat folded up in a chair. He was stoop-shouldered and looked frail. But he sometimes surprised people with sudden bursts of physical energy. In his present posture, however, all his bodily strength seemed to have retired behind his deep-set eyes, giving them an extraordinary power of penetration. He was only twenty-six, but looked thirty or more. On the whole, he was not unhandsome.

"A penny for your thoughts, Mike," said Nancy after a while, imitating the woman's magazine she read.

"I was thinking what a grand opportunity we've got at last to show these people how a school should be run."

Ndume School was backward in every sense of the word. Mr Obi put his whole life into the work, and his wife hers too. He had two aims. A high standard of teaching was insisted upon, and the school compound was to be turned into a place of beauty. Nancy's dream-gardens came to life with the coming of the rains, and blossomed. Beautiful hibiscus and allamanda hedges in brilliant red and yellow marked out the carefully tended school compound from the rank neighbourhood bushes.

One evening as Obi was admiring his work he was scandalized to see an old woman from the village hobble right across the compound, through a marigold flowerbed and the hedges. On going up there he found faint signs of an almost disused path from the village across the school compound to the bush on the other side.

"It amazes me," said Obi to one of his teachers, who had been three years in the school, "that you people allowed the villagers to make use of this footpath. It is simply incredible." He shook his head.

"The path," said the teacher apologetically, "appears to be very important to them. Although it is hardly used, it connects the village shrine with their place of burial."

"And what has that got to do with the school?" asked the headmaster.

"Well, I don't know," replied the other with a shrug of the shoulders. "But I remember there was a big row some time ago when we attempted to close it."

"That was some time ago. But it will not be used now," said Obi as he walked away. "What will the Government Education Officer think of this when he comes to inspect the school next week? The villagers might, for all I know, decide to use the schoolroom for a pagan ritual during the inspection."

Heavy sticks were planted closely across the path at the two places where it entered and left the school premises. 85 These were further strengthened with barbed wire.

Three days later the village priest of Ani called on the headmaster. He was an old man and walked with a slight stoop. He carried a stout walking stick which he usually tapped on the floor, by way of emphasis, each time he made 90 a new point in his argument.

"I have heard," he said after the usual exchange of cordialities, "that our ancestral footpath has recently been closed ..."

"Yes," replied Mr Obi. "We cannot allow people to make 95 a highway of our school compound."

"Look here, my son," said the priest, bringing down his walking stick, "this path was here before you were born and before your father was born. The whole life of this village depends on it. Our dead relatives depart by it and our 100 ancestors visit us by it. But most important, it is the path of children coming in to be born ..."

Mr Obi listened with a satisfied smile on his face.

"The whole purpose of our school," he said finally, "is to eradicate just such beliefs as that. Dead men do not require 105 footpaths. The whole idea is just fantastic. Our duty is to teach your children to laugh at such ideas."

Extract from "Dead Men's Path" by Chinua Achebe

Level 1: Comprehension

1 What was Mr Obi's objective for the school and to what extent do you think this was for the benefit of the villagers?

Level 2: Interpretation

2 What is your impression of Mr Obi as depicted in the first few paragraphs of the extract? What is your impression of his wife? Give evidence to support your answer.

Level 3: Analysis

3 **a** Explain the significance of the title of the story from which the passage is extracted and how it is central to the entire story. Give reasons for your answer.

b What is the main conflict between Mr Obi and the villagers? How does the writer effectively develop the sense of conflict between Mr Obi and the villagers in the text?

Level 4: Insight and response

4 What do you think is the writer's message at the end of this extract? What possible themes or morals could he be highlighting to his readers?

Prose Exercise 8
Four-level Question Scaffold

This passage revolves round an Asian girl who helps her American friend out of trouble.

Andy finally thought of those three magic—words—"I'm in jail."

Now it was my turn to be speechless.

So Andy said, "Have I used up my words quota yet or
5   can I say more?"

I graciously granted him permission to speak.

"They think I'm the head of a soccer gambling syndicate. I'm supposed to be like some octopus, with tentacles all over the place, in Asia, Europe, everywhere. Imagine that—little
10   ol' me. Head of a multimillion betting empire. I don't know whether to be flattered or outraged."

"Have you been charged?"

"I've been arrested under—what was that phrase again? —the Common Betting Act. They said it was a 'bookable
15   offence'. What's that in normal English?"

"It's legalese for 'You're in big trouble.'"

"So you see, I need someone to bail me out. And the police said that that someone had to be Singaporean, and over twenty-one. And I thought, hey, I've got a friend—not
20   just an acquaintance, but a *good* friend, who fits that description perfectly. Plus, she's just got her law licence."

"I'm impervious to flattery at one in the morning." But once again, I knew I had to do it. I had to rescue Andy again.

Andy was always stumbling into trouble. I don't think
he ever had a plan in his life, but if he did, it was probably
to live a life of complete cluelessness. He would do something
outrageous, after which he would flash his trademark
stricken-yet-ingenuous look: he would widen his doe-like
eyes, scrunch his mouth and flap his hands as if trying to
fend off any accusations of misconduct. "It's not my fault,"
he would invariably say, "I don't know how that broke* / I
don't know how the snot got sprayed all over your CDs* / I
didn't know you weren't supposed to smoke that in this
country* (*delete as applicable)—it just *happened.*" I was
used to getting him out of trouble. In the past few months, he
had depended on me to bail him out, in the metaphorical
sense. I didn't mind that. It's just that I never expected to
have to bail him out *literally* ...

Recently, there have been many of Andy's "It Just
Happened" incidents. Another time there was a lot of cleaning
up to do was during Andy's first MRT trip. There were these
big signs plastered all over the train station, these drawings
of a cup and a plate of steaming food, with a huge red cross
stamped across them. For those lacking the ability to interpret
visual symbols, a caption underneath warned us that the
possessors of food and drink in an MRT station would be
subjected to a five-hundred dollar fine. I told Andy to hide
his bottle of cocoa in his bag, he said, "I'm not going to let
any foreign government dictate my eating habits." So we
were standing on the platform waiting for the train and Andy
started recounting Fallensham United's latest victory, jiggling
his hands as he tried to reconstruct Varney's last-minute
winning pile driver. Of course he spilled his drink all over
the floor. He took off his T-shirt, got down on his knees and
tried to mop up the brown mess. Then this huge voice boomed
out from some hidden PA system. The cameras had been
watching us all this time, that panoptic system that governs
the public transport system. The voice said, "Will the topless
man please make his way to the Central Control Station." As
usual it was down to me to deal with the grim grey-uniformed
MRT wardens, grovelling on Andy's behalf, soothing things
over in the Singlish lingo that only the native could do—
"*Aiya,* sorry about my friend *lah.* He's *ang mo*[1], you know
what they're like. He just got off the plane, he came from this
ulu ulu town in England, very *sua-ku*[2], he doesn't know
anything. You give him chance, okay or not?"

---

[1] *ang mo: Singlish reference to a Westerner.*
[2] *sua-ku: Singlish word for "naive" or "ignorant".*

"Okay, this time *we give him chance*," the station manager said, "but next time he do this again, *we ou kong*[3] him a lot of money."

70   It was Andy's first encounter with Singlish, so after we left the control station, he asked me, "What were you talking about?"

"I told them you were this stupid white foreign country bumpkin," I said, "and they said they would let you off this
75   time, but if you litter again, they'll fine you five hundred dollars." I explained to Andy that though people like me and Eugene could speak perfect English, we reserved our 'proper' English for foreigners, job interviews and English oral exams. With friends or family, we always used Singlish, that is,
80   Singapore slang. Singlish is a type of pidgin English, where English words are arranged according to the rules of Chinese grammar, and sentences are sprinkled with the occasional Chinese, Malay and Indian words. Singlish words like 'broken' English—to foreign ears it can sound unintelligible,
85   uneducated, even crude. However, we didn't speak 'broken' English because we lacked the ability to speak the Queen's English; we spoke Singlish because with all its contortions of grammar and pronunciation, its new and localized vocabulary, Singlish expressed our thoughts in a way that
90   formal, perfectly enunciated and BBC World Service English never could. Besides, who wants to talk like some 'O' level textbook, instead of using our own language, our home language, the language of our souls?

Extract from Foreign Bodies *by Tan Hwee Hwee*

Level 1: Comprehension

1   In what ways has the narrator helped Andy over the years? Support your answer with evidence from the text.

Level 2: Interpretation

2   Why do you think the narrator continues to help Andy when he keeps getting into trouble? What is your impression of her?

Level 3: Analysis

3   Discuss how the writer uses language, tone and narrative style to create humour. Support your answer with reference to the text.

---

[3] *ou kong: Singlish term for "fine".*

4   How does the writer convey the problems foreigners face when they come to Singapore without sounding overly critical of foreigners?

Prose Exercise 9
Four-level Question Scaffold

This is an account of events which happened in the "Holocaust" during World War II when Hitler's officers were ordered to pick out sick or weaker Jews to be sent to Auschwitz—one of the largest concentration camps well-known for its gas chambers.

When it began, on the morning of Sunday, May 7, the *Appellplatz** was hung with banners: "FOR EVERY PRISONER, APPROPRIATE WORK!" Loudspeakers played ballads and Strauss and love songs. Beneath them was set a table where
5   Dr Blancke, the SS physician, sat with Dr Leon Gross and a number of clerks. Blancke's concept of "health" was as eccentric as that of any doctor in the SS. He had rid the prison clinic of the chronically ill by injecting benzine into their bloodstreams. These injections could not by anyone's
10   definition be called mercy killings. The patient was seized by convulsions which ended in a choking death after a quarter of an hour. Marek Biberstein, once president of the *Judenrat* and now, after his two-year imprisonment in Montelupich Street, a citizen of Plaszow, had suffered heart failure and
15   been brought to the *Krankenstube*. Before Blancke could get to him with a benzine syringe, Dr Idek Schindel had come to Biberstein's bedside with a number of colleagues. One had injected a more merciful dose of cyanide.

Today, flanked by the filing cabinets of the entire prison
20   population, Blancke would deal with the prisoners a barracks at a time, and when he finished with one battery of cards it would be taken away and replaced by the next.

As they reached the *Appellplatz*, prisoners were told to strip. They were lined up naked and made to run back and
25   forth in front of the doctors. Blancke and Leon Gross, the collaborating Jewish physician, would make notations on

---

* *Appellplatz : this refers to an area in a prison camp where prisoners gather for roll call.*

the card, point at this prisoner, call on that one to verify his name. Back the prisoners would run, the physicians looking for signs of disease or muscular weakness. It was an odd and humiliating exercise. Men with dislocated backs (Pfefferberg, for example, whose back Hujar had thrown out with the blow of a whip handle); women with chronic diarrhoea, red cabbage rubbed into their cheeks to give them colour—all of them running for their lives and understanding that it was so. Young Mrs Kinstlinger, who'd sprinted for Poland at the Berlin Olympics, knew that all that had been just a game. *This* was the true contest. With your stomach turning and your breath thin, you ran—beneath the throb of the lying music—for your golden life.

No prisoner found out the results until the following Sunday when, under the same banners and band music, the mass of inmates was again assembled. As names were read out and the rejects were marched to the eastern end of the square, there were cries of outrage and bewilderment. Amon [the Nazi prison commander] had expected a riot and had sought the help of the garrison of Cracow, who were on stand-by in case of a prionser uprising. Nearly 300 children had been discovered during the inspection the previous Sunday, and as they were now dragged away, the protests and wailings of the parents were so loud that most of the garrison, together with Security Police detachments called in from Cracow, had to be thrown into the cordon separating the two groups. This confrontation lasted for hours, the guards forcing back surges of demented parents telling the usual lies to those who had relatives among the rejects. Nothing had been announced, but everyone knew that those down there had failed the test and had no future. Blurred by waltzes and comic songs from the loudspeakers, a pitiable babel of messages was shouted from one group to the other. Henry Rosner, himself in torment, his son, Olek, in fact hidden somewhere in the camp, had the bizarre experience of facing a young SS man who, with tears in his eyes, denounced what was happening and made a pledge to volunteer for the Eastern Front. But the officers shouted that unless people showed a little discipline, they would order their men to open fire. Perhaps Amon hoped that a justifiable outbreak of shooting would further reduce that overcrowding.

At the end of the process, 1,400 adults and 268 children stood, hedged in by weapons, at the eastern rim of the *Appellplatz*, ready for fast shipment to Auschwitz.

Extract from Schindler's List *by Thomas Keneally*

Level 1: Comprehension

1 Explain why there was a confrontation between the prisoners and the guards in the fourth paragraph of the extract.

Level 2: Interpretation

2 **a** Why do you think music was played while the prisoners were examined?

 b What is your impression of the SS physician Dr Blancke?

Level 3: Analysis

3 **a** How would you describe the overall mood of the scene depicted?

 b Examine how the writer effectively depicts the cruel and inhumane treatment of the prisoners.

Level 4: Insight and response

4 **a** How is the use of the third person omniscient narration and the use of a distant tone effective in conveying the horrors of the holocaust without it becoming overly melodramatic?

 b Which segment of the text has created the strongest impression on you? What were your feelings as you read it and why? Give reasons for your answer.

Prose Exercise 10
Four-level Question Scaffold

The main character in this passage, Teik Lock, has been diagnosed with a rare degenerative disease which has caused him to become almost fully blind.

> As soon as she saw him, his face no longer shaded by the thick distorting lenses and now thin and empty of reflection, she began to cry.
> "So, Su Ann. Why are you crying? I'm not dead yet!"
> 5 "The doctor called. He said that ..."
> "Yes, I know what he told you. But why are you here now? You should be teaching."

"He called me in school. What happened? What's wrong with your eyes?" Even as she wept, she could not help throwing questions at him. The tears ran down her face and she licked them from her lips. "Why are you sitting alone here in the dark? You should be in the hospital. Why didn't you tell me earlier that you were losing your sight?"

"What good would it have done? Mother often said I would go blind someday, and how could you have stopped it?"

"She did not mean it." Suddenly confused, she stopped crying. Yes, there were times after their father's death when they were living with their great-aunt and their mother supported them by her sewing and by selling her special curry powders. Teik Lock always carried a book with him then; he read even in the outhouse, during meals, and while visitors were in the house. He did not seem to notice how wretched and hard life was. His nose was in a book even as he lay to sleep on the mat on the floor next to the sewing machine. Sometimes when she was tired and bitter, their mother had forbidden him to continue reading, warning him that he would go blind. Later, when she was asleep he would leave the room where they ate, lived, slept and studied to read in the compound with only the light from the moon and stars. Su Ann had spied upon him in the evening peering into the pages of a book when there was not enough light to make out his features, and she had wondered if he were actually reading the words on the page or merely deciphering his own private longings as they took shape in the indiscernible print. Finally, it was a charitable teacher who found the money to have Teik Lock's eyes examined and to buy him his first pair of glasses, a square black-rimmed pair heavy with the powerful lenses which enlarged his pupils and gave him the hideous appearance of a frog.

Was that when he began to lose his sight? Su Ann recalled that his glasses became stronger and stronger in later years. The last time she had looked through them, they were blurred and fuzzy, seeming to hinder vision rather than to improve it. The world appeared as if one were seeing it underwater, and when she snatched the glasses away from her eyes, their power persisted in her own vision, pressing in on her eyes with a painful throb.

Recalling all these events, she moved restlessly around the room. "I am going to put on the light," she said unhappily. The switch flooded the room with white light from three long fluorescent lamps. Teik Lock's gesture to his childless

marriage was never to read in the bedroom; however, after
his wife's death, he had the bright lamps installed and he
stayed more and more in this particular room, reading the
novels which he ordered from book clubs in Britain and
drinking his small tumblers of Remy Martin brandy.

The white fluorescent light made a shocking glare as it
bounced off the white undecorated walls and illuminated
brightly the stacks of books and magazines on the floor. On
the bedside table Su Ann saw only a tray with a bottle of
brandy on it. Teik Lock held a glass of brandy in his left
hand, and he put up his right hand as if to shield his eyes
from the glare.

"I am not fully blind," he said, "despite what Dr Chen
may have told you. I can distinguish between light and dark,
and I can see people and objects, although not clearly at
all."

"What can be done?"

"There is nothing to be done. He calls it a degenerative
disease. The corneas have lost their elasticity and at my age,
no operation to replace them could be helpful." His voice
was calm and light, as if he were being ironical about the
whole diagnosis.

Su Ann felt a sense of terror. "How will you live?" she
asked, then was overcome by shame at the shamelessness of
her question.

"I will live here as I have done for so long. Ah Leng will
continue to look after the house and cook for me. Fortunately,
I no longer have to work, and my pension is sufficient to
provide for me. It won't be difficult for me to manage as I
have always done."

She began to cry again.

"Ah," she wept, "if only your life had been different! If
only you had a child! If only we hadn't been so poor!"

"Come ..." he said and took a swallow of brandy. "Su
Ann, why are you crying?" He smiled in her direction and
held his glass up. "Look! Although I may not see the object
clearly, I can still feel its substance."

Extract from "Blindness" by Shirley Lim

Level 1: Comprehension

1 Give two reasons why Su Ann begins crying as soon as she
sees Teik Lock.

Level 2: Interpretation

2   What kind of person is Teik Lock? Support your answer with evidence from the text.

Level 3: Analysis

3   Why does the writer juxtapose the narration of the present with a flashback to the past? Discuss any other interesting features of the writing style and say how they contribute to your appreciation of the text.

Level 4: Insight and response

4   How does the writer convey the tragedy of Teik Lock's situation to the reader? What were your feelings as you read the extract?

Prose Exercise 11
GCE 'N' Level 2017/1 Literature in English (October 2001)

Read the passage below and answer the questions that follow it.

They travelled down with the Principal in his truck, arriving far too early for the ceremony, and spent several hours sitting in the Museum yard, waiting for the doors to open. But at last they did, and others came, teachers, people
5   from the newspapers, members of the Legislature. Then the Minister arrived in a black car and people put down their glasses of orange juice and swallowed the last of their sandwiches.

She saw her painting hanging in a special place, on a
10   room divider, and there was a small card pinned underneath it. She went with her teacher to look at it, and she saw, with leaping heart, her name neatly typed out beneath the picture: PRECIOUS RAMOTSWE (10) (MOCHUDI GOVERNMENT JUNIOR SCHOOL). And underneath that, also typed, the title
15   which the Museum itself had provided: "Cattle beside Dam".

She stood rigid, suddenly appalled. This was not true. The picture was of goats, but they had thought it was of cattle! She was getting a prize for a cattle picture, by false pretences.

20   "What is wrong?" asked her father. "You must be very pleased. Why are you looking so sad?"

    She could not say anything. She was about to become a criminal, a perpetrator of fraud. She could not possibly take a prize for a cattle picture when she simply did not deserve
25   that.

    But now the Minister was standing beside her, and he was preparing to make a speech. She looked up at him, and he smiled warmly.

    "You are a very good artist," he said. "Mochudi must be
30   proud of you."

    She looked at the toes of her shoes. She would have to confess.

    "It is not a picture of cattle," she said. "It is a picture of goats. You cannot give me a prize for a mistake."

35   The Minister frowned, and looked at the label. Then he turned back to her and said: "They are the ones who have made a mistake. I also think those are goats. I do not think they are cattle."

    He cleared his throat and the Director of the Museum
40   asked for silence.

    "This excellent picture of goats," said the Minister, "shows how talented are our young people in this country. This young lady will grow up to be a fine citizen and maybe a famous artist. She deserves her prize, and I am now giving
45   it to her."

    She took the wrapped parcel which he gave her, and felt his hand upon her shoulder, and heard him whisper: "You are the most truthful child I have met. Well done."

    Then the ceremony was over, and a little later they
50   returned to Mochudi in the Principal's bumpy truck, a heroine returning, a bearer of prizes.

Extract from The No.1 Ladies' Detective Agency
by Alexander M. Smith

1 Show how the author makes us aware of the changing feelings of Precious Ramotswe throughout this passage and make clear what those feelings were. What do you think her feelings were at the end as she rode home in the Principal's truck?

2 Show how the author's description makes it clear that the prize-giving was an important occasion.

3 Why do you think the Minister behaved as he did? Do you think he was right to do so?

The passage below tells of a boy in India who has been taught to play the bamboo flute by a master musician and describes what happens to him one night while he is playing a particular song. Read the passage carefully and answer the questions that follow it.

And now what should I see between the door and me but a black cobra! It had opened its immense hood and was swaying ecstatically. I stopped my song and rubbed my eyes to see if I was fully awake. But the moment the song ceased,
5 the cobra turned and threw a glance at me, and moved forward. I have never seen such a black cobra and such a long one in my life. Some saving instinct told me: "Play on! Play on! Don't stop." I hurriedly took the flute to my lips and continued the song. The snake, which was now less than
10 three yards from me, lifted a quarter of its body, with a gentle flourish reared its head, fixed its round eyes on me and listened to the music without making the slightest movement. It might have been a carven snake in black stone, so still it was.
15 And as I played with my eyes fixed on the snake I was so much impressed with its dignity and authority that I said to myself, "Which God would forgo the privilege of wearing this in His hair? ..." After playing the song thrice over, I commenced a new song. The cobra sharply turned its head
20 and looked at me as if to say, "Now what is all this?" and let out a terrible hiss, and made a slight movement. I quickly resumed the snake-song, and it assumed once again its carven posture.

So I played the song again and again. But however
25 great a composition might be, a dozen repetitions of it was bound to prove tiresome. I attempted to change the song once or twice, but I saw the snake stir menacingly. I vainly tried to get up and dash out, but the snake nearly stood up on its tail and promised to finish me. And so I played the
30 same song all night.

Extract from "The Snake Song" by R.K. Narayan

1 Briefly describe what the boy experiences in this passage.

2 How does the writer make the snake's appearance and behaviour interesting?

3 What feelings do **you** have for the boy when you read about his experience?

Prose Exercise 13
GCE 'N' Level 2017/1 Literature in English (October 2003)

Read the passage below carefully, and then answer the questions that follow it.

The passage describes a boy who is determined to swim through a hole and then along an underwater tunnel. He allows himself 120 seconds.

He took the edges of the hole in his hands and drew himself into it, wriggling his shoulders in sideways as he remembered he must, kicking himself along with his feet.

Soon he was clear inside. He was in a small rock-bound
5   hole filled with yellowish-grey water. The water was pushing him up against the roof. The roof was sharp and pained his back. He pulled himself along with his hands—fast, fast—and used his legs as levers. His head knocked against something; a sharp pain dizzied him. Fifty, fifty-one, fifty-two ... He was
10   without light, and the water seemed to press upon him with the weight of rock. Seventy-one, seventy-two ... There was no strain on his lungs. He felt like an inflated balloon, his lungs were so light and easy, but his head was pulsing.

He was being continually pressed against the sharp
15   roof, which felt slimy as well as sharp. Again he thought of octopuses, and wondered if the tunnel might be filled with weed that could tangle him. He gave himself a panicky, convulsive kick forward, ducked his head, and swam. His feet and hands moved freely, as if in open water. The hole
20   must have widened out. He thought he must be swimming fast, and he was frightened of banging his head if the tunnel narrowed.

A hundred, a hundred and one ... The water paled. Victory filled him. His lungs were beginning to hurt. A few more strokes and he would be out. He was counting wildly; he said a hundred and fifteen, and then, a long time later, a hundred and fifteen again. The water was a clear jewel-green all around him. Then he saw, above his head, a crack running up through the rock. Sunlight was falling through it, showing the clean dark rock of the tunnel, a single mussel shell, and darkness ahead.

He was at the end of what he could do.

Extract from Through the Tunnel *by Doris Lessing*

1   With close reference to the passage, say what impression you gain of the boy from his actions and thoughts.

2   How do the writer's words help you to experience the tension and danger of what is happening?

Prose Exercise 14
GCE 'N' Level 2017/1 Literature in English (October 2004)

The passage below tells of an incident concerning a school teacher who has taken her class of young children on a trip to a natural history museum. Read the passage carefully, and then answer the questions that follow it.

I made my way to the Hall. More children, sitting in rows on canvas chairs. An elementary class from a city school, under the control of an elderly lady teacher. A museum attendant holding a basket, and all eyes gazing at the basket.

"Oh," I said. "Is this a private lesson? Is it all right for me to be here?"

The attendant was brisk. "Surely. We're having a lesson in snake-handling," he said. "It's something new. Get the children young and teach them that every snake they meet is not to be killed. People seem to think that every snake has to be knocked on the head. So we're getting them young and teaching them."

"May I watch?" I said.

15 "Surely. This is a common grass snake. No harm, no harm at all. Teach the children to learn the feel of them, to lose their fear."

He turned to the teacher. "Now, Miss—Mrs—" he said.

"Miss Aitcheson."

20 He lowered his voice. "The best way to get through to the children is to start with the teacher," he said to Miss Aitcheson. "If they see you're not afraid, then they won't be."

She must be nearing retiring age, I thought. A city woman. Never handled a snake in her life. Her face was 25 pale. She just managed to drag the fear from her eyes to some place in their depths, where it lurked like a dark stain. Surely the attendant and the children noticed?

"It's harmless," the attendant said. He'd been working with snakes for years.

30 Miss Aitcheson, I thought again. A city woman born and bred. All snakes were creatures to kill, to be protected from, alike the rattler, the copperhead, king snake, grass snake—venom and victims. Were there not places in the South where you couldn't go into the streets for fear of the 35 rattlesnakes?

Her eyes faced the lighted exit. I saw her fear. The exit light blinked, hooded. The children, none of whom had ever touched a live snake, were sitting hushed, waiting for the drama to begin; one or two looked afraid as the attendant 40 withdrew a green snake about three feet long from the basket and with a swift movement, before the teacher could protest, draped it around her neck and stepped back, admiring and satisfied.

"There," he said to the class. "Your teacher has a snake 45 around her neck and she's not afraid."

Miss Aitcheson stood rigid; she seemed to be holding her breath.

"Teacher's not afraid, are you?" the attendant persisted. He leaned forward, pronouncing judgement on her, while 50 she suddenly jerked her head and lifted her hands in panic to get rid of the snake. Then, seeing the children watching her, she whispered, "No, I'm not afraid. Of course not." She looked around her.

"Of course not," she repeated sharply.

Extract from You Are Now Entering the Human Heart: Stories
by Janet Frame

1 How does the author help you to be aware of Miss Aitcheson's growing fear, and how she tries to control it, in this passage?

2 What reasons does the author suggest to explain Miss Aitcheson's fear?

3 With careful reference to what he says and does, give your opinion of the attendant's behaviour in this passage.

> **Prose Exercise 15**
> *GCE 'N' Level 2017/1 Literature in English (October 2005)*

Read this passage carefully, and then answer the questions that follow it.

He drove out along grassy ruts on to the road, not far from the bridge where Lucy had stood watching the eel. As he turned right, towards the town, his eyes widened and his brain whirled. The swaying, lumpy, black tower, about a

5 hundred yards ahead, close to the road, could not possibly be anything. Unless it was some structure for aerials, something to do with radar, maybe, draped in camouflage. Even when it moved, he still tried to explain it. Maybe it was a windmill, without arms, being moved—as they move whole

10 houses in America. Or maybe some film company was making a film, a horror film; it could be, and that would account for the hideous noises too. He simply did not know what to think—so he went on driving towards it.

But when it stepped out on to the road directly in front

15 of him, he jammed on his brakes.

This, he could see, was something new. This had come up all on its own out of the marsh mud. Clumps and tangles of reeds still slithered down its black length, with the slime. As it dawned on him what he was looking at, his head

20 seemed to freeze. That was his hair trying to stand on end. Tears of pure fear began to pour down his cheeks. But he was a photographer—and no true photographer ever misses a chance.

He bundled his camera with him out of the car, snatched

25 off the lens cover, and bowed over the viewfinder.

Blackness filled it. He backed away, swinging the camera from side to side, trying to squeeze the whole huge shape into the frame. But even before he got it full length he saw, in his viewfinder, that it had picked up his car. Aghast, but also overjoyed, he took shot after shot as the great figure slammed his car down on to the road, raised it high and slammed it down again, and again, and again, like somebody trying to beat the dust out of a heavy rug. The birdwatcher remembered, with a fleeting pang, the bittern's eggs. They had been nested in his cap on the passenger seat. But he forgot them as he saw the paint and glass exploding, like steam, each time the car banged down on to the road. Doors flew off, wheels bounded into the reeds, and the mouth in the head opened. As the terrible siren wail came out of that mouth, the birdwatcher turned and ran.

Fast as he ran, he wasn't fast enough. The black, mad giant bounced the twisted, steel-bright tin can of a car into the reeds, then gouged up a handful of marsh mud clotted with weedy roots.

The birdwatcher thought the swamp monster must have caught up with him and kicked him. But it was the flung mass of mud that slammed him from behind, wrapped round him and swept him many yards along the road. He struggled out of it and clutching his greasy camera, spitting out the foul black mire, and sodden, he ran for his life.

Extract from The Iron Woman *by Ted Hughes*

1 With close reference to this passage, show how the author creates a sense of fear and tension by his description of the monster.

2 Describe the emotions felt by the birdwatcher in this passage.

3 Describe and explain **your** feelings as you read this passage.

This extract from a short story by Ray Bradbury entitled "The Pedestrian" is set towards the end of the 21st century. In it, he describes the arrest of a man walking in the city. Read it carefully and then answer the questions that follow it.

On this particular evening he began his journey in a westerly direction, towards the hidden sea. There was a good crystal frost in the air; it cut the nose and made the lungs blaze like a Christmas tree inside; you could feel the cold light going on and off, all the branches filled with invisible snow. He listened to the faint push of his soft shoes through autumn leaves with satisfaction, and whistled a cold quiet whistle between his teeth, occasionally picking up a leaf as he passed, examining its skeletal pattern in the infrequent lamplights as he went on, smelling its rusty smell.

"Hello, in there," he whispered to every house on every side as he moved. "What's up tonight on Channel 4? Channel 7, Channel 9? Where are the cowboys rushing, and do I see the United States Cavalry over the next hill riding to the rescue?"

The street was silent and long and empty, with only his shadow moving like the shadow of a hawk in mid-country. If he closed his eyes and stood very still, frozen, he could imagine himself upon the centre of a plain, a wintry, windless Arizona desert with no house in a thousand miles, and only dry river beds, the streets, for company.

He came to a cloverleaf intersection which stood silent where two main highways crossed the town. During the day it was a thunderous surge of cars. The gas stations open, a great insect-rustling and ceaseless jockeying for position as the scarab-beetles, a faint incense puttering from their exhausts, skimmed homeward to the far directions. But now these highways, too, were like the streams in a dry season, all stone and bed and moon radiance.

He turned back on a side street, circling around towards his home. He was within a block of his destination when a lone car turned a corner quite suddenly and flashed a fierce white cone of light upon him. He stood entranced, not unlike a night moth, stunned by the illumination, and then drawn towards it.

A metallic voice called to him:

"Stand still! Stay where you are! Don't move!"

The police, of course, but what a rare, incredible thing! In a city of three million, there was only one police car left. Crime was ebbing; there was no need now for the police, save for this one lone car wandering and wandering the empty streets.

"Your name?" said the police car in a metallic whisper. He couldn't see the men in it for the bright light in his eyes.

"Leonard Mead," he said. The light held him fixed, like a museum specimen, needle thrust through his chest.

"What are you doing out?"

"Walking."

"Walking!"

"Just walking," he said simply, but his face felt cold.

"Walking? Where? What for?"

"Walking for air. Walking to see." There was a crackling quiet that in itself was an accusation.

"Are you married, Mr Mead?"

"No."

"Not married," said the police voice behind the fiery glare. The moon was high and clear among the stars and the houses were grey and silent.

"Nobody wanted me," said Leonard Mead with a smile.

"Don't speak unless you're spoken to!"

Leonard Mead waited in the cold night.

"Have you done this often?"

"Every night for years."

The police car sat in the centre of the street with its radio throat faintly humming.

"Well, Mr Mead," it said.

"Is that all?" he asked politely.

"Yes," said the voice. "Here." There was a sigh, a pop. The back door of the police car sprang wide. "Get in."

"Wait a minute. I haven't done anything."

"Get in."

"I protest!"

"Mr Mead."

He walked like a man suddenly drunk. As he passed the front window of the car he looked in. As he had expected, there was no one in the front seat, no one in the car at all.

"Get in."

80 He put his hand to the door and peered into the back seat, which was a little cell, a little black jail with bars. It smelled of riveted steel. It smelled of harsh antiseptic; it smelled too clean and hard and metallic. There was nothing soft there.

"Now if you had a wife to give you an alibi,' said the voice. 'But ...'

85 "Where are you taking me?"

The car hesitated, or rather gave a faint whirring click, as if information somewhere, was dripping card by punch-slotted card under electric eyes. "To the Psychiatric Centre for Research on Regressive Tendencies."

90 He got in. The door shut with a soft thud. The police car rolled through the night avenues, flashing its dim lights ahead.

They passed one house in one street moments later, one house in an entire city of houses that were dark, but this

95 particular house had all of its electric lights brilliantly lit, every window a loud yellow illumination, square and warm in the cool darkness.

"That's *my* house," said Leonard Mead.

No one answered him.

100 The car moved down the empty river-bed streets and off away, leaving the empty streets with the empty sidewalks and no sound and no motion all the rest of the chill November night.

Extract from "The Pedestrian" by Ray Bradbury

1 What impression does the writer give in this passage of life in the late 21st century?

2 What feelings do you have for Leonard Mead in the course of the passage? How has the writer created these feelings in you?

Support both of your answers by careful and relevant reference to the passage.

The following passage is an extract from a novel about a young girl called Raka, who, because of family problems, is sent to stay with her great-grandmother, Nanda Kaul, whom she has never seen before. This passage describes their first meeting at Nanda Kaul's house in Carignano. (Ram Lal is a servant.) Read it carefully and then answer the questions that follow it.

Raka meant the moon, but this child was not round-faced, calm or radiant. As she shuffled up the garden path, silently following Ram Lal, with a sling bag weighing down one thin, sloping shoulder and her feet in old sandals heavy
5   with dust, Nanda Kaul thought she looked like one of those dark crickets that leap up in fright but do not sing, or a mosquito, minute and fine, on thin precarious legs.

But "Raka" she nevertheless said, hoping somehow to relate the name to the child and wondering if she would ever
10 get used to seeing this stranger in her garden.

Raka slowed down, dragged her foot, then came towards her great-grandmother with something despairing in her attitude, saying nothing. She sucked at the loose, curly elastic of an old, broken straw hat that drooped over her closely
15 cropped head like a straw bag. She turned a pair of extravagantly large and somewhat bulging eyes about in a way that made the old lady feel more than ever her resemblance to an insect.

Turning those eyes about, Raka watched Ram Lal go up
20 the veranda steps into the house with her case, his outsized tennis shoes alternately flopping and squeaking on the stone tiles. Turning slightly, she saw a sagged-necked hen pecking beneath a bush of blue hydrangeas at some pieces of broken white china.

25 Then she raised her small, shorn head on its very thin and delicate neck and regarded the apricot trees, the veranda, Carignano. She listened to the wind in the pines and the cicadas all shrilling incessantly in the sun with her unfortunately large and protruding ears, and thought she
30 had never before heard the voice of silence.

Then it was not possible to postpone the meeting any longer and both moved a step closer to each other and embraced because they felt they must. There was a sound of

35 bones colliding. Each felt how bony, angular and unaccom-
modating the other was and they quickly separated.

"Child, how ill you have been!" Nanda Kaul exclaimed
involuntarily, leaving her hand for a moment on the hard
shield of the thin shoulder. "How ill. How thin it's made
you."

40 Raka pulled at the slack elastic with some embarrassment and rolled her eyes around to follow the flight of
the hoopoe that suddenly darted out of the tree. She saw the
old lady who murmured at her as another pine tree, the grey
sari a rock—all components of the bareness and stillness of
45 the Carignano garden.

To Nanda Kaul she was still an intruder, an outsider, a
mosquito flown up from the plains to tease and worry. With
a blatant lack of warmth she sighed "Well, better come in,"
and led her across the wavy tiles of the veranda to her room.

Extract from Fire on the Mountain *by Anita Desai*

1 What do you think Nanda Kaul is feeling during this
meeting with Raka, her great-granddaughter? Give evidence
from the passage to support your ideas.

2 By what means does the writer make you feel sympathy for
both Nanda Kaul and Raka? You should examine the
passage in detail in answering this question.

Prose Exercise 18
*GCE 'O' Level 2015 Literature
in English (November 2003)*

This passage is taken from the beginning of a short story called
"The Landlady". Billy is seventeen and has just arrived in a new
town, needing somewhere to stay. Read the passage carefully
and then answer the questions that follow it.

Suddenly, in a downstairs window that was brilliantly
illuminated by a street-lamp not six yards away, Billy caught
sight of a printed notice propped up against the glass in one
of the upper panes. It said BED AND BREAKFAST. There was

a vase of pussy willows[1], tall and beautiful, standing just underneath the notice.

He stopped walking. He moved a bit closer. Green curtains (some sort of velvety material) were hanging down on either side of the window. The pussy willows looked wonderful beside them. He went right up and peered through the glass into the room, and the first thing he saw was a bright fire burning in the hearth. On the carpet in front of the fire, a pretty little dachshund was curled up asleep with its nose tucked into its belly. The room itself, as far as he could see in the half-darkness, was filled with pleasant furniture. There was a baby-grand piano and a big sofa and several plump armchairs; and in one corner he spotted a large parrot in a cage. Animals were usually a good sign in a place like this, Billy told himself; and all in all, it looked to him as though it would be a pretty decent house to stay in. Certainly it would be more comfortable than The Bell and Dragon.

On the other hand, a pub would be more congenial than a boarding house. There would be beer and darts in the evenings, and lots of people to talk to and it would probably be a good bit cheaper, too. He had stayed a couple of nights in a pub once before and he had liked it. He had never stayed in any boarding houses, and, to be perfectly honest, he was a tiny bit frightened of them. The name itself conjured up images of watery cabbage, rapacious landladies, and a powerful smell of kippers[2] in the living-room.

After dithering about like this in the cold for two or three minutes, Billy decided that he would walk on and take a look at The Bell and Dragon before making up his mind. He turned to go.

And now a queer thing happened to him. He was in the act of stepping back and turning away from the window when all at once his eye was caught and held in the most peculiar manner by the small notice that was there. BED AND BREAKFAST, it said. BED AND BREAKFAST, BED AND BREAKFAST, BED AND BREAKFAST. Each word was like a large black eye staring at him through the glass, holding him, compelling him, forcing him to stay where he was and not to walk away from that house, and the next thing he knew, he was actually moving across from the window to the front door of the house, climbing the steps that led up to it, and reaching for the bell.

---

[1] pussy willows: blossoms found in spring, with the appearance and feel of animal fur.

[2] kippers: a type of fish eaten for breakfast.

He pressed the bell. Far away in a back room he heard it ringing, and then *at once*—it must have been at once because he hadn't even had time to take his finger from the bell-button—the door swung open and a woman was standing there.

Normally you ring the bell and you have at least a half-minute's wait before the door opens. But this dame was like a jack-in-the-box. He pressed the bell—and out she popped! It made him jump.

She was about forty-five or fifty years old, and the moment she saw him, she gave him a warm welcoming smile.

"*Please* come in," she said pleasantly. She stepped aside, holding the door wide open, and Billy found himself automatically starting forward into the house. The compulsion or, more accurately, the desire to follow after her into that house was extraordinarily strong.

"I saw the notice in the window," he said, holding himself back.

"Yes, I know."

"I was wondering about a room."

"It's *all* ready for you, my dear," she said. She had a round pink face and very gentle blue eyes.

"I was on my way to The Bell and Dragon," Billy told her. "But the notice in your window just happened to catch my eye."

"My dear boy," she said, "why don't you come in out of the cold?"

"How much do you charge?"

"Five and sixpence a night, including breakfast."

It was fantastically cheap. It was less than half of what he had been willing to pay.

"If that is too much," she added, "then perhaps I can reduce it just a tiny bit. Do you desire an egg for breakfast? Eggs are expensive at the moment. It would be sixpence less without the egg."

"Five and sixpence is fine," he answered. "I should like very much to stay here."

"I knew you would. Do come in."

She seemed terribly nice. She looked exactly like the mother of one's best school-friend welcoming one into the house to stay for the Christmas holidays. Billy took off his hat, and stepped over the threshold.

"Just hang it there," she said, "and let me help you with your coat."

There were no other hats or coats in the hall. There were no umbrellas, no walking-sticks—nothing.

"We have it *all* to ourselves,' she said, smiling at him over her shoulder as she led the way upstairs. "You see it isn't very often I have the pleasure of taking a visitor into my little nest."

95

Extract from "The Landlady" by Roald Dahl

1 Briefly explain why, in the first three paragraphs of the passage, Billy is finding it difficult to make a decision about where to stay. What impressions do you form of his character as a result?

2 What makes this passage an effective beginning for a story? How does the writer build up tension and make us feel anxious for Billy? Remember to support your answer by close reference to the passage.

Prose Exercise 19
GCE 'O' Level 2015 Literature in English (November 2004)

This passage is a short story set in a North American town in the 19th century. Read it carefully, and then answer the questions that follow it.

A man carrying a small red box in one hand walked slowly down the street. His old straw hat and faded garments looked as if the rain had often beaten upon them, and the sun had as many times dried them upon his person. He was not old, but he seemed feeble; and he walked in the sun, along the blistering asphalt pavement. On the opposite side of the street there were trees that threw a thick and pleasant shade; people were all walking on that side. But the man did not know, for he was blind, and moreover he was stupid.

5

In the red box were lead pencils, which he was endeavouring to sell. He carried no stick, but guided himself

10

by trailing his foot along the stone coping[1] or his hand along the iron railings. When he came to the steps of a house he would mount them. Sometimes, after reaching the door with great difficulty, he could not find the electric button, whereupon he would patiently descend and go his way.

The man had been out long and had walked far, but had sold nothing. Hunger, with sharp fangs, was gnawing at his stomach and a consuming thirst parched his mouth and tortured him. The sun was broiling. He wore too much clothing—a vest and coat over his shirt. He might have removed these and carried them on his arm or thrown them away; but he did not think of it. A kind woman who saw him from an upper window felt sorry for him, and wished that he would cross over into the shade.

The man drifted into a side street, where there was a group of noisy, excited children at play. The colour of the box which he carried attracted them and they wanted to know what was in it. One of them attempted to take it away from him. With the instinct to protect his own and his only means of sustenance, he resisted, shouted at the children and called them names. A policeman coming round the corner and seeing that he was the centre of a disturbance, jerked him violently around by the collar; but upon perceiving that he was blind, considerately refrained from clubbing him and sent him on his way. He walked on in the sun.

During his aimless rambling he turned into a street where there were monster electric cars thundering up and down, clanging wild bells and literally shaking the ground beneath his feet with their terrific impetus. He started to cross the street.

Then something happened—something horrible happened that made the women faint and the strongest men who saw it grow sick and dizzy. The motorman's lips were as grey as his face, and that was ashen grey; and he shook and staggered from the superhuman effort he had put forth to stop his car.

Where could the crowds have come from so suddenly, as if by magic? Boys on the run, men and women tearing up on their wheels to see the sickening sight; doctors dashing up in buggies[2] as if directed by Providence.

And the horror grew when the multitude recognized in the dead and mangled figure one of the wealthiest, most

---

[1] coping: the kerb or edge of the pavement.
[2] buggies: small horse-drawn carriages.

useful and most influential men of the town, a man noted for
55 his prudence and foresight. How could such a terrible fate
have overtaken him? He was hastening from his business
house, for he was late, to join his family, who were to start in
an hour or two for their summer home on the Atlantic coast.
In his hurry he did not perceive the other car coming from
60 the opposite direction and the common, harrowing thing
was repeated.

The blind man did not know what the commotion was
all about. He had crossed the street, and there he was,
stumbling on in the sun, trailing his foot along the coping.

"The Blind Man" by Kate Chopin

1 What different impressions of the blind man do you get
from the first three paragraphs of the story?

2 In what ways does the writer make the whole story
interesting and dramatic? Remember to support your ideas
by close reference to the story.

Prose Exercise 20
*GCE 'O' Level 2015 Literature
in English (November 2005)*

This is an extract from a novel set in the Second World War. It
concerns the crew of a Wellington bomber plane who have been
sent on a mission but are shot down over enemy-occupied
France. Franklin is the captain of the damaged aircraft. Read it
carefully, and then answer the questions that follow it.

Franklin was silent for a few moments longer. He looked
in those moments at the altimeter[1] and his speed. The air
speed was already down and was falling in irregular jerks
on the dial. The altimeter showed a little less than sixteen
5 thousand. It fell as he looked at it. In those few moments the

---

[1] altimeter: device measuring how high a plane is from the ground.

situation cleared itself finally of doubt. They had plenty of height and he was not afraid. They would lose more height, but it would, he hoped, be smooth and over a period of time. He rejected quite calmly first, the thought of getting home, and then, directly afterwards, the thought of baling out. In those few moments, making his decisions, he felt very alone and finally assured. If he had any other emotion of comparable strength it was a moment of anger; anger that a cause beyond his control and perhaps beyond his explanation should affect and change his life with violence and perhaps catastrophe.

The altimeter was down below fifteen thousand when he spoke again to the crew.

"It is the airscrew[2]," he said.

"Well, for Christ's sake," O'Connor said. "Just like that."

"Just like that," he said, "and we won't make it."

They did not answer now. He felt the moment of silence deeply. It was their confidence and did not need to be spoken. He had forgotten utterly now about the Alps, the moonlight, the boredom and even about the airscrew. A few moments of the immediate future were all that mattered. They were a division, a gap, in the lives of all of them, and it was his business to take them through it. They were waiting for what he had to say.

"Listen," he said. "I'm going to land within the next five or ten minutes. Roughly where are we, Sandy?"

"About west-north-west of the Vosges. Away south of Paris."

"Occupied or Unoccupied?"

"Unless you turn back it'll be Occupied. I'm not sure of the line."

"What's it matter?" O'Connor said. "They're all crooks."

"You're going to find that out." Franklin said.

He went on slowly and calmly telling them what to do, watching his height and his speed at the same time. The situation in these few minutes, as he reminded the crew of maps and emergency rations and the details of landing, did not once seem desperate.

"Don't do anything cock-eyed[3]," he said. "If anything happens to anybody do your best for him. Take away identification marks. Bust the kite[4] up as much as you can

---

[2] airscrew: propeller.
[3] cock-eyed: stupid.
[4] kite: slang for "plane".

317

and then start walking. Go south-west. Walk at night and go through the towns about dusk. Remember what you've been told. OK?"

50   "OK." They answered him one by one. "OK."

"OK," he said. "Pack your bags and take up stations for landing."

The face of the land in the moonlight began to show clear patterns of gold and shadow and white straight
55 intersections of road as he put the nose of the Wellington down. The land, perhaps because of the lower angle of the deeper moon, seemed everywhere of a possible and easy flatness. Coming lower, he saw here and there the white and black cube of a house in the moon. The transitory landscape
60 stopped being dead. It became real and alive with fields and roads and houses, and here and there, as he came lower still, he could see in the whiter fields the rows of shocked[5] corn.

Extract from Fair Stood the Wind for France *by H.E. Bates*

1   What impressions do you form of the character of Franklin?

2   How does the writer make the men's predicament vivid and exciting?

Remember to refer closely to details in the passage.

---

[5] *shocked: stacked in piles.*

Appendix A
A SURVEY OF SINGAPORE LITERATURE IN ENGLISH (A PERSONAL OVERVIEW)

The early years

Singaporean literature in English probably had its beginnings in the late 1950s when undergraduates in the then University of Malaya started to publish in student magazines and later in book form. Mostly, they wrote poems and among those who published early books and continued to be active were Edwin Thumboo, Ee Tiang Hong and Wong Phui Nam, the latter two being Malaysians.

Drama developed outside the university and the first few realized plays were the pioneering efforts of returned students from England, namely Lim Chor Pee and Goh Poh Seng. In the early sixties, Lim wrote and staged two plays, and Goh did the same with three plays, but the impetus they provided did not result in many more plays until nearly a decade later with practitioners like Robert Yeo, who wrote and staged his first play, *Are You There Singapore*, in 1974.

Fiction began with Goh Poh Seng's *If We Dream Too Long* (1972) and Lloyd Fernando's *Scorpion Orchid* (1976). *Little Ironies*, published in 1978 by Catherine Lim, pioneered the publication of short stories in Singapore.

In the second half of the seventies, the publisher Heinemann brought out, in quick succession, books on poetry and fiction by Singaporean (and Malaysian) writers. These publications, as well as those by Woodrose Publications, made and in some cases established the reputation of writers like Edwin Thumboo, Ee Tiang Hong, Goh Poh Seng, Robert Yeo, Lee Tzu Pheng, Chandran Nair and Arthur Yap, and introduced new writers. Kirpal Singh was an emergent name.

The anthologizing activities of Thumboo produced two important books, namely, *Seven Poets* (1973) and *The Second Tongue: An*

Anthology of Poetry from Malaysia and Singapore (1973). Important voices in fiction were Lim Thean Soo and Gopal Baratham. Both continued to publish in the eighties and well into the nineties. The developing short story scene resulted in several anthologies, such as *Singapore Short Stories*, Volumes 1 and 2 (1978), edited by Robert Yeo. It was an important period for Singapore writing.

Themes of this period

What were some of the themes of these writings? What their authors wrote about arose from their responses to the dynamic and rapid development of Singapore in the process of decolonization, independence and the making of a nation. Broadly speaking, these themes are largely political.

They can be listed as follows, keeping in mind that they are interlinked preoccupations:

- The Japanese occupation of Singapore
- Becoming a nation in Singapore
- Identity
- Race
- Urban change

For many of these writers, two defining events were deeply etched in their imagination, namely the People's Action Party (PAP) winning the general elections in 1959 to form the government of self-governing Singapore in 1959 and Singapore's secession from Malaysia to become an independent nation on 9 August 1965.

The theatre generation of the eighties and nineties

Relative prosperity and the government's nurturing of the arts in the late seventies spurred writing for the theatre. In 1985 *Emily of Emerald Hill* by Stella Kon was staged to much acclaim. In the same year, the first professional theatre company, TheatreWorks, was formed. Other companies were founded, like The Necessary Stage in 1992 and the Singapore Repertory Theatre in 1993. They provided the platform for the writing of Singaporean plays which had declined in production since the mid-sixties. New playwrights like Michael Chiang, Tan Tarn How, Ovidia Yu, Eleanor Wong, Elangovan and Haresh Sharma appeared. They wrote prolifically and brought to the writing scene issues that encouraged audiences to consider alternative views.

Themes of this generation include:

- The gay lifestyle
- Feminism

- Race
- Dissenting politics
- Generation gap

Prominent plays of this period include (the year in brackets refers to the first production): Michael Chiang's *Army Daze* (1987); *Undercover* (1994) by Tan Tarn How; *Three Fat Virgins Unassembled* (1992) by Ovidia Yu; *Dogs* (1994) by Elangovan; *Mergers and Accusations* (1994) by Eleanor Wong; and *Off-Centre* (1994) by Haresh Sharma.

At the same time, an older dramatist, born in 1939, who had up till then written only in Chinese, began to write in English. He was Kuo Pao Kun. A succession of plays beginning with *The Coffin Is Too Big for the Hole* (1985) established him as one of the most important dramatists of the period under review. Kuo's many plays addressed themes such as the individual versus society, the loss of heritage, ageing and the environment. His death in 2004 deprived Singapore theatre and the writing scene of one of its most notable playwrights.

In this period, two new novelists came into view, Suchen Christine Lim and Rex Shelley. Lim's first novel, *Rice Bowl* (1984), and Shelley's *The Shrimp People* (1992), also his first, announced the arrival of writers older than the theatre generation mentioned earlier (Shelley was born in 1930 and started writing late in his life). Shelley went on to produce a quartet of novels that extended the subject matter of Singaporean fiction. For the first time, Shelley, a Eurasian, gave voice to his community, beginning with *The Shrimp People*, which is a derogatory reference to the Eurasians as *gerago*, a colloquial reference to shrimps. Lim directly took on the theme of political dissent in *Rice Bowl*.

Amazingly, another writer of Shelley's generation, the late Goh Sin Tub, became active and, beginning with *Honour and Other Stories* (1986), published a quick salvo of short stories, novels, poetry and memoirs that made him a successful and popular writer well into the new millennium. These are collected in *One Singapore*, Volumes 1, 2 and 3. The last two were published in 2000 and 2001 respectively.

With the Singapore publication in 1995 of her novel *The Bondmaid* and its publication in New York in 1997, Catherine Lim's career as a novelist took off internationally; a number of her novels were published by Orion in England which became bestsellers locally and abroad. Two other writers of fiction who came into prominence are Philip Jeyaretnam and Claire Tham.

In poetry, a strong, new feminist voice was heard through the first book of poems by Leong Liew Geok entitled *Love Is Not Enough* (1991), while Kirpal Singh and Simon Tay continued to write, publishing *Palm Readings* (1985) and *Stand Alone* (1990) respectively. Tay also wrote short stories.

It seems a good idea now to consider the writings of those who were born in 1965, the year Singapore became an independent nation.

Among the poets are Boey Kim Cheng and Felix Cheong, both born in 1965. Boey published his first collection, *Somewhere Bound* (1989), and Cheong also published his first, *Temptation and other poems* (1998). A publishing company, Ethos Books, was willing to risk publishing new works, as Heinemann did in the mid-seventies. In the mid-nineties, many young poets began writing; several of them were friends who knew one another well and so collaborated to promote poetry anthologies. Among them are Yong Shu Hoong, Alvin Pang, Aaron Lee, Daren Shiau, Yeow Kai Chai and Paul Tan. Other poets, not of this Ethos group, include those born before 1965, like Koh Buck Song, Grace Chia and Heng Siok Tian, and younger ones, in terms of age in publication, like Alfian Sa'at, Cyril Wong and Madeleine Lee.

Born in and after 1965, most of these writers know only one government and the society that has developed under the guidance of the PAP. In their writings, they explore issues such as:

- National service
- Language
- The gay lifestyle
- The environment
- Urban change
- The education system
- Alienation, materialism and identity

An important poetry anthology which sums up very well the concerns of this generation and which was jointly edited by Alvin Pang and Aaron Lee is *No Other City: The Ethos Anthology of Urban Poetry*, published in 2000.

The narrative of Singaporean writing goes on. This is a personal survey and the author has tried at the same time to preserve a certain objectivity. Any omission is the present author's responsibility.

Robert Yeo
April 2006

Appendix B
RECOMMENDED READING

We recommend two sets of books in the following sections. They are designed to be helpful to both the teacher and the student. Teachers who wish to return to the why and how of reading poetry and prose may wish to consult the recommended books in the "Primary texts" section. The books in the "Secondary texts" section are chosen for their straightforward explanations and practical approaches to both poetry and prose.

Primary texts

1   Richards, I. A. 1924. *Principles of Literary Criticism*. London: Routledge and Kegan Paul.

2   Richards, I. A. 1929. *Practical Criticism*. London: Routledge and Kegan Paul.

In these two books, Richards, widely regarded as the inventor of practical criticism, demonstrates the principles and the methodology he devised for the close analysis of poems. See especially Part III, Chapter 1 of *Practical Criticism*.

3   Rosenblatt, Louise M. 1938. *Literature as Exploration*. London: Heinemann Educational Books.

4   Rosenblatt, Louise M. 1978. *The Reader, the Text, the Poem: The Transactional Theory of the Literary Work*. New York: Noble House.

These two books advocate the reader-response approach to literature. The first book proposes the theory and the second, a methodology. Both focus on the importance of the reader as the producer of meaning.

Secondary texts

1   Benton, Michael, and Peter Benton. 1986. *Examining Poetry*. Revised and expanded edition. London: Hodder and Stoughton.

2   Benton, Michael, and Peter Benton. 1995. *Poetry Workshops.* London: Hodder and Stoughton.

These practical books advocate response approaches to reading poetry, including using visual materials like paintings, photographs, etc. Check for the latest editions.

3   Hayhoe, Mike, and Stephen Parker. 1988. *Words Large as Apples: Teaching Poetry 11–18.* Cambridge: Cambridge University Press.

This book by two English teachers contains numerous ideas for approaching the teaching of poetry.

4   Kennedy, X. J. and Dana Gioia. 2005. *An Introduction to Poetry.* 11th ed. New York: Longman.

5   Kennedy, X. J. and Dana Gioia. 2002. *An Introduction to Fiction.* 8th ed. New York: Longman.

The instructor's manual for these classic American college and university texts is especially useful to teachers.

6   Murfin, Ross, and Ray M. Supriya. 1998. *The Bedford Glossary of Critical and Literary Terms.* New York: Bedford Books.

This is an excellent literary glossary for both teachers and students. It presents clear and up-to-date definitions of literary terms and provides detailed elaboration of these terms as well.

7   Purves, Alan, Theresa Rogers and Anne Soter. 1995. *How Porcupines Make Love III: Readers, Texts, Cultures in the Response-Based Literature Classroom.* New York: Longman.

Do not be fooled by the quirky title. It is an excellent book for teachers which takes into account the latest research and is written in a clear, accessible style.

8   Thompson, Denys. 1934. *Reading and Discrimination.* London: Chatto and Windus.

This influential little book by an English critic offers both poems and prose passages for appreciation. There are always new impressions; so check for the latest.

9   Warren, Robert Penn, and Cleanth Brooks. 1976. *Understanding Poetry.* 4th ed. New York: Holt, Rinehart and Winston.

10   Warren, Robert Penn, and Cleanth Brooks. 1959. *Understanding Fiction.* 2nd ed. New York: Appleton Century-Croft.

These two books by influential American critics present classic practical approaches to understanding poetry and prose. They offer numerous examples of poems and prose passages for analysis. There are always new impressions; so check for the latest.

Appendix C
GLOSSARY AND INDEX OF LITERARY TERMS

Alliteration The repetition of initial consonants in words next to or close to each other, for example, the repetition of the "s" consonant sound in the sentence "She sells seashells on the seashore".

Allusion This denotes a reference made in the text to a person, historical event, mythology or religion. For example, in the short story "The Secret Sharer" by Joseph Conrad, the fugitive in the story swims towards an island which he terms "Erebus". This is a reference to the Greek word meaning "hell".

Antithesis See **Juxtaposition**

Assonance The repetition of vowel sounds in words next to or close to each other, for example, the repetition of the "o" vowel sound in the phrase "So we'll go no more a-roving".

Characterization This refers to the techniques a writer employs in the construction of a character or characters in a text. There are two main forms of characterization: direct and indirect characterization.

Climax This refers to the highest point or moment of greatest excitement or tension in a text.

Conclusion The conclusion of a text usually involves the resolution (or sometimes non-resolution) of the conflict or problem posed at the beginning. Types of conclusion include the complete resolution, the ironic resolution, the twist and the revelation.

Conflict This refers to a struggle between two or more people (external conflict) or a struggle over an issue within a person (internal conflict).

Connotation The implied meaning or suggestive associations of a word, usually in a poetic context.

Consonance The repetition of consonant sounds in words. For example, the phrase "the flower lives for the praises of its people" repeats the "p" consonant sound.

Denotation The literal or specific meaning of a word.

Development In this book, this term refers to tracking the development or observing trends in the structure of a text. This practice involves spotting changes in the value or tone conveyed in repeated words or ideas as the text progresses.

Diction This refers to the choice of words employed by the writer. Writers often choose their words carefully in order to convey an implied meaning, to create a mood, to evoke a feeling or to suggest the writer's attitude towards an issue. Analysing diction involves questioning why a writer chose a specific word instead of another and then attempting to understand the connotation or implied meaning of that word.

Enjambment This term refers to the technique of letting the line in a poem run to the next line without pause; hence, the expression "run-on line/s".

Foot The basic unit of a metre.

Foreshadowing This refers to an anticipation of what is going to happen in a text before it does happen.

Genre This term refers to a category of literary works. Genres in literature may be broadly classified into poetry, prose and drama. Within these broad classifications, texts can also be further classified according to form or style such as the epic, tragedy, comedy, satire, etc.

Imagery This broadly refers to any language which allows the reader to visualize the setting or situation more clearly. Common forms of imagery include figurative language such as similes, metaphors or personification but may also include other words or associations which evoke and provoke an imaginative response in the reader such as visual imagery, tactile imagery, etc.

Irony This refers to a contradiction between two statements or between two situations.

Juxtaposition This occurs when two words or ideas opposite in meaning are close to each other. For example, we say that the writer uses juxtaposition in the sentence "My home was still in shadow; his lay in the sun." The purpose of juxtaposition is to show contrast between something and another.

Meaning According to I. A. Richards, meaning may be located by examining its four components: sense, feeling, tone and intention. *Sense* refers to the subject matter of a text, ie, what it is saying. *Feeling* refers to the emotional content of a text, ie, how a writer feels towards his subject matter. *Tone* refers to the attitude of the writer towards the reader. *Intention* refers to the effect the writer endeavours to have on the reader. The word "writer" here may refer to the speaker (in the case of a poem) and the reader is sometimes not directly addressed but implied. By examining all of these four aspects, the reader is likely to gain a greater understanding of the text's meaning.

Metaphor A metaphor is a type of imagery used to show comparison between one object (A) and another (B) where A is identified with all qualities of B. For example, a metaphor is employed in the phrase "John is a pig".

Metre This is a unit of rhythm or a reference to a particular unit.

Monologue A speech made or written by one person. There are two main forms of monologue: the interior monologue, which reveals the inner thoughts of a character, and the soliloquy, which is a dramatic monologue employed by a speaker to express his innermost thoughts aloud on stage.

Motif An object, character, or incident which recurs frequently throughout a text and which points to an issue or moral the writer may wish to highlight. One example is the recurring image of a little lost girl in the film *Schindler's List* (directed by Steven Spielberg, 1993).

Narration The process or act of recounting a story.

Narrator A character constructed by the author to communicate a story. The narrator may be omniscient or partially omniscient, reliable or unreliable.

Onomatopoeia Words which imitate real sounds such as "bang", "clang", etc.

Oxymoron A phrase or even a compound word which consists of two terms directly opposite in meaning, as seen in the sentence "They had a *bitter-sweet* romance". An oxymoron is often used to convey the paradox or a contradiction inherent in a situation.

Personification This is a type of metaphor and is employed when non-human things, such as objects, animals, a feeling or an abstract idea, are given human attributes. An example is the phrase "There was a kind breeze that morning".

Plot structure The structure of a plot refers to the manner in which events are chosen and arranged in a narrative text. The structure of a plot commonly involves three components: the introduction (involving the conflict), the body (involving the climax) and the conclusion (involving the resolution or non-resolution of the conflict).

Point of view This refers to the perspective from which a story is told. For example, a story may be told in the first person or third person perspective.

Practical criticism This term refers to the application of literary techniques to a close reading of texts. Students approach texts without having seen them before—hence, "unseen".

Pun This refers to a play on words (very commonly employed in Shakespearean plays), where words may have identical sounds but may convey different meanings or intentions.

Repetition The repetition of a word or idea in a text is often used to emphasize a point the writer is making.

Resolution See **Conclusion**.

Rhetorical questions These are questions asked not to create a response or reply but to convey the speaker's point or attitude towards an event or issue. In these questions, the answer is obvious. An example is provided when a distraught widow in mourning for her husband says, "Why did he have to die?"

Rhyme This term refers to the repetition of an identical sound, as in the beginning of Andrew Marvell's poem "To His Coy Mistress": "Had we but world enough, and time, / This coyness, lady, were no crime". When a rhyme occurs within a single line of a poem, we term this an "internal rhyme". The effect of rhyme is best seen in couplets, that is, two lines that rhyme, as in the ending couplet of a Shakespearean couplet or in the heroic couplet of the 18th century Augustan poets. Rhymes may be used to link words or ideas together to complement the meaning or mood of a text. They may also be used to create a harmonious sound effect in the text or to create disharmonious sounds.

Rhythm This term refers to the patterns of stressed and unstressed syllables or sounds within a poem.

Run-on-lines See **Enjambment**

Setting This refers to the time and place where the action occurs. Look at descriptions of the environment, the weather and the time period.

Simile This is a type of imagery often used to show comparison between one quality of an object and that of another. It can often be identified with the presence of a connecting word such as "like" or "as", as in the phrase "John is like a pig".

Style This term refers to a distinctive way of writing. If you are given an unsigned poem or passage and if you can pin it down to an author because of certain unique characteristics of the text, then in effect, you have identified the author's style.

Suspense A reader is constantly kept in suspense when what he anticipates should happen in a text is withheld from him until later on.

Symbol Symbols are objects or words which carry or convey a larger significance; for instance, they may be representative of a larger idea, issue or value.

Tension This term refers to the element of excitement (which may also involve fear or anxiety) on either the reader's or the character's part in the text.

Unseen See **Practical criticism**

Word choice See **Diction**